RECLAIMING ANISHINAABE LAW

RECLAIMING ANISHINAABE LAW
KINAMAADIWIN INAAKONIGEWIN
and the Treaty Right to Education

Leo Baskatawang

UNIVERSITY OF MANITOBA PRESS

Reclaiming Anishinaabe Law: Kinamaadiwin Inaakonigewin and the
Treaty Right to Education
© Leo Baskatawang 2023

27 26 25 24 23   1 2 3 4 5

University of Manitoba Press
Winnipeg, Manitoba, Canada
Treaty 1 Territory
uofmpress.ca

Cataloguing data available from Library and Archives Canada
ISBN 978-1-77284-025-4 (PAPER)
ISBN 978-1-77284-027-8 (PDF)
ISBN 978-1-77284-026-1 (EPUB)
ISBN 978-1-77284-028-5 (BOUND)

Cover design by Vincent Design
Interior design by Karen Armstrong

Printed in Canada

The University of Manitoba Press acknowledges the financial support for
its publication program provided by the Government of Canada through
the Canada Book Fund, the Canada Council for the Arts, the Manitoba
Department of Sport, Culture, and Heritage, the Manitoba Arts Council,
and the Manitoba Book Publishing Tax Credit.

Funded by the Government of Canada | Canadä

For the People of the Anishinaabe Nation in Treaty #3

When the waiting creatures had given up, the muskrat floated to the surface more dead than alive, but he clutched in his paws a small morsel of soil. Where the great had failed, the small succeeded.

While the muskrat was tended and restored to health, the spirit woman painted the rim of the turtle's back with the small amount of soil that had been brought to her. She breathed upon it and into it the breath of life. Immediately the soil grew, covered the turtle's back, and formed an island.

—Basil Johnston, *Ojibway Heritage*

CONTENTS

Foreword

ON THE WINDIGO, KINAMAADIWIN INAAKONIGEWIN, AND RECONCILIATION

Leo Baskatawang is unique among academics in Canada. As a veteran of the 101st Airborne with two tours of duty during the Global War on Terrorism and Operation Iraqi Freedom, he is a proven and decorated warrior. As a graduate student, he showed his passion and tenacity in crossing the country while dragging the *Indian Act* chained to his waist. We are fortunate that he has turned his formidable skills to the writing of this book. In sharing kinamaadiwin inaakonigewin, the traditional Anishinaabe law of education, Leo has given us a great gift. Once known only to Elders and insiders and only transmitted through the generations by the spoken word, the power and splendour of Anishinaabe education thought and practice is now available to all. His rigorous scholarship is matched by respect for the traditions of his nation. He has built a bridge from the knowledge keepers of Treaty 3 territory who guided him in his work to the halls of power in settler colonial society where so many terrible decisions regarding Indigenous education have been made.

As Leo observes, education was the key force of colonization, and its "greatest trick"—the loss of language—amounts to linguistic genocide (15). He writes that "colonization is a windigo, a hungry, confused, and ill predator." Residential schools, the legacy of intergenerational trauma, the Indian Act, and the continued racial discrimination of underfunding and outside control of education have been a Windigo wreaking havoc on the people of Treaty 3 and elsewhere for generations. He adds that the

Anishinaabe and others "have embedded protocols in their legal orders for identifying and dealing with Windigo-type situations and behaviours" (18). The meticulous presentation of the four orders of Anishinaabe law—from the sacred, to the traditional, to the customary, down to the most recent written temporal law—provides a step-by-step process to revitalize the legal traditions maintained by the knowledge keepers of Treaty 3. Leo's rendering of Anishinaabe laws in the pages that follow is a conscious act of resurgence, of putting the pieces shattered by the Windigo of colonization back together. In outlining kinamaadiwin inaakonigewin in a way that can be recognized and affirmed by outsiders, he confronts one of the greatest obstacles to reconciliation: "the state's inability to understand Indigenous laws and ways of being" (17).

While his focus is on the articulation and revitalization of education law for the Anishinaabe of Treaty 3 territory, the message he conveys has much wider resonance. Leo reminds us that some 70,000 children are currently enrolled in First Nations schools, experiencing institutionalized underfunding and a curriculum largely devoid of Indigenous forms of knowledge and aesthetics. Because education is an act of positioning morals, Leo asserts that an Anishinaabe school system "should be consistent with our principles of teaching and learning" and that there is value in the lessons taught by petroglyphs, the land, or the paintings of Norval Morrisseau.

The horror of Canada's history of Indigenous education was exposed by the Truth and Reconciliation Commission. It was affirmed as genocide by Pope Francis in the summer of 2022. Those of us in settler colonial society need to step aside and support a space where education no longer smothers but allows children to flourish and go on to live a good life, mino-bimaadiziwin. In setting to paper the knowledge and wisdom that gave Anishinaabe power for centuries and, in more recent times, resilience, Leo sheds light on the path that was always there but that most Canadians have been too blind to see. We are shown the foundation of a rich, relevant, and culturally grounded education system that embraces Anishinaabe values. It is also the path to what seems like a distant and uncertain goal to so many: reconciliation. I have learned much from Leo's powerful and ultimately optimistic message. I trust that you will too.

Jim Daschuk
Lumsden Beach, Treaty 4 Territory
December 2022

RECLAIMING ANISHINAABE LAW

INTRODUCTION

boozhoo
ozhaawashkozi binesi izhinikaazo
lac des mille lacs onji
adik gi-doodem[1]

First, let it be understood that *my choice* to introduce myself in my native language, Anishinaabemowin, represents a conscious, explicit act of self-determination and cultural resurgence. Like many "others" of my generation, I am not fluent in my native language.[2] This is not a happy accident. The loss of Indigenous languages in Canada and elsewhere can be attributed largely to systemic forces, imposed by a settler-colonial state, designed to erase Indigenous identity, as well as the state's constitutional obligations, in order to facilitate the dispossession of land and inherent rights of Indigenous peoples.[3] In this book, I will demonstrate how these systemic forces are constructed and maintained in a settler-colonial state through ideological apparatuses such as the education and justice systems.[4] Historically, these institutions were exceedingly detrimental to Indigenous identities, knowledges, and ways of life. That is because they were constructed primarily to establish or maintain an ideological order such as capitalism at the expense of deviant or *different* ideologies such as Indigenous relationality. Yet as the world suffers crisis after crisis—whether environmental sustainability, global warming, or the rise of pandemics—it is becoming increasingly apparent that capitalist ideologies are not only inequitable but also not sustainable for humans to live "a good life," minobimaadziwin, on the land that we all share. It is becoming equally apparent that Indigenous knowledges—best understood in their own Indigenous languages—offer principles of responsibility, respect, and reciprocity that can teach us how to live peacefully, harmoniously, and in relation to each other and the land, aki. In other words, our society as a whole stands to benefit greatly from supporting Indigenous self-determination, reconciliation, and cultural resurgence. These processes are fundamental aspects of achieving social justice in a general sense, but for the purpose of this book I will pay attention to their symbiotic relationship with Indigenous education and law. In the chapters that follow, I will explain how my people, the Anishinaabe Nation in Treaty #3, are exercising our inherent right to self-determination—particularly as it relates to education—in order to revitalize our language and laws as well as resist the processes of colonization.

In brief, the reader will find that the purposes of this book are (1) to demonstrate that the Anishinaabe Nation in Treaty #3 has its own sacred, traditional, and customary laws bound by an unwritten constitution; (2) to analyze how the imposition of settler-colonial laws has created the need to revitalize some oral laws in written form so that they can be recognized and affirmed by settler-colonial society; and (3) to discuss how recognition and affirmation of the written Treaty 3 education law by the federal government of Canada can honour some of its treaty obligations as well as fulfill its commitment to reconciliation. I write primarily within the contexts of education and law in order to demonstrate how Indigenous spiritualities, ways of life, and knowledges have been punished historically by the settler-colonial state because of the threat that they represent to the dominant ideological order. Although Indigenous knowledges have been viewed or labelled continually as marginal or inferior, their *difference*, as an alternative way of life, is why the government of Canada implemented policies such as the residential school system and enacted laws designed to erase Indigenous identities and rights, specifically via the Indian Act. Despite the attack on our ways of being, however, traditional forms of Indigenous law and knowledge have survived. This is partly the result of the advancement of "Aboriginal and treaty rights" discourse in Canada over the past forty years, but even more it is a reflection of our resilience as Indigenous peoples. In my opinion, the evolution of "Aboriginal and treaty rights" is best observed in the context of Canadian case law and "Indian" policy and Indigenous resistance to such laws and policies. In the latest development in this ongoing process, the government of Canada publicly committed to a policy of reconciliation with Indigenous nations and peoples in 2015 when Justin Trudeau was elected as prime minister on a pro-Indigenous campaign platform that promised to answer the Truth and Reconciliation Commission's (TRC) ninety-four Calls to Action as well as to implement the United Nations Declaration on the Rights of Indigenous Peoples (UNDRIP) via federal legislation. However, to fulfill its commitment to reconciliation, Canada must also respect Indigenous self-determination and cultural resurgence by recognizing and affirming traditional Indigenous laws, particularly those that relate to education. In this era of reconciliation, recognition and affirmation of Indigenous education laws such as Kinamaadiwin Inaakonigewin are important to the extent that these laws can support Indigenous self-governance, as provided for in UNDRIP, as well as serve as the legal mechanism with which to fulfill the treaty right to education promised in the Numbered Treaties. Once Indigenous education laws are recognized and affirmed by the Canadian state, corresponding Indigenous education systems can be developed, administered, and governed in accordance with our own local laws, resulting in a localized education system that is relevant for, respectful of, and responsible to local Indigenous nations. The research that I have compiled in this book will be of interest to other Indigenous nations, but for reasons that will become clear soon I have focused on the specific context of the Anishinaabe Nation in Treaty #3. Thus, in short, this book is about the recognition and affirmation of the Treaty 3 written law on education, Kinamaadiwin Inaakonigewin.

About the Author

I will now take a moment to state my *positionality*: that is, to explain who I am and how I came to be interested in the Treaty 3 education law. My name is Leo Baskatawang, and I am an Anishinaabe man from Lac Des Mille Lacs First Nation, located within Treaty 3 territory in northwestern Ontario.[5] I am told that the word *baskatawang* means "flying sand" in Anishinaabemowin, as in a desert sandstorm. I am married to Maria Nunfio, and we have three sons, Levi, Oscar, and Benjamin. I am the eldest son of Diane Baskatawang, a strong-willed anishinaabekwe. She raised me as a young single parent under the most difficult circumstances. My "father" abandoned my mother before I was born and has never been a part of my life. My grandparents, Annie and William Baskatawang, lived primarily in the tiny rural community called Valora, Ontario, near their traditional trapline. William, immensely popular among his peers, laboured for Canadian National Railways and was an excellent hunter, fisher, and trapper. Annie, in her own right, was a remarkable person. She was a three-time widow who gave birth to twelve children. She was in the best sense possible a *bush master*; she did not speak English and was the undisputed matriarch of the family.[6] Sadly, both of my grandparents were also alcoholics. That said, my mother made a decision in my infancy to flee the alcoholism that overwhelmed her parents' home. She moved us to Toronto, where she knew nobody, and at times held down three jobs just to be able to put food on the table and a roof over our heads. I was eventually enrolled in a Catholic school in which I do not recall experiencing any overt racism (I attribute this to the fact that Toronto is a highly diverse, multicultural, metropolitan city where my Indigeneity went unnoticed), but I certainly did not learn anything about my Indigenous heritage either. By the time I was eight years old, however, my mother decided that it was time to move closer to home. Over the next several years, we moved a number of times, from Toronto to Thunder Bay, then from Thunder Bay to Ignace, then from Ignace to Dryden, and finally from Dryden to Fort Frances, Ontario.

Unfortunately, despite her best efforts to make a good life for us, my mother struggled financially, mentally, and emotionally, and eventually she developed alcoholism, which made life at home very difficult. It was also during these years that I first experienced prejudice, stereotyping, and racism as an Indigenous person. These experiences included instances of being refused entry into friends' homes on their parents' orders, being benched on sports teams despite being a gifted and willing athlete, and being judged on the basis of a "treaty card." The notion of a treaty card is a common misperception in Canada, so let me just say that a treaty card as an official form of identification does not exist; it is a non-entity. The actual ID produced and recognized by the federal government is called a Certificate of Indian Status or "status card." Most important to my point, however, is that this material piece of identification, as opposed to one's own inherent knowledge of such identification, is governed in accordance with the Indian Act, not the treaties, as is commonly believed.

Although there have been times in my life when my Indigeneity has been invalidated on the basis of a false assumption of what an "Indian" is, and other times when my Indigeneity—as perceived through my appearance or behaviour—has been the subject of much racist stereotyping, I was somehow always able to focus and be successful in school. Of my entire extended family (whom I consider to be the twelve children of my grandparents, and their children, and their children's children), I have only one cousin who attended university before I did. I point out these aspects of my family history not to brag but to illuminate the long odds that many Indigenous people have to face—in addition to trying just to survive—to overcome the hardships that they experience. Yet, despite my success in high school, I soon discovered that I did not have the skills to manage my time or money to succeed at the postsecondary level, and I dropped out after a very disappointing year and a half. This was one of the major turning points in my life. I experienced a tremendous amount of self-imposed shame and guilt in letting down my family and my community, Lac Des Mille Lacs First Nation, who had sponsored my enrolment. For the next couple of years, I struggled to find my way as I worked at a series of minimum wage jobs, and eventually I moved back in with my mother, who quit drinking and now has been sober for over twenty-five years.

Following 9/11, I saw an opportunity to get my life back on track and decided to enlist in the United States Army. This option was available to me because of my possession of a Permanent Resident card—which I was eligible for as a result of my "Indian status" in accordance with Section 289 of the Immigration and Nationality Act—which my mother wisely had applied for a couple of years earlier.[7] I knew that by joining the army I would develop new skills, meet new people, and see other parts of the world—all of which held immense appeal to me. So, after completing four months of basic training in a combat unit at Fort Sill, Oklahoma, I was stationed at the prestigious 101st Airborne Division (Air Assault) in Fort Campbell, Kentucky. During my time in this unit, I completed two consecutive one-year combat tours—with the distinction of earning two Army Commendation medals—in support of the Global War on Terrorism and Operation Iraqi Freedom. My military experience instilled in me a set of core values that I still apply to my education and research today. These values can be summed up as loyalty, duty, respect, selfless service, honour, integrity, and personal courage. Following my second combat tour, and again witnessing the travesty of war, I decided to end my military career in order once again to pursue a postsecondary education—if my community would sponsor me again.

As it turned out, my community did agree to sponsor me again if I paid for the first year on my own, in order to re-establish myself as a continuing student, which I did through the Canada Student Loan program in 2008. This gesture of support from my community inspired me to dedicate my academic pursuits to the benefit of my people. I therefore endeavoured to learn all that I could about the history of Indigenous peoples in Canada, the process of colonization, and affirmative actions toward reconciliation and cultural resurgence. During this time, I met and became acquainted with literary scholar Dr. Renate Eigenbrod, who became my thesis advisor for my master's program in 2011. Under her tutelage, I became much more aware of Indigenous literature and the oral tradition, which inspired my master's thesis: "*Bawating Maywinzha*: A Long Time Ago, at the Place of Fast-Rushing Waters." The thesis is a work of historical fiction that depicts the point of colonial contact between the Anishinaabe and the French in the early seventeenth century. In the thesis, I applied the Indigenous research methodology of storytelling not only as a lens through which to understand how the process of colonization has affected Indigenous peoples negatively but also as a way to reclaim our history and demonstrate how each of us can participate actively in our cultural resurgence by telling our stories and using our languages.

Sadly, just a few weeks after my graduation in 2014, Dr. Eigenbrod passed away suddenly and unexpectedly. Her death created a void in my support system and left me unsure of how to proceed with my academic future. Initially, I thought that I would apply for law school and had begun studying for the admissions test. During one study session, however, as I was thinking about my future, I came back to an idea that I had considered during my undergrad that involved the treaty right to education. I recalled from a course that I had taken with Dr. Peter Kulchyski that the treaty right to education has not been implemented in almost 150 years since first negotiated in the Numbered Treaties. As I continued to think about this idea, I realized that a PhD program would offer better flexibility to research this topic, so in 2015 I took my idea to Dr. Kulchyski, who then agreed to supervise my doctoral program. Although this research project was intended initially to focus on the treaty right to education, and how this right could be implemented in today's society, the idea evolved after a conversation that I had in 2018 with Gary Allen, serving at the time as the executive director of the Grand Council Treaty #3. During that conversation, Gary mentioned that the Grand Council intended to revitalize Treaty 3's traditional though unwritten education law and invited me to lead the initiative. That is how I became interested in the Treaty 3 education law, Kinamaadiwin Inaakonigewin. It is important to mention, however, that in spite of the research that I have done, including my role as a member of the Technical Working Group that drafted a written form of the education law, I do not claim any personal ownership of the law, except to the extent that I accept it as a mark of my nation's self-determination to govern its own education system. Moreover, I do not claim to be an expert of the law; rather, I am a messenger for those whose knowledge far outweighs my own and for whom I try earnestly to translate and interpret to the best of my ability. In the course of my research, which consisted of conversations and gatherings with Treaty 3 Elders, educators, Grand Council staff, and other knowledge holders, a Treaty 3 archival and literature review, and analyses of historical political and legal precedents, I have come to understand Kinamaadiwin Inaakonigewin in a certain way. If the conception that I describe in the following pages is not consistent with the principles, knowledge, and logic of those whom it concerns, then I readily accept any mistakes as my own.

About the Book

I would like to take a moment to inform the reader of how this book is organized. There are four chapters that build an argument collectively that, in order to address the crisis in Indigenous education, Indigenous nations must have control of their own education systems. I argue that this can be done best through state recognition and affirmation of their respective education laws. I believe that an Indigenous-led, bilateral process would constitute an act of reconciliation in which Canada could be said finally to be honouring its treaty promises, fulfilling the Truth and Reconciliation Commission's Calls to Action, subscribing to the relevant articles of the United Nations Declaration on the Rights of Indigenous Peoples, and following principles established by its own justice system. I often refer to the TRC's Calls to Action as actions that need to be fulfilled *together* because I think that "reconciliation" is not a checklist on which each item can be checked off as done. Many of the calls to action are interrelated, and the process of reconciliation itself requires constant participation and renewal if the overarching goal of social justice is to be achieved. In other words, I do not believe that the calls are a grocery list of items that can be bought at the supermarket, and they should not be viewed as such.

In Chapter 1, "Colonization and Other Discontents," I provide a broad historical overview of colonization, which has shaped the different experiences and worldviews of Indigenous communities in terms of education. I illustrate how the processes of colonization are strikingly similar to those of the Windigo—with reference to the work of scholars such as Deborah Root, Leanne Simpson, and John Borrows—to the extent that the state and its ideological apparatuses are seen as a voracious predator with an insatiable appetite for land and resources. Drawing from the analysis of Albert Memmi in his seminal work *The Colonizer and the Colonized*, I further explain how "colonial racism" is constructed on the basis of ideological differences, particularly as related to attitudes about the land, and how such differences are exploited to the benefit of the colonizer. Although postcolonial theorists such as Albert Memmi and Frantz Fanon write within an African context of the 1950s, I believe that their analyses of the processes of colonization—as well as others, such as those by Edward Said and Paulo Freire—are worth considering today in a global context to the extent that the modus operandi of colonization remains the same everywhere: the displacement of Indigenous peoples in order to access their lands and resources for the purpose of accumulating material wealth. That said, I try my best in this book to include insights from a wide range of sources, including scholars from different Indigenous nations in Canada, such as Glen Coulthard (Dene), Harold Cardinal (Cree), and Marie Battiste (Mi'kmaq), as well as non-Indigenous scholars such as Jacques Derrida, Michael Asch, and James Tully, but whenever possible I privilege the voices of Anishinaabe scholars themselves. With regard to Memmi's insight on the components of colonial racism, my main purpose is to demonstrate that the ideological processes of colonization are still employed today in the form of capitalist enterprises, which I argue are bad not only for the environment and Indigenous peoples but also for the rest of humanity. I end this part of my analysis with a critique of the "banking" form of education in the settler-colonial system, as described by critical social theorist Paulo Freire, who argues that the settler-colonial education system is designed to produce capitalist consumers in order to leverage their habits of consumption and maintain the status quo.

In the second half of Chapter 1, I examine the concept of reconciliation and argue that it is a process that has been over fifty years in the making, beginning with the "Indian Control of Indian Education" report penned by Harold Cardinal in 1970. In this regard, I demonstrate how a flood of land claims and class-action lawsuits that began in the 1970s ultimately forced the federal government to launch the Royal Commission on Aboriginal Peoples in 1991. I argue that these events helped to expose the horrors of the residential school system, which resulted in the Indian

Residential Schools Settlement Agreement in 2006. From this settlement, the Truth and Reconciliation Commission emerged and came up with ninety-four Calls to Action that the government has since committed to fulfill in its pursuit of reconciliation. For reconciliation to occur, however, I argue that Indigenous nations must be provided with appropriate and adequate resources to govern and administer their own education systems, as provided for in the Numbered Treaties. Designing and administering their own education systems, however, is a task that requires a transformative approach to the existing form and content of settler-colonial education using *local* Indigenous pedagogical practices.

In Chapter 2, "Indigenous Laws and the State," I demonstrate how the Anishinaabe Nation in Treaty #3 has an inherent right to governance bestowed on it by the Creator at the beginning of time and since passed along by our ancestors from generation to generation through the oral tradition. This argument is based upon the teachings and literature that I received from Treaty 3 Elder and Grand Chief Emeritus Fred Kelly. It is the belief of the Anishinaabe Nation Treaty #3 that the right to self-governance was recognized in the "nation-to-nation" agreement commonly known as Treaty 3, the Northwest Angle Treaty of 3 October 1873. Although the government of Canada's written document remains the only officially recognized version of the agreement by the settler-colonial state, I demonstrate that Indigenous Elders, scholars, and other knowledge holders have long maintained that oral promises made during the negotiations have been excluded from the written text and that the "spirit and intent" of the agreement are not reflected in the state's written document. In making this argument, I draw from critical theory by Jacques Derrida to analyze what it means to "write": first, through the power or authority given to the written word, by which I mean linear, phonetic notation; second, the limitation of such a form of writing; and third, other forms of writing, including among other practices the use of language itself.

Following a brief outline of what I believe to be four distinct eras of treaty making in Canada, I explain how these practices were guided by Indigenous legal processes such as the smoking of a "peace pipe," the use of wampum, and the invocation of kinship relations. In this regard, I draw from the work of scholars such as J.R. Miller, John Borrows, and Aimée Craft. This discussion leads to an analysis of treaty interpretation and how other sources of knowledge and information—including the treaty commissioner's own transcribed notes of the negotiations, oral accounts from Treaty Elders, and the Paypom Treaty—serve to provide a better understanding of the spirit and intent of the agreement. In making this argument, I point out how these understandings have been interrupted through the force of Canadian law, specifically the Indian Act, and the residential school system. Then, building upon my argument in Chapter 1 that the politic of reconciliation essentially began in the 1970s (a politic, by the way, that gathered momentum only as a result of continuous Indigenous resistance to the Indian Act, the residential school system, and the government's general neglect of treaties), I examine how Canadian case law since has compiled a compendium of principles to be used in treaty interpretation. I take the position that, if the government of Canada were to adopt the principles established by its own justice system, such that the treaties should be interpreted as the "Indians naturally would have understood them," and that they are not frozen in time, then it would not only facilitate a greater understanding of the spirit and intent of the treaties but also provide balance to treaty interpretation through the consideration and inclusion of an Indigenous understanding of these nation-to-nation agreements. That said, if the government of Canada were to honour these principles, then it would demonstrate that it is genuinely committed to abandoning its antiquated, literal approach to treaty interpretation that has governed treaty politics for the past 150 years, in favour of a more robust, relational approach to this process.

I conclude Chapter 2 with an analysis of what it would mean for the state to honour the treaty right to education, which states "and further, Her Majesty agrees to maintain schools for instruction in such reserves hereby made as to Her Government of Her Dominion of Canada may seem advisable whenever the Indians of the reserve shall desire it."[8] In consideration of the principles established by the Supreme Court of Canada, the state's public commitment to fulfill the TRC's Calls to Action, and the implementation of the federal legislation regarding the UNDRIP, I conclude that a reasonable and justifiable interpretation of the education clause could be taken to mean that it would be *advisable* for the state to fund an Anishinaabe education system whenever the treaty partners *desire* it. I further argue that Indigenous laws, specifically Kinamaadiwin Inaakonigewin, can administer and govern an education system in a manner consistent with our own principles of teaching and learning.

Chapter 3, "Kinamaadiwin Inaakonigewin," is about the Treaty 3 Anishinaabe education law and the circumstances that gave rise to its revitalization as a written form. The impetus for this revitalization is based upon an Anishinaabe desire to have our traditional laws recognized and affirmed by the settler-colonial state so that we can establish and administer our own local and distinct education system. This is in response to the abject failure of the residential school system, as well as the public school system in Canada, to provide an education that is adequate for and relevant to the needs of Anishinaabe people in Treaty 3 territory. Drawing from meeting notes and literature over the past thirty years from Treaty 3 education archives, I outline the purpose of Kinamaadiwin Inaakonigewin and discuss seven guiding principles to be observed in the development of a written education law. This research includes analysis of Diane Longboat's "First Nations Education Law for First Nation Governments Template" as well as the government of Canada's most recent education program, the "First Nations Lifelong Learning Table" from 2018. One of the key findings of this research is that, if any indigenized education program is going to have any chance at success, then a significantly larger investment must be made to account for the expenses associated with remote, rural bush living. In attending to this concern, I highlight the need for a representative institutional entity—such as a Treaty #3 Education Commission—directly responsible for negotiating financial agreements on behalf of the Anishinaabe Nation Treaty #3 as well as for developing and administering policies, procedures, and regulations related to the implementation of the written education law. Finally, I discuss the utility of a Community Education Council insofar as having parents, Elders, and other community members involved in the administrative process of education program service and delivery within Treaty 3 territory. The chapter concludes with an analysis of the progress made in the development of the written education law, with specific reference to Treaty 3's law-making process.

In the fourth and final chapter, "Reconciliation as Recognition *and* Affirmation," I discuss and distinguish the politics of "recognition" and "affirmation" as they relate to Indigenous laws in Canada. I point out that, within the past several years, the Canadian government has taken important first steps to reconcile its relationships with Indigenous nations, including a promise to fulfill the TRC's Calls to Action and a commitment to implement the UNDRIP, but still has a lot of work to do to deliver on these promises. These steps constitute what I call a "gesture of recognition," but without concrete, observable action in the form of adequate financial resources to administer our education systems, I argue, state recognition is practically useless. Moreover, as time goes on without any meaningful resolution, I argue that frustration will continue to build, increasing the potential for escalating violence. Although Indigenous forms of protest and civil disobedience historically have been non-violent—with the reoccupation of traditional territories as well as the use of rail and road blockades, protest marches, and hunger strikes—growing frustration risks escalating the scale and frequency of such demonstrations. Thus, it is imperative that moral principles of kinship and peace and goodwill are re-established, as stated in the treaties. My argument involves an analysis of treaty negotiations, suggesting that a treaty was meant to be renewed periodically. In my analysis of the treaties, I make the case that the government of Canada's failure to honour its treaty obligations is the primary reason that there is so much dispute and discord in the Indigenous-Crown relationship. With this in mind, I argue that, if the Canadian government were to adopt a relational approach to treaty interpretation and implementation in its pursuit of reconciliation with Indigenous peoples and nations, that is, just by being considerate and respectful of the land and other worldviews, then all Canadians would benefit from healthier social, ecological, and political environments. As Gina Starblanket and Heidi Stark put it, "if we understand relationality as an analytical lens through which we recognize difference as socially and culturally produced rather than allowing the discourse of relationship to essentialize these differences in ways that confine our movements, we stand to cultivate a greater range of grounds for Indigenous identity and a broader spectrum of modes for engaging in acts of resurgence."[9]

Building upon my analysis of Kinamaadiwin Inaakonigewin in the previous chapter, I outline a two-year process by which the Treaty #3 Education Commission will develop an education plan along with education standards and a curriculum. Upon describing the breadth and scope of these tasks, I conclude that the success of this work—that is, the administration of an Anishinaabe education system, in accordance with Anishinaabe law—will depend largely on the level of cooperation from the Crown as represented by the federal government of Canada. I contend that this can be accomplished only with the requisite resources needed to administer local education programs and services. That said, by the time Kinamaadiwin Inaakonigewin is ratified and approved by a Treaty 3 National Assembly vote, the federal government must be trusted—the linchpin of this entire process—that it will do its part in this process of reconciliation. This process includes fulfilling its promises to answer the TRC's Calls to Action as well as implementing UNDRIP, which, if done in addition to observing its own court's principles of treaty interpretation, I believe would signal that we are indeed in a new era of Indigenous and Crown relations in Canada. One suggestion that I provide to advance the project of reconciliation is the establishment of a jointly appointed Crown–First Nations dispute resolution body to oversee the renewal of historical treaties.[10] I believe that this type of institution could provide a forum in which to negotiate potential funding solutions through respectful and constructive dialogue in order to properly finance Indigenous education initiatives. I conclude my analysis by suggesting that one solution for creating new revenue for Indigenous education could be to establish a new tax used for the sole purpose of fulfilling treaty obligations or perhaps even settling on a share of revenue from taxes already gathered from land-based industries. These measures have as much symbolic import as they do material import.

A Note on Terminology

The terms "Indigenous," "Indian," and to a lesser extent "Aboriginal" appear throughout this book. In reference to the other, most often I use the terms "settler-colonial" and "Western." Although I acknowledge that each term, in its own way, is inherently ideological, which generates intense emotions and is therefore problematic, I also recognize that the labels have their own unique historical context, which makes their use relevant and sometimes necessary in those contexts.[11] That said, I use the terms "settler-colonial" and "Western" to identify people and institutions that uphold and impose Eurocentric standards of anthropocentric values and beliefs (which stand in contrast to Indigenous ways of knowing) through the deployment of hegemonic state apparatuses. Although the terms "Aboriginal" and "Indian" are being effaced from public discourse, they are still given meaning through their appearance and use in state legislation, which is almost exclusively how those terms are referenced in this book. In a more general context, I most often use the term "Indigenous" because of its wider application and global acceptance, but as much as possible, I try to use the specific name of the Indigenous nation being referred to, whether that is Anishinaabe, Métis, Māori, or the like.

In other regions and by other peoples—and sometimes by themselves—the Anishinaabe are referred to as "Ojibway," "Ojibwe," or "Chippewa," dialects of the same word said to mean "Puckered Moccasin People," but in the language of Anishinaabemowin we refer to ourselves as Anishinaabe, the "descended people."[11] For that reason, I identify with and use the term "Anishinaabe." Because I was born and raised in Treaty 3 territory and am a member of a constituent "Indian band"—that is, Lac Des Mille Lacs First Nation—I also frequently use the term "Treaty 3," which most often refers to the nation-to-nation agreement by the Anishinaabe and the Crown, but it could also refer to the *land* within the territorial boundary of Treaty 3 as well as to the nation of people to whom that treaty relates, which it often does. Although my research is specific to Treaty 3, and should be regarded as such, I note again that it can also have relevance for other Indigenous nations, and therefore I invite them to apply whatever insight or knowledge gleaned from this research to their own nation-building exercises.

Two other terms that I employ throughout this work are "recognized" and "affirmed" as they pertain to "Treaty and Aboriginal Rights" in Section 35 of the Constitution Act of 1982. In the context of this book, "recognition" should be interpreted as an acknowledgement of such rights, whereas "affirmation" is the action or process by which such rights are applied. My contention is that recognition of treaty rights and Indigenous law is of little value if it is not followed up with affirmative action to support such rights and laws.

Last First Thoughts

This book was written to be of benefit to the people of the Anishinaabe Nation Treaty #3; if it represents a mere footnote in the continuing story of our national epic, then I will still be pleased. That said, it is my sincere hope that this research will also be of interest to all Canadians, whether they are Indigenous or not; as well as to government officials, policy makers, educators, administrators, and students of various disciplines, including law, education, history, political science, and Indigenous studies; and to those conducting research on the processes of reconciliation and cultural resurgence. If this book can help to advance any of these matters in the glorious pursuit of social justice, all the better.

Chapter 1

COLONIZATION AND OTHER POLITICAL DISCONTENTS

The greatest trick of colonization was convincing the colonized not to speak their own Indigenous languages. But that dubious feat was not achieved overnight. It took concerted and systematic effort, over the course of several consecutive generations, of imposing unjust laws designed to erase Indigenous languages and traditional knowledges. Indeed, for a significant portion of colonial history, many Indigenous peoples across the world have suffered tremendous physical, mental, and spiritual abuses at the hands of colonial agents, simply for belonging to a *different* culture and speaking a *different* language. In Canada, the Truth and Reconciliation Commission has reported that no fewer than 3,200 Indigenous children died in the Indian residential school system, and that tens of thousands more still suffer from intergenerational trauma as a result of what their parents and grandparents experienced in those government-funded, church-run institutions.[1] Because language is the primary means for cultural expression and dissemination of local knowledge about the land, the systematic erasure of Indigenous languages has been labelled "linguistic genocide" by some scholars.[2] As a result of these abuses perpetrated against Indigenous peoples over the past 200 years, it is estimated that over 90 percent of the world's languages will be extinct by the end of this century.[3] Of the fifty or so Indigenous languages spoken in Canada today, only three—Anishinaabemowin, Cree, and Inuktitut— are predicted to survive into the next century. To put those statistics in sharper context, sixty years ago the only language spoken in my family was Anishinaabemowin. As my mother, along with her brothers and sisters, entered the public school system, they were taught English, which soon became the dominant language spoken at home. Today neither I nor any of my cousins is fluent in Anishinaabemowin, which means that within two generations our ancestral language has been all but eradicated from our family lineage. That is the power and consequence of colonization. Although many Indigenous nations are taking up initiatives to revitalize their ancestral languages, the task is encumbered by a lack of resources to teach those languages effectively. Given that language acquisition is most often a personal choice, there is an argument to be made that the onus to learn one's ancestral language falls squarely on the individual. If not enough people take up that challenge, then the process of colonization will have run its course, and the languages—along with their respective knowledges—will be lost forever.

One of the key forces in the colonization of Indigenous peoples in Canada has been education, with the residential school system being the most obvious example. Ironically, however, it is also education that holds the greatest potential to save Indigenous languages—*if it can be transformed to represent and celebrate Indigenous worldviews, ways of knowing, and pedagogical practices.*[4] Without a significant transformation of how education is practised within Indigenous communities, the loss of Indigenous languages will be inevitable, but it might also signal the loss of Indigenous laws and legal orders, as well as knowledge about the land, which could have drastic consequences in our collective ability to come up with solutions to the global ecological crisis. Therefore, in order to address these mounting concerns, it is essential that Indigenous nations are given the means to establish and administer their own education systems. This is a call that goes back at least as far as Harold Cardinal's rebuttal to the state's proposed "White Paper" in 1970, in which Cardinal demanded "Indian Control of Indian Education."[5] However, if we consider that education was an aspect of negotiations during the time of the Numbered Treaties, then an argument could be made that the struggle for Indigenous control of Indigenous education actually dates back over 150 years. Nevertheless, the difference now is that there seems to be a new catalyst for this type of discourse. The recent work of the Truth and Reconciliation Commission of Canada—with its intensive research on the Indian residential school system and its collection of survivor testimonies of abuse and neglect—has brought forth its Calls to Action and ushered in a new era of Indigenous and Crown relations that of reconciliation. For the goal of reconciliation to be achieved, however, much work remains to be done. In this book, I propose that one way in which reconciliation can be supported is through state recognition and affirmation of the Treaty 3 education law, Kinamaadiwin Inaakonigewin. To date, one of the greatest obstacles in the pursuit of reconciliation has been the state's inability to understand Indigenous laws and ways of being. Kinamaadiwin Inaakonigewin, however, addresses that challenge, such that the Anishinaabe Nation in Treaty #3 has undertaken the task of translating the law from its oral origins into a written document, giving the law the ability to speak and write back—that is, communicate effectively—in a form of logic and language recognized and understood by the settler-colonial state that we know as Canada. This act of self-determination is representative of the resurgence of Indigenous laws and practices that many scholars have called for in postcolonial discourse.[6] At a fundamental level, the law stakes a claim to our inherent jurisdiction in education and addresses the "spirit and intent" of the treaty right to education, while also providing the necessary foundation to support an education system created by Anishinaabe people for Anishinaabe people.

On Colonization

The doctrine of Christianity—that is, in which "the pope had been given total control over the planet by God"[7]—should be considered the original justification that Western civilizations used to colonize Indigenous nations and the lands of those that they entered. From Jerusalem on to Rome, Christianity spread to the colonial nations of Spain, France, and England and from there across the world. With zeal, the colonizers carried and spread their beliefs, which eventually gave them the means to accumulate massive wealth. In fact, European colonizers believed that it was "their mission" to teach their religious and social doctrines to Indigenous peoples under their colonial tutelage.[8] By the turn of the twentieth century, they had succeeded in spreading Christianity to approximately 85 percent of the Earth's inhabited areas in the form of colonies, protectorates, dependencies, dominions, and commonwealths.[9] Resistance to colonization was met with punishing and lethal force. In *A Fair Country: Telling Truths about Canada*, John Ralston Saul points out that, "in the late fifteenth century, there are thought to have been seven to ten million [Indigenous people] in North America, two million of them in Canada. By the end of the nineteenth century, two hundred and fifty thousand were left in the United States, one hundred thousand in Canada—a depopulation of

95 percent."[10] In light of this drastic erasure, the colonizers erroneously concluded that Indigenous people soon would be extinct, leading to the notion of the "vanishing Indian."[11] As such, another ambitious campaign was launched to assimilate the survivors. Most astonishing about this history of genocide, however, is the fact that the colonizers actually believed that their assimilative campaign was somehow an altruistic gesture, an "act of generosity."[12] In Canada, such "generosity" was the justification for the establishment of the residential school system. At a global level, the great literary scholar Edward Said once remarked, "there is an unmistakable coincidence between the experiences of Arab Palestinians at the hands of Zionism and the experiences of those black, yellow, and brown people who were described as inferior and subhuman by nineteenth-century imperialists."[13] The "coincidence" or reality, as Frantz Fanon puts it, is that "Europe's well-being and progress were built with the sweat and corpses of blacks, Arabs, Indians, and Asians. This we are determined never to forget."[14] To that, one could add that Western civilizations have been good at preaching what might be considered good moral behaviour but not so good at practising such behaviour.

Western civilizations' appetite for colonial expansion has served to construct a cultural identity through reference to the other. In *When the Other Is Me: Native Resistance Discourse 1850–1990*, Métis scholar Emma LaRocque explains this identity formation as the "civ/sav dichotomy": "Everything the White man did was legitimized by 'civilization' and everything Indians did was 'explained' by their supposed savagery."[15] This dichotomous relationship is defined by the *difference* between the colonizers and the colonized and the consumption of such difference. Through this consumption of difference —accomplished through laws and policies designed to erase Indigenous knowledge and identity—the cannibalistic nature of colonization and its project of assimilation is revealed. To put it differently, colonization is a Windigo, a hungry, confused, and ill predator. With reference to a Windigo, Anishinaabe scholar Leanne Simpson has written that "the state is seen as having an insatiable hunger for natural resources, to the point where it will eventually destroy itself through over-exploitation."[16] Anishinaabe legal scholar John Borrows adds that Windigos can be either institutions or individuals who prey on Indigenous social, economic, and political infrastructures for their own material gain.[17] Observing these cannibalistic forces over many generations, the Anishinaabe—as well as other Indigenous nations—have embedded protocols in their legal orders for identifying and dealing with Windigo-type situations and behaviours.[18] Interestingly, Edward Said rose to academic prominence in the late 1970s based upon a remarkably similar theoretical discourse called "Orientalism," which he described as

> a distribution of geopolitical awareness into aesthetic, scholarly, economic, sociological, historical, and philological texts; it is an elaboration . . . of a basic geographical distinction (the world is made up of two unequal halves, Orient and Occident). . . . *[I]t is, rather than expresses, a certain will or intention to understand, in some cases to control, manipulate, even to incorporate, what is a manifestly different (or alternative and novel) world*; it is above all . . . a discourse that is by no means in direct, corresponding relationship with political power in the raw, but rather is produced and exists in an uneven exchange with various kinds of power, shaped to a degree by the exchange with power political (as with a colonial or imperial establishment), power intellectual (as with reigning sciences like comparative linguistics or anatomy, or any of the modern policy sciences), power cultural (as with orthodoxies and canons of taste, texts, values), power moral (as with ideas about what "we" do and what "they" cannot do or understand as "we" do).[19]

This "will or intention" by the Occident (the West or, plainer still, the colonizers) to control, manipulate, incorporate, and essentially cannibalize cultural difference is fed through the production and control of ideological apparatuses such as churches, schools, and courts of law, all of which enable the cannibalizing culture to establish and maintain a cultural hegemony. The use of such institutions for the purpose of marginalizing and criminalizing others constitutes an act of what could be labelled colonial racism, in which one culture assumes superiority over another culture based simply upon a binary, categorical difference.

According to Albert Memmi, colonial racism is constructed from three major ideological components: "one, the gulf between the culture of the colonialist and the colonized; two, the exploitation of these differences for the benefit of the colonialist; three, the use of these supposed differences as standards of absolute fact."[20] The main difference between colonizers and colonized used to exploit Indigenous peoples was an attitude toward the land. Whereas Indigenous peoples historically lived off the land in sustainable ways, such that there was minimal environmental impact or disruption, Western civilizations have viewed the land as a commodity, something to be transformed and used for profit: that is, for the accumulation of wealth. In one of the more memorable passages in *The Colonizer and the Colonized*, Memmi describes the difference in ideology: "Nothing could better justify the colonizer's privileged position than his industry, and nothing could better justify the colonized's destitution than his indolence. The colonized doesn't let grass grow under his feet, but a tree, and what a tree! A eucalyptus, an American centenarian oak! A tree? No, a forest!"[21] The implication, of course, is that "improving" or cultivating the land is a good thing and, in fact, a mark of civilized culture, whereas others who remain "in a state of raw nature" are primitive, uncivilized. Edward Said has also commented that this one ideological difference— that is, attitudes toward the land—almost single-handedly provided the justification "by which whole native societies who lived on American, African, and Asian territories for centuries were suddenly denied their right to live on that land."[22] Said goes on to say that the turnover in de facto authority was strikingly fast, for almost as soon as Western civilizations established their institutions they staked claims to the land, "resettling the natives, civilizing them, taming their savage customs, turning them into useful beings under European rule."[23] It was a circumstance that evokes not-so-distant memories of when race biology and social Darwinism were taught as empirical facts in class lectures.

Until the eighteenth century, the diffusion of Western progress was accomplished mainly through the Bible and churches. With the advent of the Enlightenment and the Industrial Revolution, however, Western civilizations began to explain their social progress not through religion but through science, as unquestionable proof of their superiority.[24] Although the scientific method has indeed produced vast streams of knowledge that have benefited humankind and the world, the problem, as Margaret Kovach has argued, is that this knowledge base became privileged to the extent that alternative forms of knowledge were squeezed out almost entirely.[25] To that point, Charles Darwin's evolutionary theories of "survival of the fittest" and "natural selection" were immensely influential and soon inspired an entire academic field of eugenics and ultimately became the justification for state policies of cultural assimilation. In an interesting chapter in *Indigenous Education: New Directions in Theory and Practice*,

Dwayne Donald takes Darwin's evolutionary theory a step further by suggesting that in today's society *homo economicus*, characterized by "neo-liberal understandings of innovation, progress entrepreneurship, competition, success, and well-being in the interests of building an economy," constitutes "the most natural and most developed form of human being in evolutionary terms."[26] I want to be clear in stating that Donald's analysis is less a tacit endorsement of *homo economicus* than an observation of the trajectory of Western values in today's society if such "understandings" persist without intervention.

There is a common belief that the era of colonization is over. This belief maintains that injustices committed against Indigenous peoples are historical and that the passage of time has led to changed circumstances for both the perpetrators and their victims, so there is no need to atone for these transgressions. But make no mistake, the processes of colonization are continuing in all parts of the world, to the extent that corporations are expanding their business enterprises into regions such as deserts, tundra, and rainforests, all of which were regarded previously as inaccessible or worthless but now are turning in immense fortunes.[27] This is a problem, of course, not only for local ecologies—through waste, pollution, and environmental degradation—but also for the Indigenous peoples who still depend directly on the natural environment to support their social, cultural, and spiritual ways of life. And as Canadian scholar James Tully warns in his chapter in *Resurgence and Reconciliation: Indigenous-Settler Relations and Earth Teachings*, "if 'business as usual' continues, the system will destroy the social and ecological conditions that sustain life for most human beings and for hundreds of thousands of other species and ecosystems (the sixth mass extinction)—a set of processes that is well underway."[28] In other words, if capitalism and its Windigo psychosis continue to wreak havoc, then the next extinction level event could be triggered by human ignorance and greed.

Once upon a time, Western civilizations also had a connection to the land similar to Indigenous peoples'; however, Sami scholar Rauna Kuokkanen has argued convincingly that their connection eroded with the beginning of urbanization and capitalism.[29] Karl Marx, in his immensely influential volume *Capital*, marks the beginning of capitalism as a development of thirst for new lands and resources that could be quenched only through force:

The discovery of gold and silver in America, the extirpation, enslavement and entombment in mines of the aboriginal population, the beginning of the conquest and looting of the East Indies, the turning of Africa into a warren for the commercial hunting of black-skins, signaled the rosy dawn of the era of capitalist production. These idyllic proceedings are the chief momenta of primitive accumulation. . . . In England at the end of the 17th century, they arrive at a systematical combination, embracing the colonies, the national debt, the modern mode of taxation, and the protectionist system. These methods depend in part on brute force, e.g., the colonial system. But, they all employ the power of the state, the concentrated and organized force of society, to hasten, hot-house fashion, the process of transformation of the feudal mode of production into the capitalist mode, and to shorten the transition. Force is the midwife of every old society pregnant with a new one. It is itself an economic power.[30]

This process, since identified as *primitive accumulation*, also signalled the beginning of the more common concept of private property. According to David Harvey, author of *The New Imperialism*, primitive accumulation "entailed taking land, say, enclosing it, and expelling a resident population to create a landless proletariat, and then releasing the land into the privatised mainstream of capital accumulation."[31] Given the imperative of conquest, one can see how colonization is considered to be an act of terrestrial domination in which virtually every space in the world is explored, mapped, brought under colonial control, and ultimately transformed into the likeness of the land that the colonizers left behind.

In the present day, Western science has further separated society from nature, to the extent that urbanization and technological innovation have made it increasingly difficult for people to relate to the environment. Many scholars have argued that this alienation from nature has contributed to at least some of the environmental issues that we are experiencing at a global level today.[32] The problem is exacerbated when we consider how critiques of colonial ideologies have tended to focus on people, tantamount to leaving the land to defend itself. Deborah Root has argued that this phenomenon is in fact "symptomatic of a naturalization of the dominant Western view and of the extent to which a distorting lens continues to deflect attention away from our increasing distance from the earth."[33] In a related context, there have been instances in the United States when state departments have proposed constructing parking lots around Indigenous sacred sites in order to make the sites more accessible for tourists, exactly what Joni Mitchell warns against in her sentimental but brilliant song "Big Yellow Taxi." Although the idea of building a parking lot might seem to be relatively innocuous, the loss can be quantified not in dollars or square footage but in the knowledge of a desecration of a sacred place. To put it bluntly, it is like cutting off the nose to spite the face.

"Banking" on Education

Imperialism is an unofficial social policy manifested and supported by ideological apparatuses with the aim and purpose of extending state power and influence in any given territory. In the realm of education, schools have been and continue to be conduits for disseminating the imperialist agenda. This is accomplished in a number of ways, but the most important is that it teaches the language, literature, and history of the colonizer. In Canada, the residential school system continues to stand as the epitome of how the imperialist agenda was disseminated among Indigenous peoples for much of the twentieth century. Although the last residential school closed in 1996, the public school system offers Indigenous students little relief from imperialist pedagogy and discourse. Yet, as an Indigenous person, to forgo the education available is to sentence oneself to a lifetime of hardship and poverty. As of today, Indigenous people who want to obtain jobs to earn some money and make a good living for themselves and their families almost certainly have to learn to bow to the values and customs of their colonizer. Indeed, not only are Indigenous peoples not represented in Canada's education system, but also they are being blocked from producing their own content, to the extent that school boards regulate all aspects of teaching and learning with an iron fist. As Māori scholar Linda Tuhiwai Smith points out, this has had a devastating effect on Indigenous communities since a system that already produces social inequality only exacerbates such inequality for Indigenous peoples.[34] Because schools were designed to teach students about individualism, industry, and the accumulation of wealth, the present situation seems to indicate that the education system is primed for a transformation in values as we collectively search for answers to the burgeoning ecological crisis. In that regard, Indigenous knowledge has much to offer.

The modern education system has existed, relatively unchanged, for about 200 years. The morals and principles taught in schools reflect the structural necessities required of those in positions of power for the purpose of educating and thus establishing a labour force for the production of capital projects. To that point, Louis Althusser has argued that the education system was constructed originally to be used as a state apparatus in order to reduce the cost of policing by producing law-abiding citizens.[35] Aaron Mills comments on this perverse practice of social conditioning, from an Anishinaabe perspective, in these terms:

> It was a gargantuan undertaking to build a citizenry so profoundly ignorant about its historical foundations and about the contemporary cost of sustaining its quality of life. It takes many full-time jobs to keep them misinformed, uneducated, and, once knowing, uninterested in the cost of settler-supremacy for Indigenous peoples. It's a stunning feat of public education and social engineering to have calibrated the sense of citizen entitlement that serves the state's interest, to have generated a national community that will consistently desire and even demand that its federal government offer support during humanitarian crises abroad, while maintaining a casual disinterest in Indigenous suffering in Canada.[36]

In light of these perspectives, it is perhaps easier to see how the public education system was designed to create a labour force to participate in the marketplace and its capitalist enterprises. In other words, the lessons taught at school are most often underlined with an economic imperative. In that sense, education is an act of *depositing* morals and values within students that supposedly enable them to become "productive members of society."

In his classic work *Pedagogy of the Oppressed*, Paulo Freire refers to this system as "banking education," in which there is an oppositional, authoritarian relationship between teachers and students:

> Banking education maintains and even stimulates the contradiction through the following attitudes and practices, which mirror oppressive society as a whole: a) the teacher teaches and the students are taught; b) [the] teacher knows everything and the students know nothing; c) the teacher thinks

and the students are thought about; d) the teacher talks and the students listen—meekly; e) the teacher disciplines and the students are disciplined; f) the teacher chooses and enforces his choice and the students comply; g) the teacher acts and the students have the illusion of acting through the action of the teacher; h) the teacher chooses the program content, and the students (who were not consulted) adapt to it; i) the teacher confuses the authority of knowledge with his or her own professional authority, which she [or] . . . he sets in opposition to the freedom of the students; j) the teacher is the Subject of the learning process, while the pupils are mere objects.[37]

It can almost go without saying that the banking style of education has been an ineffective method of disseminating and translating information for many Indigenous students. The very notion that youth "know nothing" and have nothing to contribute flies in the face of many Indigenous epistemologies. As such, there is a fundamental need to rethink pedagogical practices in the education system and how they might best serve Indigenous students. In response to this need, Freire suggests that a form of "libertarian education" might be more effective, in which students are taught to develop their inherent skills to think critically about how they exist in the world and ultimately to learn that the world is in a constant state of transformation.[38] According to Freire, the basis of libertarian education lies fundamentally in its drive toward reconciliation between the colonizers and the colonized. For him, "education must begin with the solution of the teacher-student contradiction, by reconciling the poles of the contradiction so that both are simultaneously teachers *and* students."[39] This idea is consistent with the more recent analysis of Linda and Keith Goulet, who have written that, "in the aspect of equality, no one is superior to or has authority over another. All knowledge is shared on equal terms no matter who is in the teaching-learning situation, whether it is adults and youth or males and females."[40]

As I stated above, the exclusion of Indigenous content, knowledge, and values in the Western education system has been harmful to Indigenous peoples as well as their communities and the land. At one level, many Indigenous students have reported that they "feel trapped" in choosing between their inherent Indigenous values and the foreign values that they are taught in schools.[41] At the community level, the lack of a relevant

education system for Indigenous peoples has led to lower rates of educational retention and success, which correspond to many other social
problems, such as unemployment, poverty, substandard housing, alcoholism and other addictions, as well as domestic violence. These adverse
social indicators are symptomatic of what some scholars call "trauma-
induced stress," which sometimes is not even detected until years or even
generations later.[42] In light of these circumstances, the need for a relevant
education system within Indigenous communities—one that respects
and honours their traditional values—is an urgent matter. It is a fact not
lost on the people themselves. Harold Cardinal raised this point over fifty
years ago in *The Rebirth of Canada's Indians*: "These schools should have
two goals: (a) providing adequate and appropriate educational opportunity, where skills to cope effectively with the challenge of modern life
can be acquired; (b) creating the environment where Indian identity and
culture will flourish."[43] Yet, even if such an education platform were to be
established, it is only one element of the much larger imperial project that
needs to be transformed, a project designed to strip Indigenous peoples
of their identity, self-determination, and connection to the land. With
regard to that point, Canadian legal scholar Peter Kulchyski has argued
persuasively that there is "a whole set of institutional plans and practices"
in the areas of "health care, housing, infrastructure, justice, family services,
and economic development," all of which "work relentlessly to underwrite
the continuing conquest" of Indigenous peoples and their lands.[44] The
Truth and Reconciliation Commission of Canada has also commented
on this issue, to the extent that it compiled a list of Calls to Action that
address a wide range of social platforms that negatively affect Indigenous
peoples in Canada. Although the government of Canada has promised to
fulfill these calls, it has yet to do so in a meaningful way. The government's
approach to dealing with the calls has been to itemize each one, as if they
were independent of each other, which to my mind is fundamentally at
odds with the spirit and intent of reconciliation.

Other Discontents

One of the main instruments used to colonize and subdue Indigenous
peoples in Canada has been the Indian Act. With its inception in 1876,
and still in effect today, the Indian Act is the federal government's legislated "Indian" policy used to "legitimize" its authority over the political,
social, economic, and cultural aspects of Indigenous peoples and their

communities.[45] Its paternalistic and patriarchal nature has reduced Indigenous peoples from sovereign, self-determining communities to "wards of the state." The Indian Act provides the state with the justification to erase Indigenous identity through its regulation of "Indian" registration, all the while appropriating Indigenous lands and resources for the state's use. As one example, Section 35 of the Indian Act describes a process by which Indigenous peoples can be removed from their communities in the "interest" of the state for the development of public works.[46] It is worth mentioning that the same political objective appears in the Numbered Treaties: "It is further agreed between Her Majesty and Her said Indians that such sections of the reserves above indicated as may at any time be required for Public Works or buildings of what nature soever may be appropriated for that purpose by Her Majesty's Government of the Dominion of Canada, due compensation being made for the value of any improvements thereon."[47] One might attempt to argue that Indigenous nations actually "agreed" to be subject to such relocation, or to the appropriation of their lands, but the logical retort to that argument would be *not without "due compensation."* In fact, this standing policy is similar to archaic notions of *terra nullius* used by colonial agents to displace Indigenous peoples from their lands, to the extent that their occupation and interest in the lands was apparently invisible to the state. For that reason, it is worth observing Article 10 of the United Nations Declaration on the Rights of Indigenous Peoples: "Indigenous peoples shall not be forcibly removed from their lands or territories. No relocation shall take place without the free, prior and informed consent of the indigenous peoples concerned and after agreement on just and fair compensation and, where possible, with the option of return."[48] It should be self-evident, but in light of these long-standing policies I state for the record that the relocation of Indigenous bodies and the appropriation of their land bases, without due compensation, are unethical and unjust practices.

When one considers how Indigenous knowledge and traditions are intimately connected to the land, then one can see how the appropriation of reserve lands through the Indian Act, and perhaps more significantly treaty-related "land surrenders," have created massive chasms in Indigenous identities with regard to how Indigenous ways of life are literally being stripped away and converted to commodities to be bought and sold. The imposition of colonial political structures such as the Indian Act has led to compromised forms of Indigenous government at odds with traditional

Indigenous values. This process has devastated traditional governance systems to the point that the adverse effects of colonization require even more colonial intervention. The irony of the situation, as Glen Coulthard points out, is that "the state's assumed position in these struggles is itself what is contested by many Indigenous claims for cultural recognition."[49] The impoverished state of many Indigenous communities governed in accordance with the Indian Act has led Indigenous scholars such as Taiaiake Alfred to conclude that "institutions and ideas that are the creation of the colonial relationship are not capable of ensuring our survival; this has been amply proven as well by the absolute failure of institutional and legalist strategies to protect our lands and our rights."[50] In other words, Indigenous nations do not want more colonial intervention; rather, they want reconciliation with and resurgence of their traditional practices and epistemologies.

Unfortunately, as unsuccessful as foreign social, economic, and political governance structures have been in Indigenous communities, they are maintained through a combination of coercion and consent. Coercion exists in the sense that Indigenous leaders must do something, with whatever means available, to manage the issues in their communities. In another way, Howard Adams suggests that, because Indigenous peoples are unable to resist the structures placed before them, they become conditioned to accept inferiority as a natural way of life.[51] In *Red Skin, White Masks: Rejecting the Colonial Politics of Recognition*, Coulthard helps to explain this circumstance: "Where colonial rule is not reproduced through violent force alone, the maintenance of settler-state hegemony requires the production of what he [Fanon] liked to call 'colonized subjects': namely, the production of the specific modes of colonial thought, desire, and behavior that implicitly or explicitly commit the colonized to the types of practices and subject positions that are required for their continued domination."[52] To reiterate, "colonized subjects"—sometimes unwittingly—*internalize* colonial thought, desire, and behaviour, facilitating an *implied* consent to their continued domination. Sadly, this is exactly what the colonial regime expects and wants to happen. Coulthard continues that "the long-term stability of a colonial system of governance relies as much on the 'internalization' of the forms of racist recognition imposed or bestowed on the Indigenous population by the colonial state and society as it does on brute force."[53]

In *The Wretched of the Earth*, Frantz Fanon writes that "poverty, national oppression, and cultural repression are one and the same. After a century of colonial domination culture becomes rigid in the extreme, congealed, and petrified."[54] His analysis suggests that state apparatuses, such as the Indian Act, stifle cultural growth and heterogeneous identities. Indeed, Indigenous peoples are commonly depicted in Western literature and media as members of a "timeless traditional culture." From this perspective, Indigenous peoples appear as though they "need" colonial intervention in terms of a moral uplifting to enable their progress toward a recognized and acceptable form of civilization. In contrast, Western civilizations are presumed to possess a fluid, dynamic, and progressive culture that adapts effortlessly to the passage of time. Yet any cultural adaptation undertaken by Indigenous nations to improve their social and economic conditions is commonly viewed as "disingenuous" and "inauthentic" and consequently met with unwarranted criticism and resistance. As Linda Tuhiwai Smith explains, at the heart of such a view as inauthenticity "is a belief that Indigenous cultures cannot change, cannot recreate themselves and still claim to be Indigenous. Nor can they be complicated, internally diverse or contradictory. Only the West has that privilege."[55]

This concept of "timelessness," given its ubiquitous stature in today's society, deserves further analysis. Simply stated, it is not just benign rhetoric but also has significant real-world ramifications. As Deborah Root points out, timelessness "can be valorized and used to underpin a romanticized view of non-Western people, but more commonly it appears as a sign of inferiority and stasis. This has obvious political implications, as it ignores both the transformations that occur and have always occurred within traditional societies and the reality of what change means in a colonial or neocolonial situation."[56] As a prime example, an Indigenous nation might be accused of being disingenuous if it were to codify some of its traditional laws, on the grounds that writing is not a traditional practice for an oral people. In another way, the Indian Act is also strongly implicated in this idea of timelessness with regard to how it maintains a stranglehold on "Indian" identity. With a fundamentally basic—and much maligned—blood quantum formula, the state gets to determine who is eligible for "Indian status," with the end goal of assimilating all "Indians" through legislative extinction. Despite these regulations, Indigenous peoples have been able to escape such extinction because many have subverted the meaning and representation of such policies in their favour.[57] In this way, "Indians" made having a rather arbitrary "status" a constant and visible reminder of the obligations of the state to its treaty partners.

In the context of education, timelessness can be observed time after time when curriculums focus too much on certain aspects of traditional Indigenous material culture, such as bows and arrows, canoes, totem poles, dreamcatchers, igloos, and many other material objects. With such an emphasis on material culture, there is a notion that, if Indigenous people are not wearing buckskin and feathers, they can hardly be considered Indigenous. In this way, schools are complicit in maintaining a settler-colonial hegemony by keeping their focus on the material culture of a people subjected to racism and discrimination instead of expanding their curricular offerings to include more fundamental components of Indigenous knowledge and practices. Moreover, John Borrows has argued that, when Indigenous peoples are put in a situation in which they must subscribe to a pre-existing set of values, doctrines, principles, and laws that have a fundamental a priori criterion, their right to self-determination is diminished.[58] Yet it needs to be said that, despite the immense pressure on Indigenous peoples to remain the same or frozen in time, many of us have actively resisted that false categorization. As Frantz Fanon once said, "we believe the conscious, organized struggle undertaken by a colonized people in order to restore national sovereignty constitutes the greatest cultural manifestation that exists."[59]

Reconciliation

Albert Memmi was right when he said that "we have no idea what the colonized would have been without colonization, but we certainly see what has happened as a result of it."[60] The truth is, as a result of colonization and its Windigo manifestations, many aspects of Indigenous culture—including languages, laws of governance, traditional practices, and relationships to the land—have been severely attacked. To heal these wounds, Indigenous nations must be able to determine for themselves which steps need to be taken. And, if we agree that education is fundamental to understanding, interpreting, and establishing values within society, then control over its institutions must be an integral component of the survival of Indigenous cultures. Fortunately, within the past twenty-five years, a new generation of critical thinkers and Indigenous scholars has emerged to contest the Western canon and neo-liberal ideology of education, helping many Indigenous nations to take important strides to reclaim their self-determination. These scholars are now asserting that "we will no longer be the subjects of objective study; we are the subjects of our own knowledge creation. When we claim our location, we become congruent with Indigenous world views and knowledge, thus transforming our place within research."[61]

In Canada, there is general consensus among Indigenous scholars that the move toward "Indian Control of Indian Education" began in 1969 as a response to the *Statement of the Government of Canada on Indian Policy*, commonly referred to as the "White Paper."[62] Among the issues cogently refuted was the explicit proposal to eliminate treaty rights and all other rights related to special or separate "Indian status." Although the sentiment for the extinguishment of "Indian status" was not new, this veiled progeny still proved to be ugly. The White Paper, as Thomas King has pointed out, draws easy comparisons to the state's previous efforts to assimilate Indigenous peoples in the 1920s, when Duncan Campbell Scott—head of Canada's Department of Indian Affairs from 1913 to 1932—said that "I want to get rid of the Indian problem. Our objective is to continue until there is not a single Indian in Canada that has not been absorbed into the body politic and there is no Indian question, and no Indian department."[63] The difference in 1969, however, was that the state's initiative actually served as a catalyst for the establishment of enduring, or lasting, pan-Indigenous organizations such as the National Indian Brotherhood (NIB), which ultimately became the Assembly of First Nations (AFN).[64] Although such pan-Indigenous institutional mechanisms are inherently flawed political structures, to the extent that it is nearly impossible for a single institutional body to represent adequately the full diversity of all Indigenous nations, they still have an important role—and have had some success—in advocacy on a full spectrum of Indigenous issues. Some of these successes include facilitation and coordination of national and regional discussions, advocacy campaigns, federal legal and policy analysis, and development of communication channels with Canadian governments, the private sector, and the general public.[65]

In response to the White Paper, the Indian Association of Alberta—with support from the National Indian Brotherhood—developed a "Red Paper," published in 1970, that extensively discussed issues related to Indigenous education, including its jurisdiction and control. The Red Paper was a key catalyst in the state's decision to shelve its legislative assimilative agenda temporarily. In addition to arguing for "Indian Control of Indian Education," the Red Paper contended that it was the federal government's fiduciary responsibility to provide adequate funding for education as a result of the treaties that the government had signed. Kanien'kehá:ka scholar Frank Deer also notes that the Red Paper "frequently asserted the importance of traditional perspectives on First Nations life (particularly language and culture), [and] has led to such institutional changes as band-managed schools on First Nations, post-secondary and university educational programs that focus on Indigenous issues, and agencies devoted to Aboriginal child welfare services."[66] Emma LaRocque adds that the movement also served as inspiration for the birth of Native resistance literature: "On the heels of Cardinal came, first, a steady stream of socio-political commentaries, then poetry, and autobiographies."[67] To LaRocque's point, Indigenous-authored books such as *Half-Breed* (1973), *In Search of April Raintree* (1983), and *Slash* (1988) have been instrumental in cultivating a growing awareness of Indigenous history and politics in Canada.[68] The keen eye will note that all three of those books were written by women, a testament to their presence, strength, and influence in Indigenous literature and culture.

In 1991, following a flood of land claims, class action lawsuits, and Indigenous protests, the Royal Commission on Aboriginal Peoples (RCAP) was established to investigate a litany of issues regarding Indigenous peoples' complex status in Canada. In addition to an overwhelming backlog of litigation, the commission was spurred on by recent events, notably the Oka Crisis—essentially about an armed stand-off regarding the proposed development of a golf course on Mohawk burial grounds—and Elijah Harper's filibuster with the Meech Lake Accord. According to Glen Coulthard, Indigenous leaders "overwhelmingly opposed the Meech Lake deal because it failed to recognize the political interests of First Nations."[69] After a five-year investigation, a 4,000-page RCAP report was finally published in 1996. The report noted that in virtually every institutional office that the commission investigated—whether it was education, child and family services, or the justice system—the state was responsible for perpetrating deliberate as well as inadvertent harms against Indigenous peoples by encroaching on their ways of life and ignoring the needs of their communities. It concluded that "in every sector of public life there is an urgent need to liberate Aboriginal initiatives by making room for Aboriginal institutions."[70] RCAP also made forty-four recommendations on Indigenous education, each one pointing to a different issue that Indigenous nations faced in the state's existing education system. Some of these recommendations included "increasing the number of Aboriginal people in education leadership; administrative and support positions; increased access to all levels of education; curriculum that includes Aboriginal perspectives and worldviews; involvement of Elders; Aboriginal language classes; increased mechanisms for family and community involvement and education to combat racism."[71] Unfortunately, the significance of these recommendations was muted by the fact that the state chose to ignore RCAP almost entirely. There is some irony then that, when the Truth and Reconciliation Commission released its final report in 2015 the state praised it enthusiastically, even though the Calls to Action echoed many of the recommendations made by RCAP almost twenty years earlier. Regarding that fact, the TRC's tenth Call to Action states that:

> We call on the federal government to draft new Aboriginal education legislation with the full participation and informed consent of Aboriginal peoples. The new legislation would include a commitment to sufficient funding and would incorporate the following principles:
>
> i.   Providing sufficient funding to close identified educational achievement gaps within one generation
>
> ii. Improving education attainment levels and success rates.
>
> iii. Developing culturally appropriate curricula.
>
> iv. Protecting the right to Aboriginal languages, including the teaching of Aboriginal languages as credit courses.
>
> v.   Enabling parental and community responsibility, control, and accountability, similar to what parents enjoy in public school systems.
>
> vi. Enabling parents to fully participate in the education of their children.
>
> vii. Respecting and honouring Treaty relationships.[72]

One can only hope for the sake of Indigenous communities that have to contend with chronic underfunding and lack of representation within the education system that the state's response to the TRC's Calls to Action will be more substantial than it was for RCAP.

Throughout the 1990s and early 2000s, Indigenous grievances continued to pile up, particularly in relation to the claims of abuse and negligence suffered in residential schools. Unable to skirt the issue any longer, the state came to terms on an Indian Residential Schools Settlement Agreement (IRSSA) in 2006, developed in concert with the AFN and other Indigenous organizations, survivors, and several Christian denominations. At over $5 billion, the IRSSA is the largest class action settlement in Canadian history; it has five components: the Common Experience Payment; the Independent Assessment Process; the Truth and Reconciliation Commission; Commemoration; and Health and Healing Services.[73] The agreement was widely publicized in Canadian media and even elicited a formal apology from Prime Minister Stephen Harper in 2008. In part, the apology stated that, "in the 1870s, the federal government, partly in order to meet its obligations to educate aboriginal children, began to play a role in the development and administration of these schools."[74] The problem, however, as some scholars have pointed out, is that the apology was rather hollow in the sense that it framed the harms and wrongdoings of the residential school system as things of the past and said and did nothing about addressing the structural injustices that continue to inflict harm on Indigenous people.[75] Thomas King has also pointed out that "there was nothing in the apology about treaty violations. Nothing about the theft of land and resources. Nothing about government incompetence, indifference, and chicanery. Nothing about the institutional racism that Aboriginal people have endured and continue to endure."[76] To King's point, whether we are talking about treaty violations, the Indian Act, the White Paper, or the residential school system, each policy sought to subjugate Indigenous peoples and communities, with the ultimate goal of eliminating our rights as people distinguishable from the rest of Canadian society. As such, each one of those policies deserves an apology of its own backed up and affirmed by an appropriate course of action for reconciliation. As King says, "in real life, we expect apologies to be accompanied by a firm purpose of amendment. . . . But in the political world, apologies seem to have little to do with responsibility, and it appears that one can say 'I'm sorry,' and 'I'm not responsible,' in the same breath."[77]

Despite harmful policies that have destroyed Indigenous languages and traditional practices over the past 150 years, many Indigenous people in Canada still have hope that education can liberate their future lives, and they are determined to see education fulfill its potential. However, as Leanne Simpson argues, if reconciliation is going to be considered a worthwhile objective, then it cannot be focused solely on the residential school system; instead, it must be responsive to "the broader set of relationships that generated policies, legislation and practices aimed at assimilation and political genocide."[78] Reconciliation, in this regard, must also account for the state's treaty obligations as well as support Indigenous nations' goals to revitalize our languages, oral histories, and traditional practices in governance and law—all of which were attacked and nearly destroyed by Windigo-type forces.

In *Decolonizing Education: Nourishing the Learning Spirit*, Marie Battiste offers several recommendations for achieving constitutional reconciliation between Indigenous nations and the state. In addition to being an advocate of Indigenous pedagogical practices and the inclusion of Indigenous content within education curriculums, Battiste contends that Aboriginal and treaty rights should be recognized and affirmed by the state as creating "constitutional educational jurisdictions."[79] I interpret this to mean that the treaty right to education should be the basis upon which Indigenous nations have exclusive jurisdiction over the education of their members. If that is so, then recognizing and affirming Indigenous education laws would be instrumental to understanding and acknowledging the scope and depth of such jurisdiction. Battiste further argues that, "combined with antiracism, anti-oppressive, decolonizing, and reconstructing of Aboriginal education, the constitutional provision for affirming Aboriginal and treaty rights offers Indigenous Services Canada and provincial and territorial education systems a framework for renewing First Nations education in Canada."[80] Frank Deer also notes that the development and implementation of education initiatives related to reconciliation must be congruent with the identity of the local community and go beyond curriculum amendment and course content. According to Deer, "pedagogical practices, school climate, community involvement, and language should also be amended to reflect the character of the local community in an effort to address the contested spaces in which Indigenous identity development is situated."[81] In other words, given the vastly different circumstances of Indigenous peoples throughout Canada, it must be recognized that, if Indigenous education is to be reconciled, it ought to take different forms for different nations; a "one size fits all" approach will not work. Hence the need for different Indigenous education laws.

Indigenous peoples are working hard to implement our cultural values and knowledges into existing education systems. Yet, as long as the state continues to maintain its paternalistic control of education, more often than not it is still delivered in a way that ignores Indigenous knowledge. Rauna Kuokkanen has identified this issue as "epistemic ignorance" and observed that it arises at both the institutional level and the individual level, to the extent that Indigenous knowledge continues to be excluded from curriculums on the basis that there is a lack of interest in or understanding of Indigenous cultures.[82] In relation to that, Linda and Keith Goulet have argued that the failure to make changes to curriculums and education programs is also a failure to ensure success for many Indigenous youth.[83] When state institutions fail to show respect for Indigenous knowledges or engage in healthy, responsible relationships as a principle of reciprocity, they are activating their unconscious epistemic ignorance. As Michelle Pidgeon has pointed out, "honouring the principle of reciprocity is not just about offering a one-time program and checking the 'done' box; for many Indigenous communities, it is an ongoing commitment to provide relevant programs and services that evolve with the needs of the community."[84] That is, the reconciliation of Indigenous education is not a list of items that can be checked off as "done"; rather, it is an active process of engagement and unwavering persistence done with the knowledge and input of Indigenous peoples.

Self-Determination

When we think of terms such as "social and political sovereignty" in a colonial context, self-determination is often the basis of those considerations. However, the omnipresence of structural power imbalances necessarily means that the principle of self-determination for Indigenous peoples has been dependent largely on the concentration of colonial relations through a constant cycle of negotiation and compromise with the state. However, in order for self-determination to have any meaningful and positive impact within Indigenous communities, Taiaiake Alfred contends, "we need authentic ideas and intellectual tools" drawn from the heritage of Indigenous peoples, "physical infrastructure, and reinforcement of community cohesion in communications and media and education."[85] Although I agree that maintaining and even revitalizing Indigenous intellectual traditions is important in the quest for self-determination and reconciliation, as Indigenous scholars, policy analysts, and legal practitioners, we must be careful with how the term "authentic" is wielded in academic and political discourse since "authenticity" also carries the notion of "inauthenticity" against which the former is evaluated. As Deborah Root has pointed out, the question of authenticity presupposes "the existence of someone doing the deciding, who presumably is able to stand above the action and choose the good, someone who is likely to be our old friend, the Western subject."[86] Fortunately, the growth of Indigenous scholarship over the past couple of decades has meant that we have begun to assert our knowledge and power and are no longer allowing others to speak in our stead. As Shawn Wilson explains in *Research Is Ceremony: Indigenous Research Methods*, "we are beginning to articulate our own research paradigms and to demand that research conducted in our communities follows our codes of conduct and honours our systems of knowledge and worldviews."[87] When it comes to education, Indigenous peoples must have a voice in articulating the standards and principles that accompany the centring of Indigenous knowledge in any education system as well as the means and resources to demonstrate how our vision for education supports self-determination and the healing of our communities.

There is a fundamental link between self-determination and quality Indigenous education; one cannot exist without the other. Hence, in constructing an education plan based upon Indigenous knowledge, the first principle should be to revitalize Indigenous languages. The main reason for doing so is that every language represents a different knowledge system, and, if any language is lost, then that piece of knowledge is erased indefinitely. The preservation and maintenance of Indigenous languages are thus vital to our collective understandings of place and how we might be able to live harmoniously in an ever-changing global climate. That is not to say that Indigenous people should not learn English, for all of us must navigate our way within a predominantly Western society in which English is the primary language spoken. As Emma LaRocque explains,

> we are in the twenty-first century, and English is as much our
> birthright as our Indigenous languages. English is in many
> respects our new "native" language, not only because English
> may become the only language known to future Native gen-
> erations but also because it has become the common language
> through which we now communicate. English is now serving
> to unite us, and, in many ironic respects, serving to decolonize

us. . . . Since we have a painful and political relationship with
this language, we attend to the task of "reinventing the enemy's
language" as Native American poet Joy Harjo so aptly put it.[88]

Beyond the inclusion of Indigenous languages within education curriculums, however, there also has to be a commitment to other aspects
of our cultures and histories, such as traditional land-based and spiritual
practices, ceremonies, and contributions to Canadian society.

To support such an initiative, all education institutions would be wise
to welcome Elders, knowledge keepers, and workers competent in our
languages and traditional practices and recognized as pedagogical experts.
Elders and other traditional knowledge holders represent a network of
human resources that can support and reinforce the goals of teaching
and learning with students in a culturally responsive way. Parents, too,
must have the right to be involved and make decisions about the lives of
their children, their education, and the values that they grow up with in
their preparation for life. Research by Sheila Cote-Meek has shown that
Indigenous students have spoken at length of the value of having access
to Elders and community members, as well as traditional ceremonies,
medicines, and other culturally relevant supports in their schools, which
has helped them to deal with ongoing colonial violence.[89] Not only are
these measures easy to implement in schools, they are also consistent
with Article 13(1) of the United Nations Declaration on the Rights of
Indigenous Peoples: "Indigenous peoples have the right to revitalize, use,
develop and transmit to future generations their histories, languages, oral
traditions, philosophies, writing systems and literatures, and to designate
and retain their own names for communities, places and persons."[90] On
that note, I mention here that the Canadian government recently drafted
UNDRIP legislation that received royal assent in June 2021, and I will
discuss that development in more detail in the following chapter.

Recently, an academic debate has emerged over the politics of
Indigenous inclusion within dominant education paradigms. Some scholars have suggested that a strong policy of inclusion of Indigenous peoples
at all levels of the administrative ladder is required by governments and
education institutions to lead a successful Indigenous education program.
On one side of the debate, scholars say that "a robust policy of positive and
qualitative inclusion of Indigenous peoples in the societal sphere will have
a significant long-term impact on the forward movement of Indigenous

peoples."[91] On the other side, scholars such as Sandy Grande have pointed out that liberal models of democracy and education use the "politics of inclusion" as an accomplice for the broader project of assimilation.[92] Such models apparently "ignore the historic economic, and material conditions of 'difference,' conspicuously averting the whitestream gaze away from issues of power."[93] Inclusion, in this context, constitutes a "melting pot" that beckons the martyrdom of Indigenous knowledge. Rauna Kuokkanen adds that, when a school includes a course on Indigenous history or readings on Indigenous issues, "it is not building a new knowledge edifice—in terms of transformation, it doesn't amount to much more than changing furniture in the classroom."[94] That is, Indigenous peoples' struggle with education is not necessarily about inclusion in terms of what might be considered enfranchisement in the "new world order" but about the Indigenous project of self-determination and how our knowledges, practices, and peoples are included in the delivery of education programs. There is little doubt that settler-colonial education institutions—including all levels of teachers, administrators, and students—could benefit from some "red pedagogy" in their otherwise black-and-white curriculums; a little colour could go a long way toward repainting a dreary educational picture, but it must be done in such a way that it respects the people who provide that knowledge.[95]

The project of self-determination need not be inimical to Western knowledge and science. Indeed, self-determination, in the context of education, is not about rejecting all theory and/or research on Western knowledge; rather, as Māori scholar Linda Tuhiwai Smith explains, it is about "centring our concerns and world views and then coming to know and understand theory and research from our own perspectives and for our own purposes."[96] Anishinaabe scholar Leanne Simpson adds that "our children live in a very different world than their pre-colonial counterparts, and they have to be able to live and function in (at least) two worlds, so complete immersion into pre-colonial parenting traditions is not only impossible, it is also not desirable."[97] The challenge, then, is to develop what Marie Battiste calls a "trans-systemic" level of analysis and methodological practice that reaches "*beyond* the two distinct systems of knowledge to create fair and just educational systems and experiences so that all students can benefit from their education in multiple ways."[98] Generally speaking, it stands to reason that, if a healthy union between Western and Indigenous knowledges can be achieved in educational settings, then all students stand to benefit from a robust multidisciplinary form of education, particularly in the fields of environmental sciences, humanities, and arts. James Tully, for one, has called this objective "the most important pedagogical task of the twenty-first century if we are to have a sustainable shared future."[99] Thus, if we are to live harmoniously with each other, then all respective knowledges must be respected and cared for—life does not exist within a vacuum.

Political Discontent

Ever since the beginning of the colonial relationship, Western knowledge—as observed through the social institutions of education and law—has always been valorized, whereas Indigenous knowledge has been denigrated. As Frantz Fanon once said, "the customs of the colonized, their traditions, their myths, especially their myths, are the very mark of this indigence and innate depravity."[100] Yet Western myths and folklore have been and continue to be accepted—and even venerated—as rich and dynamic aspects of their histories, serving as the backbones of their cultures. A primary reason for this is the value that has been attributed to the written word. There is a sense of superiority given to a written text that supersedes the oral tradition in terms of how these different sources of information are measured as forms of empirical knowledge. John Ralston Saul has also observed that in Canada and the United States there is an unhealthy obsession with written texts in academic institutions, to the extent that credible sources become increasingly more exclusionary as one ascends the hallowed ranks of academia.[101] Not only do written texts serve to embody or express what is best in society, but also they define what is acceptable and legitimate in society, insofar as mass culture is concerned. Janice Acoose sheds more light on this social phenomenon in her book *Iskwewak: Neither Indian Princesses nor Easy Squaws*: "More than literary art belonging to an unreal or metaphysical realm whose aesthetic qualities please the reader, literature is powerfully political because it persuades and influences the oftentimes unsuspecting reader. Because it absorbs and conforms, in varying degrees, to place of origin, political and nationalistic agenda, literature manifests ideology and expresses the dominant group's economic, philosophic, religious, and political codes and conventions."[102] To reiterate, the writing of literature, as well as history and law, is a political act that not only influences but also maintains social order and hierarchy. It is a striking reminder of what Gerald Vizenor once quipped: "What has been published and seen is not what is heard or remembered in oral stories."[103]

Although academic institutions might see themselves as being neutral, or part of an inclusive international community, it is clear that schools at all levels are implicated in the historical processes of imperialism and colonization—but they are not alone. Advocates of the justice system have long insisted that the law is impartial, neutral, and free from or above moral complicity, but as Anishinaabe legal scholar John Borrows points out, it is not. In *Law's Indigenous Ethics*, Borrows explains that lawyers and judges often make "implicit appeals to truth, faith, belief, speculation, logic (which always involves emotional calibration of how we perceive the world)" and are in fact "omnipresent in Canadian legal reasoning."[104] Borrows goes on to suggest that even the Supreme Court does not occupy a neutral space in its decision-making processes, for historically it has placed economic imperatives above Indigenous peoples' concerns about land-based and cultural appropriation. According to Borrows, "the Court's own assumptions, tenets, and actions spread world views about life's purposes despite their seeming silence as to these questions, or other claims to the contrary."[105] To understand better the inherent biases of institutions of law and education and the power structures that they support, it is important to consider how they determine which information counts as truth and knowledge, as well as how such information is produced and whose interests are served by it, and in doing so one likely will find that the sources of information that they support are definitely not neutral.

Despite decades of dispossession and exclusion, Indigenous oral traditions continue to be vibrant sources of knowledge and have more than enough potential to find solutions to complex legal questions and educational issues. As I have shown above, however, the dispossession and exclusion of Indigenous knowledges were, and continue to be, justified through the establishment and enforcement of racist laws and policies designed to deny Indigenous self-determination. The presence of these laws and policies has made the pursuit of Indigenous control of Indigenous education a political endeavour, especially when we consider that such education will be designed to support Indigenous nations' social, economic, and political aspirations. Nevertheless, in spite of whatever challenges might arise from the state, in terms of contesting settler-colonial hegemony, I expect that Indigenous nations will continue to push for localized education systems that align with their values and interests, so that our histories, ceremonies, and traditional practices are not forgotten. In that regard, Sandy Grande has argued that Indigenous education must make no claim to political neutrality but steadfastly engage in "a method of analysis and social inquiry that troubles the capitalist, imperialist aims of unfettered competition, accumulation, and exploitation."[106] Gina Starblanket and Heidi Stark have argued similarly that the key to presenting Indigenous knowledge is to place it in contrast to tools or systems of oppression:

> It is most useful to understand Indigenous modes of relating as presenting a *challenge* to modernity that calls into question its hegemonic claims and highlights the destructive and oppressive nature of its inherent logic by way of contrast, while also creating specific opportunities to bring forward the values and precepts underlying our traditional laws and values within contemporary contexts. Rather than getting discouraged by the seeming futility of enacting past practices in the present, we might instead understand these practices as the embodiment of values and beliefs that were given life in the past in relation to particular contexts, that have lived on in spite of efforts explicitly aimed at their erasure or assimilation, and that can continue to be given life anew.[107]

It is worth noting that this assertion has been met with some resistance from non-Indigenous educators who have complained that Indigenous education is taught with bias.[108] But as Rauna Kuokkanen has pointed out, this form of resistance is an example of the push toward "racelessness" within education programs in Canada, which have the effect of maintaining Western normativity and settler-colonial dominance.[109] Shawn Wilson likewise adds to this insight, stating that culture "is an important part of how all people think and know (not just Indigenous people). Once we recognize the importance of the relational quality of knowledge and knowing, then we recognize that all knowledge is cultural knowledge. The foundations of this cultural knowledge guide the way that our societies come to be formed."[110] In other words, it is impossible for the production and dissemination of knowledge to be acultural or non-political, but perhaps we can mitigate the negative effects of these circumstances just by being aware of and respecting our relationality with each other and the land that we share.

The Assembly of First Nations has estimated that there are about 70,000 Indigenous youth living in their communities and attending community schools across Canada who do not have access to the same standard of education programs and services available to non-Indigenous students. As evidence of this fact, a report from the Fraser Institute in 2013 found that on average provincial governments spent about $10,000 per student on education, whereas the federal government spent only about $7,000 per Indigenous student.[111] Consequently, a pre-existing achievement gap actually has widened because of increased investment in non-Indigenous populations, whereas Indigenous communities continue to face chronic underfunding. According to Dawn Zinga, "the national and provincial trends indicate that Indigenous youth ages 12–18 tend to leave school before completing high school, and drop-out rates among Indigenous youth aged 15 and over are reported at 40% in comparison to 13% rates for their non-Indigenous counterparts."[112] Exacerbating this problem is the fact that the Indigenous population in Canada is experiencing a boom, which means that more Indigenous youth will be in classrooms at all levels in the future. In light of these statistics, it seems to be obvious that, if the state is serious about achieving equity in educational achievement, then a commitment to the principle of equal funding must be adopted. Linda and Keith Goulet similarly have pointed out that equity can be achieved only when there is equality "in staff salaries and benefits as well as infrastructure, including up-to-date technologies; quality curriculum resources, including those that support Indigenous languages and cultures; specialized programming to support students with special needs; and access to specialized programs to expand student life choices in science, sports, and the arts."[113] Notwithstanding the Goulets' otherwise valid point is the fact that isolated northern and remote Indigenous communities—which I discuss in more depth in Chapter 3—will require even more funding than urban areas to provide the same quality of education.

Transforming the Education System

For Indigenous nations to achieve their goals in education, a "transformative model of redistribution" must be pursued. In addition to extra funding, Glen Coulthard explains, transformative models of education seek to "correct unjust distributions of power and resources *at their source*; that is, they not only seek to alter the *content* of current modes of domination and exploitation, but also the *forms* that give rise to them."[114] The first step in this transformative process should involve a thorough examination of every subject at every grade level in every school in order to determine how and to what extent the current content and pedagogical practices reflect the presence of Indigenous knowledge. As Jean-Paul Restoule and Angela Nardozi have pointed out, "the notion that Indigenous content belongs only in a specific grade level or a particular subject area is a privileged one, and one that takes for granted the dominance of Euro-Western perspectives on all subjects, not just history and social studies."[115] Training on cultural sensitivity is needed too. After receiving such training, educators (both administrators and teachers) should also examine themselves through a process of self-reflection—which includes an honest interrogation of one's own prejudices—to ensure that the status quo and the systems that perpetuate ideological views rooted in colonization are dismantled.[116] In *Dancing on Our Turtle's Back: Stories of Nishnaabeg Re-Creation, Resurgence and a New Emergence*, Leanne Simpson describes what a process similar to this looks like from an Anishinaabe perspective: "*Biskaabiiyang* is a verb that means to look back. In this context it means 'returning to ourselves,' a process by which Anishinabek researchers and scholars can evaluate how they have been impacted by colonialism in all realms of being. Conceptually, they are using *Biskaabiiyang* in the same way Indigenous scholars have been using the term 'decolonizing'—to pick up the things we were forced to leave behind, whether they are songs, dances, values, or philosophies, and bring them into existence in the future."[117]

Another way in which educators can help to transform the education system is through active engagement with the community and attendance at appropriate social events, which would facilitate better communication with parents, Elders, and other Indigenous community members in order to address outstanding educational issues. As public intellectuals, educators at all levels of education are saddled with an enormous responsibility to excel in teaching, research, and service. Within the context of Indigenous education, however, educators also bear a responsibility to ensure that their education programs are relevant directly to and centred on the needs of local Indigenous communities. To put it differently, educators carry a heavy burden in the pursuit of decolonization since they are literally on the front line of the transformational process.

At the institutional level, traditional customs and ceremonies should be respected and honoured on all campuses and schoolgrounds. Frank Deer has commented that the integration of Indigenous identity and knowledge within education institutions can be enhanced "by school-based interventions that include language exploration, content, and academic themes and topics that are reflective of Indigenous knowledge and traditional pedagogies."[118] The inclusion of traditional customs and ceremonies can be considered a form of creating space—physically, theoretically, and conceptually—in education institutions. As Patricia Johnston points out, it is a process that includes "the active recognition and practice of worldviews and knowledge bases that are distinctly Indigenous, which encompass the ways in which Indigenous Peoples think about the world, articulate their relationships with it, and aspire to their own self-determinations and developments."[119] Johnston further suggests that "creating space" is also about "vacating space" by members of dominant groups and accepting Indigenous peoples' inherent rights to ownership of their own knowledges, cultures, and worldviews. In this regard, vacating space is about "recognizing that those referred to in the 'walk' (research), the 'talk' (policy), and the 'chalk' (teaching) might like to occupy those spaces themselves."[120]

Summary

In Paulo Freire's immortal words, "the pedagogy of the oppressed is a pedagogy which must be forged *with*, not *for*, the oppressed (whether individuals or nations) in the incessant struggle to regain their humanity."[121] This "incessant struggle," as discussed, is predicated on "difference." In being defined literally by our difference, our very existence as Indigenous peoples is thus dependent on the survival of what makes us different, but this difference includes more than just cultural practices; it also includes how we use our land base, apply our laws, and govern our communities. Properly understanding and appreciating our difference from Western society means recognizing and respecting the fact that different histories exist and can support different pathways to alternative forms of knowledge. When it comes to addressing the "epistemic ignorance" that prevails within today's social institutions, Rauna Kuokkanen argues that the primary issue is gaining the *acceptance* of Indigenous "intellectual conventions" as well as the protection of this knowledge from the practices and discourses that historically have excluded and marginalized them in ideological apparatuses.[122] The difference of Indigenous knowledges offers an alternative to a neo-liberal, capitalist understanding of the world with regard to the establishment of healthy relationships between peoples and the land built upon principles of reciprocity and respectful coexistence. Leanne Simpson has pointed out that Anishinaabe strategies for dispute resolution, restorative justice, and international diplomacy have been consistent throughout history and aim "to restore balance, justice and good health to our lands and our peoples based on respect for our sovereignty, independence and jurisdiction over our territories."[123]

The process of colonization—with its Windigo psychosis—has severely damaged Indigenous social institutions. Decolonization has been slow and arduous, especially as we work within institutional structures of the dominant culture, but one way to subvert the power of these institutions is to revitalize our traditional laws and practices. And, as Simpson has forcefully argued throughout her career, "we do not need funding to do this. We do not need opportunity to do this. We need our Elders, our languages, and our lands, along with vision, intent, commitment, community and ultimately, action."[124] The key to Indigenous cultural resurgence rests in the hands of our own people, who can identify the ways in which we can use our traditional laws to eradicate our systemic oppression. That said, our cultural resurgence does not mean a return to the past, an impossible undertaking anyway; rather, it is the recreation of cultural and political autonomy that we enjoyed in the past in order to support the well-being of our people today. In the last analysis, Indigenous peoples' own laws and traditions of governance can and should be applied in the pursuit of reconciliation and decolonization. These tools and practices can lead not only to creative but also to culturally respectful, responsible, and relevant solutions to complex problems, particularly in the field of education. In this chapter, I have shown that Indigenous languages have been under constant threat and that there is a dire need to transform the existing education system in Canada. One way in which this can be accomplished is through the revitalization and application of Indigenous laws, which will provide Indigenous nations—particularly the Anishinaabe Nation of Treaty #3—with the foundation required to establish our own education system, according to our own traditions of governance and self-determination. In the following chapters, I will provide further justification for this process as well as discuss what an Indigenous education law might look like for those who wish to pursue it.

Chapter 2

INDIGENOUS LAWS AND THE STATE

Self-determination cannot be given or taken away. It is an act of conviction that resides in the heart of every individual, and it is cultivated through the cohesion of community values, customary practices, and education. From a collective standpoint, self-determination is the means by which nations exercise their right to freedom in the face of tyranny and oppression. As John Borrows and James Tully have observed, self-determination "is deployed by communities as a force for reclaiming and reconnecting with traditional territories by means of Indigenous ways of knowing and being. These individual and collective powers include the resurgence of governance, Indigenous legal systems and languages, economic and social self-reliance, and sustainable relationships with the ecosystems that co-sustain all life and well-being."[1] Despite seditious attempts by the Canadian state to undermine Anishinaabe governance and cultural sovereignty through Windigo-type mechanisms such as the Indian Act and the residential school system, the will of our people—and *others* around the world—is alive and strong.[2] For the Anishinaabe Nation in Treaty #3, the strength of our conviction is in the knowledge that all sacred gifts, including our cultural sovereignty and nationhood, as well as our inherent jurisdiction to governance, are bestowed on us by the Creator and our ancestors. According to Treaty 3 Elder Fred Kelly, this truth is preserved and maintained in our unwritten constitution. Elder Kelly says that our constitution is derived from our knowledge of "the four directions, four levels of sky, four layers of earth, the feathers, the four drums, the four lodges, petroglyphs and pictographs, songs, dances, birchbark scrolls and in so many other sacred things, places and ceremonies."[3] That said, it is our position, as the Anishinaabe Nation in Treaty #3, that our cultural sovereignty and right to self-determination were recognized in the "nation-to-nation" agreement with the Canadian state, known commonly as Treaty 3, the Northwest Angle Treaty of 3 October 1873.[4] The treaty established a unique constitutional relationship, which simultaneously established the Anishinaabe Nation in Treaty #3 as a distinct nation. As Elder Kelly says, "the principal effect of the Treaty is the sharing of sovereignty. By making the Treaty with Canada, the Nation acknowledged the sovereignty of the Queen and effected the exercise of its jurisdiction accordingly. By making the Treaty with the Nation, Canada acknowledged the sovereignty of the Nation and effected the exercise of its jurisdiction accordingly."[5] This point is substantiated by the fact that, during the Treaty 3 negotiations, Treaty Commissioner Alexander Morris told Treaty 3 leaders that "I wish to treat with you as a Nation, not as separate bands."[6] In this chapter, I will show that several forms of external jurisprudence, including Canadian case law, the United Nations Declaration on the Rights of Indigenous Peoples, and the Truth and Reconciliation Commission's Calls to Action, all support our right to autonomous governance, especially as it relates to the treaty right to education. That said, it is the will of the Anishinaabe Nation in Treaty #3 to exercise this right through a revitalization of our traditional education law, Kinamaadiwin Inaakonigewin, in a written form. We believe that this will enable our people to establish our own education system for the benefit of our children, and our children's children, so that they can live a good Anishinaabe life, mino-bimaadziwin.[7]

On Writing

In the previous chapter, I discussed how cultural difference was used to exploit, manipulate, and expropriate Indigenous peoples' relationships with their lands, thereby facilitating the construction of cultural identities for both the colonizers and the colonized. With most Indigenous nations being primarily oral cultures, one way by which colonization achieved its capitalist ends was through the written word. According to the eminent critical theorist Jacques Derrida, "it has long been known that the power of writing in the hands of a small number, caste, or class, is always contemporaneous with hierarchization, let us say with political *différance*; it is at the same time distinction into groups, classes, and levels of economico-politico-technical power, and delegation of authority, power deferred and abandoned to an organ of capitalization."[8] Cultural anthropologists have long assumed that there are societies with writing and those without it, and it is the presence of writing that gives societies the glorified status of "civilization." As one example of this fact, in *Tristes tropiques*, Claude Lévi-Strauss writes that, "after eliminating all other criteria which have been put forward to distinguish between barbarism and civilization, it is tempting to retain this one at least: *there are peoples with, or without, writing*; the former are able to store up their past achievements and to move with ever-increasing rapidity towards the goal they have set themselves, whereas the latter, being incapable of remembering the past beyond the narrow margin of individual memory, seem bound to remain imprisoned in a fluctuating history which will always lack both a beginning and any lasting awareness of an aim."[9] Thus, in his estimation, it is the absence of recognizable writing—that is, linear, phonetic notation—that makes Indigenous peoples uncivilized or barbaric and therefore justifies their exploitation. Put another way, no writing equals no history, and no history equals no law. In this regard, settler-colonial common laws, treaties, and construction of canons of recognized knowledge systematically have enabled Western civilizations, through their state apparatuses, to prevent Indigenous nations from being sovereign, free peoples and to make them slaves and prisoners on their own lands.

In *Of Grammatology*, Derrida rejects the claim that there are societies without writing, because for him writing is inscribed within the structure and use of a society's language.[10] To that point, Anishinaabe legal scholar Aimée Craft explains that Anishinaabe law is not codified, but it is taught through the oral tradition, such that laws are "infused and contained in the *Anishinabemowin* language and passed down through the teachings related to *mino-bimaadiziwin* (leading a good life)."[11] Thus, it is the *structure* of Anishinaabemowin—being verb based, so that every word is not just a word but also a concept or an idea or a way of life—and the way that it is *used* that give the language a presence of writing. That said, if writing can be conceived of as something other than linear and phonetic notation, perhaps as a *device to articulate history and law*, then we can see, as Derrida does, that "no reality or concept would therefore correspond to the expression 'society without writing.'"[12] To put this idea in better context, Peter Kulchyski, in his aptly titled article on "bush writing," has argued that trails on a trapline constitute a form of writing, as does the name of any given location or a design on clothing or a housing structure, each of which has a set of local stories and knowledge attributed to its being.[13] Furthermore, if we consider language as a form of *exchange*, such that it is employed through human interaction, and that there is always some level of give and take, then we can also see that there are economic connotations by which language is given a property of law. According to Derrida, the word *economy* comes from the Greek words *oikos* and *nomos*, which literally translate into the term "property" or "exchange law": "Among its irreducible predicates or semantic values, economy no doubt includes the values of law (*nomos*) and of home (*oikos*, home, property, family, the hearth, the fire indoors). Nomos does not only signify the law in general, but also the law of distribution (*nemein*), the law of sharing or partition (*partage*), the law as partition (*moira*), the given or assigned part, participation. . . . Besides the values of law and home, of distribution and partition, economy implies the idea of exchange, of circulation, of return."[14] In other words, not only is there no reality that corresponds to the idea of *societies without writing*, but also we can conclude that *there are no societies without their own laws*. By virtue of possessing and using their own languages, Indigenous nations effectively practise their own laws. As Treaty 3 Elder Fred Kelly pointed out to me, "the Constitution of Great Britain is not written, and many other constitutions are not written. Our traditional constitution is also not written. Before the treaty, there was no need to explain the constitution, the people just lived it. Now it is becoming an urgent matter of survival. That is why it must be taught and relearned."[15] *Writing*, in the common sense of the word, is therefore not a necessary element of law; more so, it is a useful instrument to communicate between laws or different languages.

The Anishinaabe Nation in Treaty #3

The oral tradition, in Anishinaabemowin, affirms that our laws and ways of knowing the world were given to us by the Creator "when Kizhe Manito came down through the star constellation, Paagonekishig, the Hole in the Sky."[16] Etymologically, the word *anishinaabe*, meaning "man," is derived from the word *niisinaabe*, meaning "descended." It is said that the Creator, upon descension, provided the Anishinaabe with "original instructions," which came to be recognized as "sacred law." Indigenous legal scholar Diane Longboat explains that "sacred laws speak of the origins of life and creation and the evolution of human beings with their gifts, duties and responsibilities, moral and ethical codes of behaviour, challenges to the human spirit, and ceremonies and medicines to strengthen the journey of life."[17] In Anishinaabemowin, "sacred law" means Kagagiwe Inaakonigewin, which represents the first order of Anishinaabe law. Kagagiwe Inaakonigewin forms the basis of the Anishinaabe constitution, the sanctity of which is preserved in the oral tradition and is thus forbidden to be written (in the narrow sense of phonetic notation). As Elder Kelly says, "the oral constitution is an invaluable cultural and legal asset. It is sacred and not a matter for negotiation. The Anishinaabe citizens must see that Canada's insistence on a written constitution will not be necessary. The constitution should remain unwritten."[18] This view is supported by Justices A.C. Hamilton and C.M. Sinclair in *The Justice System and Aboriginal People: Report of the Aboriginal Justice Inquiry of Manitoba*: "There were and are Aboriginal laws. There were and continue to be Aboriginal governments with lawmaking powers and with provisions to enforce those laws. There were and are Aboriginal constitutions that are the supreme 'law of laws' for some Aboriginal peoples and their nations."[19] With regard to Kagagiwe Inaakonigewin, Elder George Kakeway further explains that the Creator, Kizhe Manito, "gave us the sacred duty to provide care and protection for all life on the lands, in the soil, skies, and water in our territory."[20] Elder Kakeway also says that sacred law provides our people with instructions on how to practise disciplines such as "medicine, science, technology, engineering, health, transportation, food security, economy, weather readings, environmental concerns, mining, forestry, animal harvesting, fishing, water conservation, land restoration, climate change, kinship and social customs."[21] In short, Kagagiwe Inaakonigewin provides the Anishinaabe with our worldview and the knowledge with which to sustain our way of life on the "land," aki.

The second of four orders of Anishinaabe law is Kete Inaakonigewin or "traditional law." Like sacred law, traditional law is not permitted to be "written," in the common use of the term. Kete Inaakonigewin is observed by Anishinaabe Elders and traditional knowledge holders who participate in ceremonial and spiritual practices such as the sweat lodge and shaking tent. There are several organized Anishinaabe societies, such as the Midewi'win, Waabanowin, and Jiisakiiwin, that are custodians of sacred law and traditional law. These societies have been maintained over many generations—even throughout the time that such organizations were banned under the Indian Act in the early part of the twentieth century—and are dedicated to the preservation and protection of traditional Anishinaabe laws as well as to the maintenance of cultural protocols in ceremonies and special events.

The third order of Anishinaabe law is Anishinaabe Inaakonigewin or "customary law." It is most often practised by community members who maintain a strong connection to the land through the maintenance of customary practices such as fishing, hunting, trapping, and food harvesting. Some important principles of Anishinaabe Inaakonigewin are key reference points for our beliefs on environmental sustainability, which include do not take more than what is needed, use all of which is taken, hunt and fish during the appropriate seasons, and ensure that the next generation can also enjoy the bounty of the land. Unlike sacred law and traditional law, deeply rooted in creation and tradition, as their names imply, Anishinaabe Inaakonigewin can be adapted for contemporary circumstances, and some aspects of it may be written down, as opposed to being maintained strictly through ceremony, storytelling, and other traditional practices.

The fourth order of Anishinaabe law is Ozhibiige Inaakonigewin, which translates into "written temporal law." As the last order of law, the distinguishing feature of Ozhibiige Inaakonigewin is its phonetic form of representation. Apart from its written form, its most important aspect is that it must conform to, and be consistent with, all of the principles inherent to the other three orders of Anishinaabe law. Written temporal laws are most often employed to harmonize with the administration of other laws (e.g., Crown laws). According to the Grand Council Treaty #3, the traditional government of the Anishinaabe Nation in Treaty #3, "in modern times, we have felt the need to write down some especially important laws given the shared jurisdiction of territory and people in the 55,000 square miles dealt with under Treaty #3."[22] Following Elders' gatherings in Kay-Nah-Chi-Wah-Nung at Manito Ochi-waan on 22 and 23 April 1997 and on 31 July 1997, the first written temporal law— Manito Aki Inakonigaawin or the "Great Earth Law"—was approved and petitioned for ratification by the National Assembly of Chiefs. Accordingly, the Anishinaabe Nation in Treaty #3—with the approval of Elders in traditional ceremony and subsequently ratified by the National Assembly—officially proclaimed this law effective on 3 October 1997. Manito Aki Inakonigaawin establishes that the Anishinaabe Nation in Treaty #3 "maintains rights to all lands and water in the Treaty # 3 territory commonly referred to [as] Northwestern Ontario and south-eastern Manitoba. Accordingly, any development in the Treaty # 3 Territory such as, but not limited to, forestry, mining, hydro, highways and pipeline systems that operate in the Treaty # 3 Territory require the consent, agreement and participation of the Anishinaabe Nation in Treaty # 3."[23] The Anishinaabe Nation in Treaty #3 is currently in the process of developing and ratifying several other written temporal laws relating to our inherent jurisdiction of governance. Two of them address child care and health care within our nation. Another law being developed, and the focus of this book, is Kinamaadiwin Inaakonigewin or education law.

Indigenous peoples have yearned, for many years, for an education system that respects our traditional knowledge and values, ever since it has become clear that the existing system in Canada does not meet our needs and desires. Parents, Elders, as well as community leaders have all noticed that many of our youth experience a sense of isolation, rejection, and anxiety when they attend the public school system, which does not reflect our cultural value system. As I mentioned in the previous chapter, those negative experiences often lead to poor academic performance. Adding to this problem is the unwillingness of the government of Canada to reach an agreement that would support constructive changes to the education system for the benefit of Indigenous youth. Dene scholar Glen Coulthard argues that this is because the state wants to "facilitate the 'incorporation' of Indigenous people and territories into the capitalist mode of production."[24] Given the state's reluctance to adopt any transformational measure in the field of education on its own merit, I will discuss some historical events that support Indigenous nations' inherent rights to education—including the jurisdiction to govern and administer our own education systems—that I hope will serve as justification for addressing these concerns meaningfully.

On Treaties

There are four distinct eras of treaty making on the land now known as Canada. The first era is the *Precontact Era*, which predates the era of colonization and is distinguished by the fact that it is still preserved, maintained, renegotiated, and resettled through the oral traditions of many Indigenous nations today. Two of the most prominent examples of treaties from this era are related to the formation of the Three Fires Confederacy, a long-standing alliance among the Anishinaabe, Odawa, and Potawatomi Nations dating back to a meeting at Michilimackinac on Manitoulin Island in 796 AD, and the Haudenosaunee Confederacy, initially composed of the Mohawk, Oneida, Onondaga, Cayuga, and Seneca Nations, until the Tuscarora Nation joined the confederacy in 1722.[25] All across Turtle Island—which is to say North America—there are many more such nation-to-nation agreements.

The second era of treaty making could be considered as the *Peace and Friendship Era*, which sometimes involved written agreements between colonial agents (mostly English and French) and various Indigenous nations east of the Mississippi River. On its official website, the government of Canada acknowledges that it signed such treaties with the Mi'kmaq, Maliseet, and Passamaquoddy Nations before 1779.[26] Other treaties from the Peace and Friendship Era include the Kaswentha (1613) and the Treaty of Niagara (1764), each represented by its own wampum belt, which, I note, constitutes another form of Indigenous writing. Regarding the Kaswentha, Audra Simpson explains in *Mohawk Interruptus: Political Life across the Borders of Settler States* that, though it was negotiated initially between the Haudenosaunee and the Dutch, the Kaswentha was recognized in fact by other Indigenous and European nations—including the English and French—"and in their earliest stages, the United States and Canada."[27] In addition to being internationally recognized, another important aspect of Peace and Friendship treaties is that they did not involve land transfers, and usually, they did not include any other payments besides gift distributions.

The third era of treaty making, and the one of most relevance to this book, is the *Confederation Era*. This era most often refers to the post-Confederation Numbered Treaties but includes treaties such as the Robinson-Huron and Robinson-Superior Treaties from 1850, notably because the Robinson Treaties were the templates for the Numbered Treaties. Collectively, these treaties have written documents officially recognized by the state, and they are distinguished by a phrase similar to "the Indians inhabiting the district hereinafter described and defined, do hereby cede, release, surrender and yield up to the Government of the Dominion of Canada for Her Majesty the Queen and Her successors forever, all their rights, titles and privileges whatsoever, to the lands included within the following limits," as is written in Treaty 3.[28] The Confederation Era treaties are especially notable because they are the means by which the Confederation of Canada—by right of the royal monarch in Great Britain—validated its previously illegitimate claim to sovereignty, which had depended on racist doctrines of "discovery" and "terra nullius." I will discuss these treaties at more length in the pages that follow.

The fourth era of treaty making in Canada is the *Modern Era*, which began with the James Bay and Northern Quebec Flood Agreement in 1975. So-called modern treaties are settlement agreements with the government of Canada that sometimes began as lawsuits by Indigenous nations in the form of comprehensive land claims. Whereas Confederation Era treaties are silent on issues of Indigenous self-governance, Modern Era treaties are distinguished by the legalism employed to limit Indigenous nations' rights. As Peter Kulchyski explains, "while comprehensive land claims are constitutionally defined as treaties, and hence have constitutional status and protection, a clause in the self-government section of the claim ensures that the whole section does not have such protection, nor does any agreement negotiated as a result of the section."[29] According to Kulchyski, "some of the highly paid staff on the ironically named Justice Department in the federal government came up with a two-word solution to that problem and the solution then found its way into all the land claims that followed. All their Aboriginal claims, *if any*. Even in the moment of surrender of Aboriginal title, the very instant of extinguishment that so much energy is spent achieving, the government has not entirely recognized that such title ever existed or had legal force."[30]

The legalism by which the Canadian state continually attempts to strip Indigenous nations of their inherent rights is a strategic hallmark that has come to define treaties in both the Confederation Era and the Modern Era. Nevertheless, the process continues as Indigenous nations continue to stack up comprehensive land claims in the hope of reaching a fair agreement that recognizes their inherent rights to self-governance and self-determination. In this regard, there have been substantial changes in the comprehensive land claims process, as well as in federal policy that has benefited Indigenous nations, since 1975. As one example, newer settlement agreements such as the Nisga'a Final Agreement (1998) now include constitutionally protected self-government agreements, as long as the Indigenous nation agrees to the application of Canada's Charter of Rights and Freedoms. It is worth noting that in every era of treaty making Indigenous nations relied on their own laws and protocols—as much as on what has been written—when negotiating these nation-to-nation agreements and that these practices were observed and adhered to by the nations that they treated with, including the Canadian state.

Many people in Canada are aware that a treaty relationship exists between the federal government and Indigenous peoples, and some probably even know about the tumultuous history of the treaties, but very few understand that they actively contribute to the frayed relationship simply by maintaining the status quo. A number of scholars, both non-Indigenous and Indigenous, have pointed out that much of the discord in the treaty relationship has to do with a fundamental gap in mutual understanding of what treaties actually represent or signify.[31] Similarly, Aimée Craft has argued that this discord stems from the uncoordinated operation of two distinct legal systems in treaty making, interpretation, and implementation.[32] As a result, many Canadians believe that treaties are merely documents that catalogue limited sets of rights in exchange for title to specific tracts of land. Harold Cardinal has argued, conversely, that, "to Indian people, the actions of the colonial powers in entering into treaties with Indian peoples were an acknowledgement of sovereignty and a recognition of Indian rights to the land."[33] The notion of rights in treaties is prevalent in treaty discourse and rightly so. John Borrows and Michael Coyle, among other scholars, assert that "treaties first and foremost are concerned with right relations between First Peoples and settler governments."[34] For these scholars, this means asking what is right in the treaty? (as in what is just and moral) as opposed to asking what are rights in the treaty? (as in cataloguing a list of rights). Mark Walters helps to articulate this emerging discourse as such: "To claim a right is not always the same thing as seeking right. To ask what rights one has is to ask what one is owed by others, an inquiry that looks backward to an *a priori* conception of rights, whereas to ask what is right between people seems to involve asking what it is that they should do in relation to each other, an inquiry that *looks forward* towards establishing just relationships."[35] From this perspective, one can see that treaties were intended to establish peace and friendship between Indigenous nations and the Crown through principles of mutual respect and trust. To understand *what is right* in treaties, however, it is important to have a historical frame of reference upon which to base that inference.

A Brief History, Part 1: Treaty Making in Canada

In a Canadian context, the era of colonization began in 1534 with Jacques Cartier, the first to meet and establish economic trade relations with Indigenous nations in current-day Quebec and the Maritimes. It is important to note that the provinces did not exist as such at that time since they were under the authority and control of the Indigenous nations that occupied those lands. In the following decades, British and Dutch settlers and merchants joined their French counterparts in what became a very lucrative fur trade with Indigenous nations. Less commonly understood, however, is that the economy of the fur trade was actually practised under the authority of local Indigenous laws and protocols. As I noted previously, one of the earliest treaties negotiated during this time was the Kaswentha between the Haudenosaunee and the Dutch. In an article for the *Journal of Early American History*, John Parmenter explains that the Kaswentha

> may best be understood as a Haudenosaunee term embodying the ongoing negotiation of their relationship to European colonizers and their descendants; the underlying concept of *kaswentha* emphasizes the distinct identity of the two peoples and a mutual engagement to coexist in peace without interference in the affairs of the other. The Two Row Belt, as it is commonly known, depicts the *kaswentha* relationship in visual form via a long beaded belt of white wampum with two parallel lines of purple wampum along its length—the lines symbolizing a separate-but-equal relationship between two entities based on mutual benefit and mutual respect for each party's inherent freedom of movement—neither side may attempt to "steer" the vessel of the other as it travels along its own, self-determined path. A nineteenth-century French dictionary of the Mohawk language defined the very word for wampum belt (*kahionni*) as a human-made symbol emulating a river, due in part to its linear form and in part to the way in which its constituent shell beads resemble ripples and waves. Just as a navigable water course facilitates mutual relations between nations, thus does *kahionni*, "the river formed by the hand of man," serve as a sign of "alliance, concord, and friendship" that links "divergent spirits" and provides a "bond between hearts."[36]

However, as British influence ascended in the latter half of the seventeenth century, these earlier treaties were soon forgotten by the new colonial powers. This is evident from the fact that the British Crown started drafting its own legislation regarding land rights without any consultation with the Indigenous nations that inhabited those lands. The primary example is the Royal Charter drafted by the British Crown in 1670. It illegitimately granted to the Hudson's Bay Company (HBC) title to and benefits, including monopoly trading privileges, of an enormous tract of land consisting of the entire drainage basin of Hudson Bay occupied by several Indigenous nations, including the Anishinaabe in Treaty 3 territory. Despite the illegitimate authority granted by the British Crown, the HBC actually operated its business, de facto, in accordance with Indigenous laws of the land at the time. As John Ralston Saul explains, "the rituals of [the HBC's] yearly negotiations with Indigenous Nations wherever they traded were lengthy, formal, filled with exchanges of information and presents, formal pipe smoking, and the leaving behind of such things as the grand calumet pipe—to be smoked again the next year as a sign of long-term continuing negotiation."[37] As a principal feature of Indigenous law, it is worth considering the significance of the pipe ceremony, with its relationship to tobacco and treaty making.

The smoking of tobacco in a pipe ceremony is a spiritual event that symbolizes a sworn oath, a contract or exchange, or what might be understood better as a proper act of law. In that regard, it has been said by some Indigenous Elders that when there is a pipe ceremony, the smoke that rises from the pipe acts as a signal to the Creator to bear witness to the event that is taking place, which obligates everyone participating in the ceremony to be respectful and honest. Jacques Derrida similarly notes that "tobacco is a symbol of . . . the agreement [*engagement*], of the sworn faith, or the alliance that commits the two parties when they share the two fragments of a *symbolon*, when they must give, exchange, and obligate themselves one to the other."[38] As a highly revered and recognized symbol of honour, justice, and law, the smoking of tobacco obligates one to keep one's word. This means that, for European merchants and settlers who participated in pipe ceremonies with Indigenous peoples, failure to abide by the law could have had grave consequences such as hostile conflict, starvation, and/or death. As J.R. Miller notes, it was the "commercial ambitions [of European settlers] that compelled them to adapt themselves to the Indigenous Nations who outnumbered them and exceeded them in locally relevant knowledge and economically essential skills."[39] Thus, we can say that, when European settlers adapted themselves to Indigenous nations' systems of exchange or economic trade, they were complying in fact with Indigenous law.

Following the establishment of the Royal Charter of 1670, the next key event in pre-Canadian history was the "Great Peace" of Montreal in 1701, which was represented by the Dish with One Spoon wampum. With approximately 1,300 Indigenous representatives from forty different nations in attendance, John Ralston Saul points out, the goal of this Peace and Friendship treaty was to establish "a continuous equilibrium of shared interests and shared welfare."[40] The phrase used to express that intention was that everyone would "eat from a common bowl," meaning that everyone ought to benefit and get sustenance from the land that we share. Despite its grand ambitions, the Great Peace was short-lived since a growing American national identity necessitated the construction of another colonial document in 1763, called the Royal Proclamation. That document, still recognized today under s.25 of the Canadian Charter of Rights and Freedoms, explicitly states that any negotiation with "Indians of any Lands" must be done by representatives of the highest political offices and in a public gathering:

> We do, with the Advice of our Privy Council strictly enjoin and require, that no private Person do presume to make any purchase from the said Indians of any Lands reserved to the said Indians, within those parts of our Colonies where, We have thought proper to allow Settlement: but that, *if at any Time any of the said Indians should be inclined to dispose of the said Lands, the same shall be Purchased only for Us, in our Name, at some public Meeting or Assembly of the said Indians,* to be held for that Purpose by the Governor or Commander in Chief of our Colony respectively within which they shall lie.[41]

With regard to the Royal Proclamation, it has been argued that Indigenous nations did not cede their rights and title to any of their lands or their right to self-government, primarily on the basis that Indigenous nations did not participate in or consent to the drafting of the document.[42] As news spread along the "moccasin telegraph"—that is, by word of mouth—among Indigenous nations of the implications of the Royal Proclamation, there was significant unrest in "Indian country" as leaders from many

Indigenous nations questioned the validity of such a document. As a result of this backlash, the British Crown—as represented by Superintendent of Indian Affairs Sir William Johnson—agreed to host a meeting the following year that over 2,000 Indigenous representatives attended and that since has become known as the Treaty of Niagara.

From an Indigenous perspective, the purpose of the meeting was to reaffirm the validity of the Kaswentha, such that Indigenous nations would continue to retain control over their lands and people without interference from the British Crown. During the meeting, Johnson and Indigenous leaders reached an agreement for peace and friendship given that colonial governments would not have authority over Indigenous nations. The validity of this agreement was signified by another wampum belt created to mark the importance of the occasion. At the gathering, Johnson was noted as interpreting the wampum belt as "a large Belt, with two Men holding it fast on each side and a Road through it. 'To the Western Nations,' in particular, he said, 'I desire you will take fast Hold of the same, and never let it slip, to which end I desire that after you have shewn [sic] this Belt to all Nations you will fix one end of it with the Chipaweighs at St. Mary's [Sault Ste. Marie] whilst the other end remains at my House.'"[43]

Undoubtedly, the presentation of the wampum belt would have opened and closed with a pipe ceremony in order to sanctify the peace and goodwill of the event, which again demonstrates the application of Indigenous law. As Miller explains, "using these Indigenous devices to record the important pact for Indigenous Nations was an example of the bicultural practice that by now was common in eighteenth-century treaty making. The protocols involved were ones of which the Indian superintendent was a master."[44] In their landmark book *Bounty and Benevolence: A History of Saskatchewan Treaties*, Arthur Ray, J.R. Miller, and Frank Tough agree with an argument put forth by John Borrows that, when read together, the Royal Proclamation and the Treaty of Niagara constitute a formal agreement "between First Nations and the Crown that positively guarantees First Nations the right of self-government."[45] Thus, there should be little doubt that the Treaty of Niagara was an archetypal event in pre-Canadian history. According to Anishinaabe legal and treaty scholar Aimée Craft, "the *Proclamation* and the Treaty of Niagara set the terms for the relationship between the Crown and Indigenous people, and set the stage for the negotiations of the future treaties."[46] In other words, the Treaty of Niagara was the foundation upon which future treaties and ultimately the Canadian state were built.

Over the next 100 years after the Treaty of Niagara, the social landscape in Canada changed dramatically. The rapid influx of Western settlers and their increasing westward expansion eventually pushed Indigenous peoples to the margins of society. The collapse of the fur trade, coupled with famine and disease, had decimated Indigenous populations. The shift in balance enabled Western settlers to establish more permanent settlements and ultimately introduce their own systems of governance and law. Although Indigenous nations and the British Crown maintained a relatively peaceful relationship throughout this time, the precipitous shift in authority culminated in the Confederation of Canada on 1 July 1867. Within a few years following Confederation, the newly formed government of Canada moved quickly to validate its claim to "sovereignty" over the lands acquired illegitimately by the Hudson's Bay Company via the Royal Charter back in 1670. The result of this arrangement was the "Rupert's Land transfer," which took place in 1870. Opposition among Indigenous peoples to the transfer was immediate and fierce, led by Louis Riel in the Red River Resistance, which eventually culminated in the Manitoba Act of 1870.[47] The Red River Resistance is also significant in the sense that it again signalled to the colonial government the importance of recognizing and accommodating Indigenous land title. The following year the Canadian government entered treaty negotiations with the Anishinaabe of the Red River Valley in what would eventually become Treaty 1, the Stone Fort Treaty. I note here that the first negotiations for the Numbered Treaties actually took place at the Northwest Angle of Lake of the Woods, in what is now Treaty 3 territory, but the state representatives, led by Wemyss Simpson, were unable to negotiate a settlement and therefore went back to Winnipeg to negotiate the Stone Fort Treaty instead.[48]

The Stone Fort Treaty formally concluded on 3 August 1871 after several days of difficult negotiations. Like all other formal diplomatic negotiations and economic transactions with Indigenous nations up to this time, Treaty 1 (like the other Numbered Treaties that followed) was conducted in accordance with Indigenous law—but with a few new wrinkles. John Ralston Saul explains that, "once treaties began to be put on paper, the methodology of the early negotiations was an almost exact continuation of the Hudson's Bay Company approach, which . . . had been shaped by indigenous approaches to how civilized people should deal with one another. Highly ritualized, lengthy, filled with formalized statements of purpose, these negotiations were not about clarity and completion. They were about ongoing and developing relationships."[49]

Although the smoking of tobacco and the pipe ceremony remained prominent features of the event, the terms of the treaty were partially written down at best, but there remains much controversy about what was actually agreed. Aimée Craft argues that the written texts of the Numbered Treaties are nothing more than a prewritten set of instructions delivered from Ottawa.[50] As such, they have been constant sources of consternation for Indigenous peoples and woefully insufficient as representations of *truth*, especially as *sole representations* of truth, as more or less regarded by the government of Canada today. The problem with a written text is that it is merely a signifier, a representation of the truth. Accordingly, whenever the representation is interpreted differently, a deliberation must take place to decide the meaning of the text. And, as Jacques Derrida has pointed out, "one cannot abstract from the written text to rush to the signified [of what] it *would mean*, since the signified is here the text itself."[51] Yet, with regard to the Confederation Era treaties, state officials heretofore typically considered *only* the written document as a representation of truth. As a result, many of today's socio-economic and -political problems in Indigenous communities have arisen from this narrow field of interpretation. In 2007, for example, the Ontario Ipperwash Inquiry determined that "the existence of long-standing, unresolved treaty disputes is perhaps the most important indicator of the potential for an occupation or protest."[52]

Treaty Interpretation

According to Alexander Morris, the treaty commissioner and Crown representative for Treaties 3 to 6, the principal features of the treaty were "*the relinquishment to Her Majesty of the Indian title*; the reserving of tracts of land for the Indians, sufficient to furnish 160 acres of land to each family of five; providing for the maintenance of schools, and prohibition of the sale of intoxicating liquors on the reserves, a present of three dollars per head to the Indians and the payment to them of an annuity of three dollars per head."[53] This point of view is complicated, however, by the fact that the historical record is filled with testimony from treaty witnesses who maintain that the written text of the treaty does not correspond to what was agreed to verbally. Several scholars have noted that there is no evidence that the notorious extinguishment clause was even mentioned at the negotiations and "much less that the Indigenous parties had agreed to cede and surrender their lands."[54] It has long been contended by virtually all Indigenous nations across Canada, since ink was first put to paper, that the treaties were a device with which to *share the land*, not transfer ownership of it. For Indigenous nations, the concept of "fee simple" title was incomprehensible since it was utterly incompatible with their world-views. The land, as one's *mother*, is not for sale; to put it differently, it is impossible to own one's mother, even more so to sell her. This notion is articulated by renowned Anishinaabe historian Basil Johnston:

> The principle of equal entitlement precludes private ownership. No man can own his mother. This principle extends even into the future. The unborn are entitled to the largesse of the earth, no less than the living. During his life a man is but a trustee of his portion of the land and must pass on to his children what he inherited from his mother. At death, the dying leave behind the mantle that they occupied, take nothing with them but a memory and a place for others still to come. Such is the legacy of man: to come, to live, and to go; to receive in order to pass on. No man can possess his mother; no man can own the earth.[55]

With this in mind, it should be clear that Indigenous leaders were ne-gotiating not the transfer of land ownership but complex concepts of coexistence on the land.

Myriad references to *kinship relations* during the treaty negotiations, such as the land or Earth as mother, the queen or Crown as mother, and the treaty commissioner as brother, demonstrate the importance of relationships to Indigenous people, as repeatedly invoked during the negotiations. Kinship relations comprise a fundamental element of many Indigenous epistemologies that perhaps could be summed up best as "all our relations." Writing for the *Kamloops Daily News*, the late Richard Wagamese articulated this concept: "When you say those words you mean everything that you are kin to. Not just those people who look like you, talk like you, act like you, sing, dance, celebrate, worship or pray like you. Everyone. You also mean everything that relies on air, water, sunlight and the power of the Earth and the universe itself for sustenance and perpetuation. It's recognition of the fact that we are all one body moving through time and space together."[56]

Within an Anishinaabe context, Aimée Craft adds that "there is no fiction in Anishinabe kinship. The Anishinabe are kin to the rocks, the trees, the animals, the birds, the fish, to each other, and to 'the other.'"[57] Thus, by invoking kinship law through a proper ceremony, Indigenous nations and Western settlers were made family and consequently inherited sacred obligations of alliance and goodwill to each other. In *Two Families: Treaties and Government*, Cree Elder Harold Johnson writes that, "when my family adopted your family, we became relatives, and that cannot be undone. A bond far stronger than any contractual obligation holds us together. Your law of contract and treaty allows for breach and remedy. The Creator's law does not allow for any breach whatsoever. Failure to comply had consequences, and no matter how severe the failure, the promise never becomes null and void; the consequences just keep getting greater and greater."[58] Thus, Indigenous *kinship law* defines the level of relationship, maintains calls for renewal, establishes responsibility, and demands reciprocity.

Although one might be inclined to interpret words such as *brother* and *relatives* as loose metaphors, or perhaps as mere figures of speech, Michael Asch argues that, by invoking kinship relations through a proper ceremony, and "by becoming family members, all have become members of the same ethical community, that is, the community within which promises are kept."[59] John Borrows also points out that the "relational aspect of the treaty-making venture is irrefutably manifested by the frequency with which, across the country, both sides' negotiators used language of kinship in describing the intended goal of the treaty process."[60] This point is further substantiated by Michael Coyle: "The fact that Crown representatives took such pains historically to adopt relational metaphors in treaty-making is a reflection of the fact that the clarification and building of relationships were central to Indigenous perspectives on treaty-making."[61] Given how extensively kinship law was invoked during these formal proceedings, it is imperative that the treaty relationship is reimagined and honoured in a good way today, which means observing our kinship relations and treating one's family members with respect and keeping one's word.

The difference in ideology and epistemological beliefs between Indigenous nations and the settler-colonial state might have caused some confusion during treaty negotiations, but it does not mean that

Indigenous nations did not understand the value of the land. It is true that social, economic, and political forces compelled many Indigenous nations to sign the best deal that they could, but each strove to maintain the integrity of its worldview and sense of self-determination. To put it differently, Indigenous nations were neither gullible nor ignorant in terms of understanding the importance of negotiating reasonable terms in the Numbered Treaties. They knew exactly what was at stake and negotiated the best terms that they could under the most difficult circumstances. Harold Cardinal illustrates this point best in his seminal work *The Rebirth of Canada's Indians*:

> When the white man's commissioner came to sign treaty, one of the elders took off his coat, put it on the ground, then scooped up a pile of earth and put it on the cloak. He said to the commissioner, "You want to buy our land, this is how you have to buy it. When I go to your store to buy anything, you weigh it and charge so much by the pound. If you have money enough to buy our land on that basis, then we can deal." And the reply, according to our elders, was, "The land you have is so valuable that I never would have enough money to pay for it on that basis. The five dollars that we give you is not payment for your land; it's an annual and continuing token of our recognition of the partnership that we are entering into."[62]

During the Treaty 3 negotiations, Chief Mawedopenais is on record telling Treaty Commissioner Alexander Morris that "the sound of the rustling of the gold is under my feet where I stand; we have a rich country; it is the Great Spirit who gave us this; where we stand upon is the Indians' property, and belongs to them."[63] Observed in this context, it is evident that Anishinaabe leaders understood that the value of the land was so high that it could not possibly be bought with cash and therefore conducted negotiations with the aim of securing rights—such as the right to education—that would enable them to carry on their traditional ways of life as well as participate in the practices of Western society if they so wished. Thus, with regard to reconciling the treaty relationship, in terms of establishing what is *right*, as in what is fair and just, the state must provide appropriate or "due compensation" to the Indigenous nations that agreed to open up their lands for settlement, in exchange for "what allowance they are to count upon and receive from Her Majesty's bounty and benevolence," as stated in the treaties.[64] As Michael Asch states, this involves rejecting "a path that disavows the obligations passed down to us" and instead taking the high road, which begins "with honouring the commitments made on our behalf by our forebears."[65]

The Paypom Treaty

Written transcripts of the treaty negotiations provided by Alexander Morris in *The Treaties of Canada* show that Anishinaabe leaders were very wary of how the treaty was being transcribed. They repeatedly asked for someone who knew their language and customs to draft the document. One Chief at the Treaty 3 negotiations said, for example, that it is not "to my convenience to have a stranger here to transact our business between me and you. It is a white man who does not understand our language that is taking it down. I would like a man that understands our language and our ways. We would ask your Excellency as a favour to appoint him for us."[66] In fact, another document was drafted during the negotiations that has since become known as the Paypom Treaty.[67] The document, unique to Treaty 3, lists eighteen terms of the treaty agreement—three of which are mysteriously omitted from the text—as recorded by Joseph and August Nolin at the request of Chief Powasson. Although copies of the Paypom Treaty can be viewed online, the whereabouts of the original handwritten document are unknown. Nevertheless, one of the most important observations regarding the treaty is that it does not mention anything about the extinguishment clause—supposedly the main purpose of the treaty—which lends support to the argument that this clause was not discussed at the negotiations. That said, the Paypom Treaty does not mention anything about education or hunting and fishing rights either, which are included in the Crown's document. Although it is not known for certain why these latter clauses were omitted from the treaty, we know beyond a reasonable doubt that they were definitely discussed during the negotiations. Treaty Commissioner Morris is on the public record stating that "it may be a long time before the other lands are wanted, and in the meantime you will be permitted to fish and hunt over them. I will also establish schools whenever any band asks for them, so that your children may have the learning of the white man."[68] It is noteworthy in this transcribed account that Morris does not suggest that establishing schools is "advisable" to the government, as written in the Crown's document, only that it will be done "whenever any band asks for them." I will come back to this point in the section on "The Treaty Right to Education."

The *Canadian Encyclopedia* notes that the Paypom Treaty differs from the Crown's document of Treaty 3 in other significant ways: "First, the Paypom Treaty includes two signatures that the original does not—those of Joseph Nolin and August Nolin. Second, it includes the four verbal promises excluded from the written text of Treaty 3."[69] According to Wayne Daugherty, who wrote a research report on Treaty 3 for the Department of Indian and Northern Affairs Canada (now Indigenous Services Canada), the four verbal promises recorded in the Paypom Treaty are the following:

1. If their children that are scattered come inside of two years and settle with you, they will have the same privilege as you have.
2. The English Government never calls the Indians to assist them in their battles but he expects you to live in peace with red and white people.
3. If some gold or silver mines be found in their reserves, it will be to the benefit of the Indians but if the Indians find any gold or silver mines out of their reserves they will surely be paid the finding of the mines.
4. You will get rations during the time of the payment every year.[70]

The most likely explanation of why these terms were excluded from the Crown's version of the treaty, as I mentioned earlier, is that the document had been drafted already before the negotiations took place. Indeed, in an 1895 letter to Deputy Minister of Indian Affairs Hayter Reed, S.J. Dawson wrote that "I was one of the commissioners appointed by the Government to negotiate a Treaty with the Saulteaux tribe of the Objibbeway Indians and as such was associated with Mr. W.M. Simpson in 1872, and subsequently acted in the same capacity with Lieut: Governor Morris and Mr. Provencher in 1873. The Treaty was practically completed by myself and Mr. Simpson in 1872, and it was the draft we then made that was finally adopted and signed at the Northwest Angle of the Lake of the Woods in 1873."[71]

Another important aspect of the Paypom Treaty is a postscript memo in which Elder Paypom explains how he came to possess the document. In the memo, Paypom states that "Linde was a photographer and a friend to the Indian people. One day, about forty or fifty years ago, he told me he had a paper and the Government wanted to buy it from him. He said they would give him $5,000.00 for it. But he wanted me to have it, 'for your children' he said."[72] It is unclear precisely who offered Linde the money and when for the document, how the document became known to the government, or even why the government would pay such a substantial fee for it, but Paypom obviously thought that it was important to obtain since "the paper had on it the promises made to the people by the Government, and they were breaking those promises."[73] If nothing else, the very existence of the Paypom Treaty raises questions about the veracity of the Crown's version of the treaty. At a more fundamental level, different accounts of the treaty negotiations such as this have led to over a century of misunderstanding of and uncompromising resistance to treaty interpretation between Indigenous nations and the Canadian state.

A Brief History, Part 2: Political Subordination

When we consider how Canada has blossomed into an exceedingly prosperous nation as a result of the treaties to which it agreed, it is a terrible and indefensible shame that its treaty partners have suffered tremendous harms and injustices. For this reason, it is crucial to examine critically the colonial foundation upon which the Canadian state was built. As mentioned above, the 1870s comprised a period of social and political upheaval for Indigenous nations in Canada. The collapse of the fur trade was a major factor in the demise of Indigenous ways of life, but so was industrialization and the imposition of Canadian law. Of key importance to this circumstance was the Indian Act established by Parliament in 1876. On the one hand, the state appeared to be acting in good faith through the treaty process in order to provide a "hopeful future" for Indigenous nations.[74] On the other, the state seemed to be using the Indian Act to take away any such future from them. One method of doing so was to erase "Indian" identity altogether, a feat accomplished by legislating who gets to be recognized as an "Indian" and who does not, without any messy bloodshed. Throughout the first half of the twentieth century, the government of Canada tried, ambitiously, to do just that by disqualifying as many Indigenous people as possible from their birthright: "Indian status." In a process known commonly as *enfranchisement*, Indigenous people would be stripped of their Indian status if they served in the Canadian armed forces, if they earned a university degree, of if they lived off-reserve for an extended period of time; or, in the case of women, if they married a non-Indigenous man. Although the policy has been amended several times, registration for Indian status remains restrictive, as Pamela Palmater explains: "The ultimate effect of the legislation, despite changes in official policy with regard to assimilation, is to reduce the number of people the government must be accountable to in terms of protection, treaty obligations, land rights, self-government, and other Aboriginal rights, including a whole series of culturally specific programs and services that are provided today."[75] With regard to the treaty relationship, the Indian Act unabashedly violates the nation-to-nation agreement by delegating provincial authority over a wide range of social, economic, and political platforms, including education. This can be observed most clearly in Section 88 of the Indian Act: "Subject to the terms of any treaty and any other Act of Parliament, all laws of general application from time to time in force in any province are applicable to and in respect of Indians in the province, except to the extent that those laws are inconsistent with this Act or the *First Nations Fiscal Management Act*, or with any order, rule, regulation or law of a band made under those Acts, and except to the extent that those provincial laws make provision for any matter for which provision is made by or under those Acts."[76]

John Borrows, among others, has also argued that "the federal government's 'transfer' of legislative responsibility from itself and First Nations to provincial governments is a significant derogation from a First Nations–derived constitutional narrative."[77] With regard to education, the major consequence is that Indigenous education standards and curriculums must conform to, or be compatible with, provincial education standards and curriculums—undermining Indigenous nations' inherent self-determination—but as I will discuss in more depth in Chapter 4, Indigenous nations are finding ways to subvert Canadian law. At a more fundamental level, the unilateral imposition of the Indian Act, as a colonial construct, exemplifies the state's presumed authority to dictate Indigenous affairs, as though Indigenous nations are non-human entities incapable of governing themselves and exercising self-determination. It is a presumption that demonstrates the imbalance of power that Indigenous nations are still confronted with today, distributing power to the settler-colonial state while oppressing the self-determining authority of Indigenous nations.

During the tumultuous period of the 1870s, once treaties were negotiated, the commitments made to Indigenous nations were soon forgotten by the state. Alexander Morris, for his part, often pleaded with members of the federal government to make them aware of the complex circumstances of the treaty negotiations and the delicate diplomacy needed to reach a final agreement with each nation. As one example, Morris wrote a letter to Secretary of State Joseph Howe stating that the government "should maintain constant communication with these tribes, and see that all the provisions of the treaty are rigidly carried out. . . . It is of the utmost importance to retain the confidence and maintain the friendliest relations with the Indians."[78] In a biography of Morris, Canadian scholar Robert Talbot notes that "Morris clearly suspected that the government was attempting to plead ignorance of its previous commitments in order to shirk its treaty responsibilities."[79] Despite the efforts of Morris to hold politicians in Ottawa accountable to their treaty obligations, those politicians had already decided to proceed with a policy of assimilation in which Indigenous peoples would be forced to conform to a new way of life or be punished by Canadian law. This was exemplified in 1879 when Edgar Dewdney was appointed to the "all-powerful" position of Commissioner of Indian Affairs for the North-West Territories. Upon his ascension to that prestigious position, Dewdney adopted a policy that he called "sheer compulsion" in which he would routinely and callously withhold food rations and farming and agricultural equipment from Indigenous communities in order to break their political will.[80] Meanwhile in Ottawa, when questioned by the opposition party about the government's fraudulent activities in the plains and northwest territories, John A. Macdonald reportedly said: "It cannot be considered a fraud on the Indians because they were living on Dominion charity ... and, as the old adage says, beggars should not be choosers."[81]

That said, an anecdote from a schoolteacher—identified as Father Cochlin—who taught students from Poundmaker's Reserve in Treaty 6 territory helps to elucidate what effect the state's "sheer compulsion policy" really had on Indigenous communities: "I saw gaunt children, dying of hunger, come to my place to be instructed. Although it was 30–40 degrees below zero their bodies were scarcely covered with torn rags. . . . The hope of having a little morsel of good dry cake was the incentive which drove them to this cruel exposure each day. . . . The privation made many die."[82] Cochlin's account is substantiated by the fact that, during the 1883–84 winter alone, three communities in Treaty 6 territory—The Mosquito, Grizzly Bear Head, and Lean Man—reported that fifty children died, representing one-sixth of their total population.[83] There are similar alarming statistics for other Indigenous communities across Canada. In fact, the historical record is filled with evidence that proves the state's "Indian" policies were devised not only to keep Indigenous nations under the thumb of the state, but ultimately to strip them of their treaty rights through legislative if not actual extinction.[84] In view of these (de)pressing circumstances—which say nothing about the residential school system that followed—it is astonishing to think that Indigenous nations would even want to continue to push today for a relationship based upon peace, mutual respect, and mutual benefit.

Treaty Case Law

Treaty litigation in Canadian courts has a long history that mostly has been unfavourable to Indigenous nations. The first case of significant consequence was *St. Catharines Milling and Lumber Co. v. R.* in 1888. At issue in this case were treaty lands thought to be within Rupert's Land when the federal government negotiated Treaty 3 with the Anishinaabe in 1873. At the time, Canada presumed to be entitled to administer treaty lands, under the auspices of the treaty, and its legislative authority under Section 91(24) of the Constitution Act, 1867 ("Indians and Lands reserved for Indians"), and therefore granted a permit for a timber berth to St. Catharines Milling and Lumber Company, subsequently challenged by Ontario. As the case made its way through the Chancery Division, the Court of Appeal, the Supreme Court of Canada, and finally the Judicial Committee of the Privy Council, at no time were the Anishinaabe of Treaty 3 ever consulted or even approached to participate in the proceedings. Nevertheless, the highest court, the Judicial Committee of the Privy Council, affirmed the lower courts' ruling in a decision delivered by Lord Watson:

> The tenure of the Indians was a personal and usufructuary right, dependent upon the good will of the Sovereign. The lands reserved are expressly stated to be "parts of Our dominions and territories"; and it is declared to be the will and pleasure of the sovereign that, "for the present," they shall be reserved for the use of the Indians, as their hunting grounds, under his protection and dominion. There was a great deal of learned discussion at the Bar with respect to the precise quality of the Indian right, but their Lordships do not consider it

necessary to express any opinion upon the point. It appears to them to be sufficient for the purposes of this case that there has been all along vested in the Crown a substantial and paramount estate, underlying the Indian title, which became a plenum dominium whenever that title was surrendered or otherwise extinguished.[85]

In short, "their Lordships" determined, per the Royal Proclamation, that Indigenous title existed only as a "usufructuary right," such that Indigenous people could use the land as "their hunting grounds" and that this title would be "extinguished" once the treaty commenced. The decision was based upon a statutory interpretation of the Royal Proclamation that utilizes a textual approach in which statutes are interpreted according to their plain wording and ordinary meaning.[86] Unfortunately, the textual approach, as Aimée Craft points out, "yields a lot of faith in the judges interpreting the statute" to be "impersonal and objective,"[87] but as I have shown, such objectivity often was absent in late-nineteenth-century Canada in matters related to Indigenous peoples and nations. The irony of the matter is that, had the federal government won this case, the entire land base of the property in question would have remained with Indigenous nations. As an aside, one would think that having an Elder or two provide testimony on the dominion's behalf would have helped its case. That no Indigenous treaty signatories were approached about this case shows how little Indigenous peoples were thought of in those days. Nevertheless, *St. Catharines Milling* proved to be the benchmark ruling on Indigenous title in Canada for more than eighty years and had repercussions still felt to this day.

Entering the twentieth century, Indigenous peoples were bombarded with a litany of amendments to the Indian Act and changes to regulations aimed to deny their self-determination. Such amendments included but were not limited to the forced attendance of "Indian youth" at residential schools (1884); a ban on "all dances, ceremonies and festivals that involve the wounding of animals or humans, or the giving away of money or goods" (1895); the forced removal of Indigenous people from "reserves near towns with more than 8,000 residents" (1905); and a ban on anyone "from soliciting funds for Indian legal claims without a special license from the Superintendent-General" (1927).[88] It was not until 1951, when the Indian Act was amended again, that the most onerous regulations related to Indigenous ceremonies and the right to retain legal counsel against the government were no longer prohibited by law.

Following the amendments in 1951 to the Indian Act, another case—*Calder v. British Columbia*—made its way to the highest court in Canada in 1973. This time the action was brought forward by Frank Calder and the Nisga'a Nation Tribal Council for a declaration that Indigenous title to certain lands in the province had never been extinguished lawfully since they were not part of any treaty. In the decision, six of the seven Supreme Court judges recognized that the Nisga'a possessed "Aboriginal title" at some point in time, but they were split on whether that title was still valid or had been extinguished lawfully. On the matter of extinguishment, Justice Judson—writing for one of the three-justice pluralities—reasoned that Aboriginal title had been lawfully extinguished through a series of laws passed by Governor James Douglas and the government of British Columbia and therefore moved to dismiss the Nisga'a appeal. In a stirring dissenting opinion, however, Justice Emmett Hall—writing for the other three-justice plurality—questioned whether a "competent legislative authority" had enacted *specific legislation revealing "clear and plain" intention to extinguish Indigenous title* and concluded that this had not happened, which in their opinion meant that the Nisga'a still had Indigenous title in 1973.[89] The seventh and deciding judge, Justice Pigeon, did not render a decision on the substantive issues of the case related to Aboriginal title and instead focused on the fact that the Nisga'a did not receive proper permission—in the form of a "writ"—from the attorney general to sue the provincial government and therefore moved to dismiss the appeal. The Nisga'a ended up losing the case based upon that technicality. Despite the unfortunate outcome of the case, Justice Hall's argument was so persuasive that it compelled the federal government to form a comprehensive land claims process in which the state first had to gain consent from Indigenous nations before it could claim sovereignty over unceded lands. In the following years, the government of Canada formally recognized and affirmed "Aboriginal and treaty rights" in Section 35 of the Constitution Act, 1982, also stating that "'treaty rights' includes rights that now exist by way of land claims agreements or may be so acquired."[90]

Over the past forty or so years, Canadian courts have developed a staggering edifice of case law related to Aboriginal and treaty rights. A few of the key cases during this time include *R. v. Taylor and Williams I* (1981), *R. v. Sparrow* (1990), *R. v. Sioui* (1990), *R. v. Badger* (1996), and *R. v.*

Marshall (No. 1) (1999), each of which has established important precedents with regard to how Aboriginal and treaty rights are to be interpreted in Canada. Although there has been progress toward a more equitable construction of treaty interpretation, the courts, more often than not, still demonstrate a high level of deference to settler-colonial worldviews. In *R. v. Sioui*, for example, the Supreme Court of Canada determined that "even a generous interpretation of the document . . . must be realistic and reflect the intention of both parties, not just that of the Hurons. The Court must choose from among the various possible interpretations of the common intention the one which best reconciles the Huron's interests and that of the *conqueror*."[91] Even if we put aside the fact that the courts believe that the Hurons were "conquered," and concentrate on what the "common intention" of the treaty was, we are still left with the conundrum of reconciling the difference between two opposing worldviews. In a dissenting opinion in *R. v. Marshall (No. 1)* (1999), Supreme Court Justice Beverley McLachlin compiled a list of principles drawn from previous case files that is meant to help address this issue. According to Justice McLachlin,

1. Aboriginal treaties constitute a unique type of agreement and attract special principles of interpretation.
2. Treaties should be liberally construed and ambiguities or doubtful expressions should be resolved in favour of the aboriginal signatories.
3. The goal of treaty interpretation is to choose from among the various possible interpretations of common intention the one which best reconciles the interests of both parties at the time the treaty was signed.
4. In searching for the common intention of the parties, the integrity and honour of the Crown is presumed.
5. In determining the signatories' respective understanding and intentions, the court must be sensitive to the unique cultural and linguistic differences between the parties.
6. The words of the treaty must be given the sense which they would naturally have held for the parties at the time.
7. A technical or contractual interpretation of treaty wording should be avoided.

8. While construing the language generously, courts cannot alter the terms of the treaty by exceeding what "is possible on the language" or realistic.

9. Treaty rights of aboriginal peoples must not be interpreted in a static or rigid way. They are not frozen at the date of signature. The interpreting court must update treaty rights to provide for their modern exercise. This involves determining what modern practices are reasonably incidental to the core treaty right in its modern context.[92]

At first glance, Justice McLachlin's principles of treaty interpretation seem to be fair and reasonable, but the reality is that they are far from complete. Worse yet, some of the principles are drawn from the United States Supreme Court decision in 1899 in *Jones v. Meehan*, which famously stated that,

> in construing any treaty between the United States and an Indian tribe, it must always be borne in mind that the negotiations for the treaty are conducted, on the part of the United States, an enlightened and powerful nation, by representatives skilled in diplomacy, masters of a written language, understanding the modes and forms of creating the various technical estates known in their law, and assisted by an interpreter employed by themselves; that the treaty is drawn up by them and in their own language; that the Indians, on the other hand, are a weak and dependent people, who have no written language and are wholly unfamiliar with all the forms of legal expression, and whose only knowledge of the terms in which the treaty is framed is that imparted to them by the interpreter employed by the United States. . . . The treaty must therefore be construed, not according to the technical meaning of its words to learned lawyers, but in the sense in which they would naturally be understood by the Indians.[93]

In short, this ruling epitomizes the "civ/sav dichotomy" that Emma LaRocque has written about in *When the Other Is Me*. According to LaRocque, that dichotomy is "the systematic construction of self-confirming 'evidence' that Natives were savages who 'inevitably' had to yield to the superior powers of civilization as carried forward by Euro-Canadian civilizers."[94] Put another way, Western or settler-colonial society is consistently represented in texts as being progressive, industrious, and civilized, whereas Indigenous nations and people are represented as being timeless, uncultivated, illiterate, and savage. With this in mind, it cannot be just ignored that Justice McLachlin draws inspiration for her principles of treaty interpretation from a clearly racist decision rendered by Justice Gray. The first element of this racist doctrine to observe is the fact that the United States is considered to be an "enlightened and powerful nation"; "Indians, on the other hand, are a weak and dependent people." This can be deconstructed in many ways, but for the sake of brevity let me just say that it is not an enlightened nation that breaks the socio-economic backs of others for no reason other than greed. The second element to note is that, as far as the United States—and Canada should be included in this analysis—are "masters of a written language" in relation to Indigenous nations, supposedly "wholly unfamiliar with all the forms of legal expression," this is another example of the racial and ideological bias within the justice system that I spoke of in Chapter 1. That said, to his credit, Justice Gray does make the critical point that treaties "must be construed" as they would "naturally be understood *by the Indians*" since the state had every other conceivable advantage in the treaty process. Justice McLachlin also concedes that in her second point above. As flawed and biased as the court system has been to Indigenous nations, there still seems to be enough reason to hope that a fair and balanced understanding of the treaties can be reached eventually, as long as the common intention of the signatories can be identified.

To discover the common intention of a treaty, Indigenous legal scholars have consistently argued that one must look beyond the words of the written text. Aimée Craft points out, as one example, that "privileging the text of the treaty gives undue weight to the Crown perspective and puts the Crown signatory in the privileged position of the 'legislator.'"[95] Moreover, as I mentioned previously, it is well documented in the historical record, as well as the oral tradition, that a number of verbal promises were made during the negotiations that did not make it into the written text of the treaty. For this reason, the negotiations with which each treaty was signed must be a fundamental component of how these agreements are to be interpreted properly. In support of this view, Leonard Rotman states that "treaties are time[-] and context-specific, and must be examined in light of the circumstances under which they arose, including the Crown's and the Indigenous people's understandings of their terms. . . . One must observe their *spirit and intent*, which includes the substance of the negotiations between the Crown and the Indigenous peoples *leading up* to the conclusion of the treaties."[96] To reiterate, what was said and what was done at the negotiation table are just as important as the treaty itself and need to be recognized as such.

The absence of consensus, in terms of how historical treaties should be interpreted, has led legal experts to consider other principles to help with this unenviable task. In *R. v. Badger*, for example, Supreme Court Justice Cory, writing for the majority, opined that "certain principles apply in interpreting a treaty. First, treaty represents an exchange of solemn promises between the Crown and the various Indian nations. Second, the honour of the Crown is always at stake; the Crown must be assumed to intend to fulfill its promises. No appearance of 'sharp dealing' will be sanctioned."[97] It has been argued additionally that "extrinsic evidence" such as oral testimony should be considered in the task of treaty interpretation. This view has its roots in the *Delgamuukw v. British Columbia* decision in 1997 in which Chief Justice Antonio Lamer, writing for the majority, stated that, "notwithstanding the challenges created by the use of oral histories as proof of historical facts, the laws of evidence must be adapted in order that this type of evidence can be accommodated and placed on an equal footing with the types of historical evidence that courts are familiar with, which largely consists of historical documents."[98] These are important developments in Canadian jurisprudence that create the potential to facilitate a greater understanding of the spirit and intent of the treaties by putting the oral tradition on "an equal footing" with the written word. Most importantly, they are further justification for rejecting the state's antiquated literal approach to treaty interpretation, which has dominated treaty discourse for over 150 years. That said, let us now analyze what a principled but balanced approach to treaty interpretation looks like with regard to the education clause in the Numbered Treaties, with specific reference to Treaty 3.

The Treaty Right to Education

The education clause in the Numbered Treaties is a rather nondescript line that reads "and further, *Her Majesty agrees to maintain schools for instruction in such reserves hereby made as to Her Government of Her Dominion of*

Canada may seem advisable *whenever the Indians of the reserve shall desire it.*[99] There are two key elements of this clause: one is the notion that schools will be maintained by the Crown; the other is that the schools will be built whenever the "Indians" ask for them or "shall desire it." Elders of the Anishinaabe Nation in Treaty #3 have long argued that the written text of the treaty differs in content and context from notes and memories of the treaty negotiations maintained respectively by the Paypom Treaty and the oral tradition. The dispute stems mostly from the phrase "may seem advisable," which the state has taken to mean that the establishment of schools must seem advisable to the government of Canada. In contrast, Anishinaabe Elders and their elected leaders have maintained that "the actual promise spoken by Lt. Gov. Morris during the Treaty negotiations did not include any provision that the Government, following a Band request to establish a school, would have to deem it 'advisable.'"[100] In other words, the promise of education, as articulated at the treaty negotiations, is not limited to what the state thinks is appropriate. In *The Rebirth of Canada's Indians*, Harold Cardinal seems to speak for all Indigenous nations that signed treaties: "The Indian position is that all education, irrespective of level, was prepaid by our treaties, and consequently we are entitled precisely to that—all education."[101] More recently, Indigenous scholars such as Blair Stonechild have argued that the first part of the education clause, "agrees to maintain schools," should be interpreted to mean that the government will finance the schools to be built.[102] Regarding the second part of the clause—"whenever the Indians of the reserve shall desire it"—it has long been contended that the decision to establish schools on reserves rests with the communities.[103] From these perspectives—as well as what has been written by Alexander Morris himself—one can deduce that there was no authority delegated to the government of Canada to establish the content of the education system: that is, Indigenous nations retained the right of self-determination to inform the nature and scope of any such education system. Because the Supreme Court of Canada has said that any "ambiguities or doubtful expressions should be resolved in favour of the aboriginal signatories,"[104] it is reasonable to conclude that interpretation of the education clause, as provided by treaty Elders and other scholars, should be taken into account upon its implementation.

The matter of the education clause has not been litigated yet in court, for the courts have said repeatedly that these issues should be dealt with in a fair political process, meaning that the state and Indigenous treaty signatories are urged to reach a settlement to the satisfaction of both parties without court intervention. Although much time has passed, and very little has been resolved, recent political developments—which I will discuss at more length in the following section—such as the election of a Liberal federal government have brought renewed hope that the treaty relationship can still be reconciled. That said, it has been nearly 150 years since the signing of Treaty 3, and the treaty right to education still has not been implemented properly. It is nothing short of an insult to all Indigenous peoples in Canada that the state, as represented by Prime Minister Stephen Harper, would even attempt to justify the residential school system as a way of fulfilling "its obligation to educate Aboriginal children."[105] The legacy of the residential school system, as a system of genocide, has been researched and studied extensively, so I will keep my discussion of it brief.[106] The main point is that the residential school system was a Windigo, manifested to give the state the authority to remove forcefully Indigenous children from their homes, strip them of their cultural identities, and assimilate them into the norms and values of settler-colonial society. As a case in point, in 1883, during a debate in the House of Commons, Minister of Public Works Hector Langevin was recorded as saying that "if you wish to educate these children you must separate them from their parents during the time that they are being educated. If you leave them in the family they may know how to read and write, but they still remain savages, whereas by separating them in the way proposed, they acquire the habits and tastes—it is to be hoped only the good tastes—of civilized people."[107]

As a result of this view, in addition to a lack of funding and supervision, there were many incidents of rape and murder of Indigenous children—as well as awful living conditions—during this odious stretch of Canadian history that make the residential school system one of the most heinous social policies in human history. Conditions were so terrible in these "schools" that many children were compelled to run away in the middle of winter and sometimes froze to death trying to get back home.[108] Let it suffice to say that the residential school system was far from anything that Indigenous nations had imagined when they secured the right to education, nor was there any choice in the matter.[109] In short, it was a unilateral policy imposed by the federal government, whose singular goal was to eliminate "Indians" and our treaty rights from its legislative ledger. That said, in April 2022, a delegation of Indigenous peoples from all across

Canada travelled to Vatican City, where they met the head of the Catholic Church, Pope Francis, who issued an apology for the church members' role in the abuse of Indigenous children who attended residential schools. Although Indigenous leaders such as Phil Fontaine have called the apology an "important step" in the path toward reconciliation, it remains to be seen if the Catholic Church will do anything else to atone for the abuses committed under its watch.[110] After all, it is nothing short of ironic that the pope's apology came on April Fool's Day.

As I have discussed throughout the first two chapters of this book, the government of Canada has failed egregiously in administering education policy for Indigenous nations. There is now a heavy responsibility to atone for those mistakes. One way to do that is by "respecting and honouring Treaty relationships," as called for in the Truth and Reconciliation Commission's final report.[111] With regard to treaty rights that have not yet been implemented, such as education, it is important to bear in mind the principle that "treaty rights of aboriginal peoples must not be interpreted in a static or rigid way. They are not frozen at the date of signature. The interpreting court must update treaty rights to provide for their modern exercise. This involves determining what modern practices are reasonably incidental to the core treaty right in its modern context."[112] In observing this principle, it does not take much imagination to envision the education clause to mean that it would be *advisable* for the state to fund an Anishinaabe education system whenever its treaty partners *desire* it. Such a simple interpretation would be "guided by the spirit and intent of the original treaty relationship, one that respects inherent rights, treaty jurisdictions, and . . . the decisions of our courts," exactly what has been articulated by Prime Minister Justin Trudeau himself.[113] Accordingly, if an education system is to be established as the implementation of the treaty right to education, then it must be recognized and affirmed that it will be the Indigenous nations that signed treaties that will articulate the standards, curriculum, and general governance of the education system, in accordance with our own laws not only to meet our education needs but also to promote our healing and self-determination.

The United Nations Declaration on the Rights of Indigenous Peoples

In 2015, the Liberal Party of Canada was elected into government office on the strength of an ambitious but nonetheless pro-Indigenous policy agenda that included a commitment to implement the United Nations

Declaration on the Rights of Indigenous Peoples. I note first that the
UNDRIP has been criticized by some scholars, including Peter Kulchyski,
who has argued that "aboriginal rights are not human rights."[114] According
to Kulchyski, Aboriginal rights are different from human rights because
the former are grounded in the protection of land-based and cultural
practices of Indigenous peoples. Therefore, if the two terms become
conflated, there is an inherent risk that "Aboriginal" peoples will lose the
protections that make them different. That said, the UNDRIP has also
been criticized by some Indigenous peoples themselves on the grounds
that "no consensus was ever reached on the majority of the Preambular
Paragraphs and Articles or on the document as a whole."[115] Nevertheless,
the UNDRIP is more generally recognized as a global human rights instrument that sets out the minimum standards for the survival, dignity,
and well-being of Indigenous peoples around the world.

For greater clarity, the UNDRIP consists of forty-six articles that
recognize the basic human rights of Indigenous peoples, including our
right to self-determination, passed in a formal General Assembly in 2007.
The UNDRIP states that, in exercising our right to self-determination,
Indigenous peoples "have the right to autonomy or self-government in
matters relating to their internal and local affairs, as well as ways and
means for financing their autonomous functions."[116] Moreover, the
UNDRIP recognizes that "Indigenous peoples have the right to maintain
and strengthen their distinct political, legal, economic, social and cultural
institutions, while retaining their right to participate fully, if they so
choose, in the political, economic, social and cultural life of the State."[117]
Given that Indigenous nations—particularly the Anishinaabe Nation in
Treaty #3—understand the treaty relationship in accordance with our own
principles and systems of law, these articles provide a foundation upon
which to enact and enforce those laws in matters related to the treaty.
Article 37, in particular, states that Indigenous nations have the right "to
the recognition, observance, and enforcement of treaties" and that states
must "honour and respect such treaties, agreements, and other constructive arrangements."[118]

With regard to education, the UNDRIP clearly states that "Indigenous
peoples have the right to establish and control their educational systems
and institutions providing education in their own languages, in a manner
appropriate to their cultural methods of teaching and learning."[119] For the
Anishinaabe Nation in Treaty #3, our law related to education is called

Kinamaadiwin Inaakonigewin. Like all other Anishinaabe laws, it is informed by Anishinaabe principles and derived from sacred and traditional
laws, and it is classified as Ozhibiige Inaakonigewin or "written temporal
law." Kinamaadiwin Inaakonigewin is the focus of the following chapter,
and I mention it here because it is the law by which the Anishinaabe
Nation in Treaty #3 interprets the treaty right to education, and it will be
the means by which we govern and administer an Anishinaabe education
system. For now, if one considers that the state has tried and failed disas-
trously (on multiple occasions) to administer an effective education policy
for Indigenous peoples, then perhaps we can agree that Indigenous peoples
should finally be given the opportunity to establish our own education
systems, in accordance with our own laws, cultural values, and beliefs in a
way that is enshrined in Canadian law. Article 18 of the UNDRIP provides
a means to accomplish this by recognizing that "Indigenous peoples have
the right to participate in decision-making in matters which would affect
their rights, through representatives chosen by themselves in accordance
with their own procedures, as well as to maintain and develop their own
indigenous decision-making institutions."[120] As previously discussed, all
Indigenous nations, which obviously includes the Anishinaabe Nation in
Treaty #3, already possess decision-making institutions that govern and
administer the laws of our peoples. This is significant because, if the state
acts in good faith in the fulfillment of the obligations set out in its own
Canadian Charter of Rights and Freedoms, then the adoption of federally recognized and affirmed UNDRIP legislation can provide a strong
foundation upon which to implement treaty rights as well as to fulfill the
Truth and Reconciliation Commission's Calls to Action.

Several months after the federal election in 2015, a private member's
bill, Bill C-262: An Essential Framework for Implementation of the
United Nations Declaration on the Rights of Indigenous Peoples, was
tabled in Parliament by NDP MP Romeo Saganash and won majority
support in the House of Commons by a vote of 206 to 79.[121] In a public
statement dated 4 May 2016, the Assembly of First Nations endorsed Bill
C-262, noting that it "sets out the key principles that must guide implementation of the *Declaration*" and, most importantly, that it "provides
clear public affirmation that the standards set out in the *UN Declaration*
have 'application in Canadian law.'"[122] However, just when it seemed that
Indigenous and state representatives were on the same page, and working
together to draft and implement pro-Indigenous legislation, the inevitable

happened: "The bill died in the Senate after being blocked by Conservative senators."[123] Conservative Senator Scott Tannas explained the reasoning to CBC News: "I support the UNDRIP in its entirety, with the exception of the word that gives me heartburn, which is 'consent.' What does that mean? If it turns out that consent equals a veto or anything approaching a veto for Indigenous people over activities and projects affecting their traditional lands, then we need to know that before we vote on this bill and bring it into law."[124]

Despite the apparent impasse within Senate chambers, the UNDRIP bill was revived at the provincial level when British Columbia passed Bill 41: Declaration on the Rights of Indigenous Peoples Act in December 2019, which essentially mirrored its federal predecessor. On the hotly debated word *consent*, Premier of British Columbia John Horgan said that "free prior and informed consent is not the end of the world" and that adding the UNDRIP legislation would create more certainty in the province because it enshrined Indigenous rights in law.[125] Within days of the province's motion to support UNDRIP, the territorial government of the Northwest Territories did the same thing and became the second government in Canada to write the declaration in law. In the aftermath of another federal election in 2019, Minister of Justice David Lametti and Minister of Crown-Indigenous Relations Carolyn Bennett stated that "our government has committed to co-develop legislation, to implement the legislation," with the goal of passing it by the end of 2020.[126] To the government's credit, on 3 December 2020, the minister of justice and attorney general of Canada, with support from the minister of Crown-Indigenous relations, indeed introduced Bill C-15: An Act Respecting the United Nations Declaration on the Rights of Indigenous Peoples to the House of Commons. Following that, in June 2021, Bill C-15 received royal assent, giving it the force of law in Canadian jurisprudence. This obviously marks a historic milestone given that Bill C-15 is Canada's first substantive step toward ensuring that federal laws actually reflect the standards set out in the UNDRIP.

As presently constituted, Bill C-15 presents two key goals: one is to affirm the UNDRIP as a universal international human rights instrument with application in Canadian law; the other is to provide a framework for the government of Canada to implement the declaration. A couple of the notable clauses of Bill C-15 include Section 5, which requires the government of Canada to take all measures necessary to ensure that Canada's federal laws are consistent with the declaration and to do so in consultation and cooperation with Indigenous peoples. To achieve that goal, Section 6 requires the minister designated by the federal cabinet to prepare and implement an action plan to achieve the objectives of the UNDRIP in consultation and cooperation with Indigenous peoples and other federal ministers. The action plan, supposed to be made public, must be completed "as soon as practicable" and no later than two years after Section 6 comes into force.[127] To provide for accountability and transparency in implementing the act, the minister must also prepare a publicly available annual report on the government of Canada's progress in ensuring that Canada's laws are consistent with the UNDRIP as well as on the minister's progress in completing the action plan. Questions remain, however: to what extent will Indigenous peoples be involved in the action plan, and what will this piece of legislation mean for "Aboriginal and treaty rights" for Indigenous peoples in Canada?

One of the reasons, perhaps the only reason, that the Canadian state made a push to legislate the UNDRIP—after deriding it for years under a Conservative government—is because it is featured so prominently in the Truth and Reconciliation Commission's Calls to Action, also part of the Liberal Party's electoral platform in 2015. Indeed, recognition of the UNDRIP is explicitly called for in sixteen of the ninety-four Calls to Action, including in Calls 43 and 44: "We call upon federal, provincial, territorial, and municipal governments to fully adopt and implement the *United Nations Declaration on the Rights of Indigenous Peoples* as the framework for reconciliation," and "we call upon the Government of Canada to develop a national action plan, strategies, and other concrete measures to achieve the goals of the *United Nations Declaration on the Rights of Indigenous Peoples*."[128] Significantly, the Truth and Reconciliation Commission also called "on the federal government to draft new Aboriginal education legislation with the full participation and informed consent of Aboriginal peoples." This legislation is supposed to include a commitment to "sufficient funding" while "respecting and honouring Treaty relationships."[129] With regard to that point, it is worth considering that a First Nations education act was in fact introduced in the House of Commons in 2014, but it failed to pass, partly because of Indigenous opposition to the proposed legislation. That said, the calls to action should not be considered an exhaustive list of measures that could be adopted in the pursuit of reconciliation. As Metis scholar Laura

Forsythe points out, "in the seventeen calls the TRC presented on education, other than encouraging consultation and participation with First Nations on the creation of new Aboriginal education legislation, there is no call to recognize the inherent right of First Nations to control education, nor is there a mention of jurisdictional issues that require partial or full transfers of authority to First Nations. Therefore, the TRC's contribution to support the journey to assert Indigenous educational sovereignty is strikingly minimal."[130]

To Forsythe's point, it is also worth noting that there is no call from the TRC for the federal government to recognize and affirm the treaty right to education. Despite these shortcomings, even if the calls to action are satisfied as is, and the new UNDRIP legislation is adopted in good faith, these political initiatives can still go a long way toward recognizing and affirming the treaty right to education in a way that truly respects and honours an Indigenous understanding of the treaty relationship. Indigenous laws are vital to this understanding, and they have the capacity to govern and administer an education system in a manner consistent with our own principles of teaching and learning.

Summary

In this chapter, I have demonstrated that Indigenous nations had their own laws prior to colonial contact and that these laws continue to be observed and practised in all diplomatic negotiations today as they did in the past. In addition to asserting cultural sovereignty through an oral constitution, Indigenous laws provide principles on duties and responsibilities associated with moral and ethical codes of behaviour and the governance of a nation, so they are marks of self-determination. Until recently, Indigenous laws were not codified in written texts but taught through the oral tradition. Historical circumstances with colonizing nations, however, created a need to harmonize Indigenous laws, so that they can be recognized and understood by settler-colonial society, and to help with the administration of settler-colonial laws that relate to Indigenous peoples and education. This work is bolstered by the development of treaty principles in Canadian case law, as well as the adoption of the UNDRIP, and Canada's commitment to reconciliation. In the following chapter, I will discuss how the Anishinaabe Nation in Treaty #3 is developing a written law in education, Kinamaadiwin Inaakonigewin.

Chapter 3

KINAMAADIWIN INAAKONIGEWIN

Education is the primary means for the transmission of cultural values, history, and law in all societies. As an institution of knowledge production, dissemination, and acquisition, an education system is always governed by and accountable to a relevant and corresponding education law. Canadian laws and regulations, however, particularly as they relate to education, have been extremely detrimental to Indigenous nations. Nevertheless, in Canada, the state continues to be responsible for administering education programs for Indigenous peoples, even though its history of failed policies has produced a legacy of calamitous social conditions in Indigenous communities marked by poverty, alcohol and drug addiction, and domestic violence. As a case in point, I will share a brief anecdote of my family history.

My mother's generation of family members, which includes her eleven siblings, grew up in the bush, on my grandmother's trapline during the 1950s and through the 1970s. The only language spoken at home was Anishinaabemowin, so they did not learn to speak English until they attended the Ontario education system, in which they all struggled immensely. None of the twelve children graduated from high school, which I believe contributed to an overwhelming sense of self-loathing and boredom quickly drowned by alcoholism. The alcoholism reached a peak in the late 1970s and throughout the 1980s and was responsible for countless acts of domestic violence. As my mother and her siblings began having children during this time, the combination of lack of education, alcoholism, and poverty made parenting within my family extremely dysfunctional. Although my cousins and I were all fortunate enough to be born and raised with English as our first language, which made our adjustment to mainstream society a bit easier, we all struggled to cope with issues at home. So merely being in attendance at school was exceedingly difficult—let alone trying to do well in school. Therefore, as I discussed in the Introduction, only me and one other cousin successfully navigated the provincial education system and went on to earn post-secondary degrees. On the other hand, for all of my other cousins—as well as my own brother and sister—who did not finish their education, they all struggle to make ends meet on a month-to-month basis, which makes going to school hard for their children.[1]

The fact is, because of systemic circumstances that all Indigenous families have to deal with, there is a false belief in mainstream society that Indigenous peoples are dull and incompetent, which means that they cannot and should not govern their own education systems. Yet, if colonial institutions of education have failed to produce the law-abiding, productive citizens who are coveted, then it stands to reason that local Indigenous institutions could be more effective in producing such citizens. In *Like the Sound of a Drum: Aboriginal Cultural Politics in Denendeh and Nunavut*, Peter Kulchyski points out that Indigenous nations have produced "a clearly defined vision" of governance structures "that is coherent, workable yet working towards the achievement of ideals that correspond with prominent critical notions of social justice."[2] To that point, Leanne Simpson adds that "the act of visioning for Nishnaabeg people is a powerful act of resurgence, because these visions create *Shki-kiin*, new worlds."[3] In other words, envisioning processes for social change is the first step toward actualizing social change. However, as Kulchyski goes on to say, that Indigenous concepts of social justice remain "a vision and not an actuality is a testament to the failure of the dominant political system, not to the lack of definition or the unpreparedness" of Indigenous nations.[4] Thus, for reconciliation to occur, Indigenous nations' visions for education must be turned into realities.

As I discussed in Chapter 1, one of the main factors that contributes to Indigenous peoples' woeful social conditions has been an absence of Indigenous content in education programs, which has led to low achievement rates for Indigenous youth. As far back as 1975, Indigenous scholars such as Howard Adams were asserting that these low rates are because Indigenous students have difficulty relating to the foreign curriculum.[5] Another cause of concern has been the state's continuous attempts to jam square pegs into round holes by using a one-size-fits-all approach

to Indigenous education. The failure of settler-colonial education policies underlines the need for Indigenous control of Indigenous education
systems as well as Indigenous representation on local school boards of
provincial systems. Fortunately, many education programs across the
country are trending in the right direction as increasingly more Indigenous
nations are exerting more self-determination in their local curriculums
and programs of study. Thus, in this new era of reconciliation, Indigenous
nations have even more reason to hope that our woes in education will
soon be relieved. If the state follows through with its commitments to
fulfill the Truth and Reconciliation Commission's Calls to Action and
to implement the UNDRIP federal legislation in a good way, then these
will be important steps toward honouring its long-overdue obligations to
the treaty right to education. Indigenous nations will then have another
catalyst with which to facilitate the construction of our own education
systems, in accordance with our own education laws. This chapter will
provide an overview of Anishinaabe law-making processes and discuss
how our education law, Kinamaadiwin Inaakonigewin, will govern an
Anishinaabe education system as well as interact with provincial and
federal education laws in Canada.

On Writing Oral Laws

Since time immemorial, the oral transmission of Anishinaabe sacred,
traditional, and customary laws has been sufficient legal practice to govern our people; however, the imposition of Western forms of law have
brought forth the need to revitalize our legal traditions in a way that
accommodates the written word. Revitalizing our laws—a process called
Ozhibiige Inaakonigewin or "written temporal law"—enables our people
to communicate more effectively our legal traditions in a way that can be
recognized and understood by settler-colonial society as well as provide a
basis on which we can articulate our understanding of our treaty relationship with the Crown. Although the translation of our laws into English
might seem to be an obvious or natural development, it is in fact an imprecise science and a complicated endeavour, especially if considered in
the context that writing is permanent and that, once something is written,
it has a tendency to be locked or frozen in time. In *Research Is Ceremony*,
Shawn Wilson helps to explain this conflict: "Writing ideas down fixes
them as objects that can be taken out of context of time and relationship.
As fixed objects, ideas lose the ability to grow and change, as those who

hold relations with the ideas grow and change themselves. They lose their relational accountability."[6] To Wilson's point, Anishinaabemowin is a language based upon relational thought; it is both flexible and malleable, and subject to change, making it somewhat open to interpretation. As one example of this fact, at an education gathering that I attended while conducting research in Hayward, Wisconsin, at the Lac Courte Oreilles Ojibwe School for the Grand Council Treaty #3 for the development of the Treaty 3 education law, a local teacher explained how they were developing new words in Anishinaabemowin that describe technological innovations. However, given that Anishinaabemowin is a verb-based language, there are very few nouns to work with, which makes the translation of English nouns a very complicated process. Nevertheless, one English word that the educators had worked on was *projector*, translated as "that one that emits light onto the wall."

The process of translating Anishinaabe concepts into English is further complicated by the fact that a standardized orthography has yet to be achieved. Although the double-vowel system is becoming more common, as can be seen in texts such as *Talking Gookom's Language: Learning Ojibwe*, it is still in a nascent stage of development.[7] As of today, if one were to ask three different Anishinaabe language speakers about kinamaadiwin, which I translate very loosely here as "education," one would likely receive three different orthographic representations of the word, accompanied by three different definitions. For example, a more precise translation of kinamaadiwin might be "the process by which we practise teaching and learning." Similarly, with regard to the word inaakonigewin—which I have plainly interpreted here as "law"—I have been informed by language expert and Treaty #3 Elder Patricia Ningewance that the literal translation of the word is "the way a stick is pointed towards." She says that the word most likely evolved from the pipe ceremony, where pipe carriers are known to raise their pipes in reverence and gratitude to the Creator, who provides all things (including our laws). All this is to suggest that kinamaadiwin inaakonigewin might be better translated as "the process by which we practise teaching and learning, according to the rules provided to us by the Creator."

Bearing in mind that language is central to a culture's distinctive knowledge and value system, the difference between Anishinaabemowin and English is as vast as our respective cultural epistemes. This fact alone introduces substantial interpretive and translational issues between the two languages. Thus, the challenge of arriving at a national-level consensus on a written law is immense since such a task is far more complex than defining any one word. Cree scholar Tasha Hubbard explains that "placing Indigenous concepts over Western European concepts is a difficult exercise, and the tendency is to dismiss Indigenous concepts, or to label them as metaphors rather than as a reflection of the Indigenous world."[8] Simply put, Anishinaabe legal concepts do not translate easily, or even satisfactorily, into a foreign language, particularly one as linguistically different as English. Nevertheless, given the state of our communities, and what is at stake for our future, it is a task more than worth attending to; it is one of utmost urgency. The task is not to validate our law but to preserve the integrity of our language and traditional knowledge as well as to protect the culture and future of our people.

On Nationalism

The challenge of achieving national consensus on a written law stems, in part, from the existence of regional dialects of the Anishinaabe language and from regional differences in local histories and needs as a result of unique geographical, sociological, economic, and political circumstances. Although Anishinaabe from different regions might identify as such, and even communicate effectively in the same language, Anishinaabemowin, the unique geo-socio-eco-political factors of each *community*—let alone region—constitute a unique identity and warrant a claim to nationhood, hence *First Nation*. Yet, notwithstanding First Nations' inherent rights to local autonomy, self-governance, self-determination, and/or sovereignty, any community is likely to find it difficult to advocate on behalf of itself and therefore *self-determine* a good reason (common language, history, values, goals, aspirations, etc.) to join a larger entity for the sake of better political representation, access to resources, and lower costs for social infrastructure and public works. In the context of education, think schools, transportation, teachers, and administration of services, among other considerations.

The most significant and divisive geo-socio-eco-political factor among the Anishinaabe seems to be the practice of treaty making that took place throughout the Confederation era. During that time, the Anishinaabe occupied a vast tract of land consisting of much of the Hudson Bay watershed and the basin of the Great Lakes. The expanse of our region can be traced back to the "Seven Fires Prophecy" (sometimes referred to as the

"Eight Fires"), an intergenerational saga that forms part of an extensive Anishinaabe oral tradition. As Leanne Simpson explains, "the prophecy of the Seventh Fire foretold of a time when the most oppressive parts of the colonial regime would loosen and Nishnaabeg people would be able to pick up the pieces of their language, culture and thought-ways and begin to build, in essence, a resurgence."[9] According to Anishinaabe historian Edward Benton-Banai, the first prophet said the following to the people:

> In the time of the First Fire, the Anishinabe nation will rise up and follow the Sacred Shell of the Midewiwin Lodge. The Midewiwin Lodge will serve as a rallying point for the people and its traditional ways will be the source of much strength. The Sacred Megis will lead the way to the chosen ground of the Anishinabe. You are to look for a turtle-shaped island that is linked to the purification of the Earth. You will find such an island at the beginning and end of your journey. There will be seven stopping places along the way. You will know that the chosen ground has been reached when you come to a land where food grows on the water. If you do not move, you will be destroyed.[10]

Thus, over the span of many generations, the Anishinaabe migrated from the northeastern coast of North America into the heartland of the Canadian Shield around the Great Lakes. In the course of this diaspora, there were seven "major stopping places" at which some families settled, whereas others continued to move farther west.[11] To be sure, at each local place was a unique ecology—whether on the east coast, the eastern woodlands, the subarctic, or the plains—that spawned different regional practices influenced by the local ecologies and cultures with which the people interacted. However, as colonial legislators subsequently moved in and began treating with different "bands" of Anishinaabe (or "Indians" as they were called) in the nineteenth century, distinct political entities were forged, paving the way toward unique identities of nationhood. Thus, with each treaty, through the stroke of a pen, a new Anishinaabe Nation was born, distinctively dyed by its own ink.[12] Through this piecemeal process, some Anishinaabe communities were united, whereas others were separated by arbitrary borders facilitated by treaties. In other words, a once united Anishinaabe Nation was formally divided into several distinct political and national entities, with the Anishinaabe Nation in Treaty #3 being one of those entities. Treaty 3 territory encompasses twenty-eight Anishinaabe communities over 55,000 square miles of land, and though all of the communities are politically connected by the treaty, not all of them have the same geo-socio-eco-political concerns. Northern and remote communities such as Saugeen and Wabauskang, for example, have much more expensive living costs, making it impossible for their local governments to deliver the same quality of social services to their people on budgets on par with more urbanized communities.

The influence of colonization has had different effects at different times for different Indigenous nations. For that reason, within the context of the Anishinaabe Nation in Treaty #3, the education law will apply only to those communities or First Nations that subscribe to it. For those communities that do not subscribe to Kinamaadiwin Inaakonigewin, they will have the opportunity to opt out and develop a separate or different law that meets their educational needs.[13] That said, the development of such national laws is a key expression of self-determination, and it is a precursor to the grand goal of liberation: that is, freedom from colonial oppression. As Howard Adams explains, "such nationalism is linked to or contains within itself . . . a progressive political ideology that serves to advance the social awareness of oppressed native people regarding their colonized circumstances, as well as directing the cultural revolution."[14] It is also worthwhile considering the words of Frantz Fanon: "We are dealing with a strategy of immediacy which is both all-embracing and radical. The objective, the program of every spontaneously formed group is *liberation at a local level*."[15] Thus, the development of "nationalism" through national laws can be considered a process in which a localized governing body takes direct action against an oppressive regime on behalf of peoples possessing a common history, language, and desire for freedom. Nationalism, in the final analysis, is a force driven by a people's shared struggle for self-determination.

Beginning in the 1950s and carrying through the rest of the twentieth century, the residential school system left in its wake a vacuum in Indigenous education programming within Treaty 3 territory as well as across Canada. As the residential school system disintegrated, Indigenous youth were registered in the public education system, which employed its own Windigo-type agenda. Although some of these youth found hardearned success, many others struggled to find meaning and comfort in another foreign education system that did not represent their cultures or even provide basic infrastructure within their communities to support their educational needs. Some families were forced to relocate in order to send their children to school, whereas others who remained in their communities or lived in other rural areas were faced with long commutes to and from school. These circumstances, among other socio-political factors, led to a surge of Indigenous youth placed in non-Indigenous foster homes, a phenomenon which has since been labelled the "Sixties Scoop." As Bonita Lawrence explains, "even when children were placed in 'good' homes, they were raised in ignorance of their culture, with no knowledge of their own identity, and few defenses against the racism of outsiders—or foster family members. The practice of obscuring the Native heritage of adoptees appears to have been too common to be dismissed as a 'mistake.'"[16] On a personal note, I had one Anishinaabe friend placed in a "good" foster home with a very affluent white family in the 1980s. I remember being over at his house to eat dinner one evening and being amazed at the size of the house—they even had two pet scarlet macaws!— but more so puzzled about why we "Indian kids" had to eat at a separate table. Only later did I come to understand that such a privilege was apparently reserved for "civilized" individuals. Suffice it to say that Seneca did not learn anything about his Anishinaabe heritage at that house.

Back in 1964, Harry Hawthorn led a federal government–sponsored study to assess the "contemporary situation" of Indigenous nations in Canada. Two years later Hawthorn released his report, *A Survey of the Contemporary Indians of Canada: A Report on Economic, Political, Educational Needs and Policies in Two Volumes*. One of the major findings in the report was that Indian "children are required to enter school and urged by parents and teachers to do well, but their stay there is often marked by retardation and terminated by dropping out; although ever more Indian children attend school and stay longer, the increasing national educational levels provide another receding horizon."[17] Over fifty years later, it is clear that the public education system is still not working for Indigenous peoples, for dropout rates continue to be higher, and socio-economic indicators such as poverty and crime demonstrate substandard community wellness. Such conditions prompted leaders in Treaty 3 territory to establish the Treaty 3 Anishinaabe Education Secretariat in 1991, with the goal of designing, implementing, and controlling an Anishinaabe education system. Building upon this initiative, Treaty 3 Elder Fred Kelly penned his own report for the Grand Council Treaty #3 in March 1994,

"A Treaty-Based, Community-Driven Model of Self-Government in Education and Language and Culture," the first document that articulates the need for a written Treaty 3 education law. In that report, Kelly asserts that jurisdiction is the fundamental aspect of ownership and control in the governance of education. According to him, jurisdiction "is the law-making capacity of the owners which immediately and directly rests within the primacy of the First Nations," and it must be "promulgated within the context of the inherent right of self-government."[18] Therefore, as Kelly goes on to argue, it is the responsibility of the Grand Council Treaty #3, in concert with the federal and provincial governments, to "enable and facilitate the recognition of a national [education] law within Treaty 3 territory."[19] The federal government ultimately stymied these early efforts at policy reform by cutting off funding to the Treaty 3 Anishinaabe Education Secretariat in 1997 as one measure to reduce the national deficit. Despite this setback, the development of a national Treaty 3 education law remained a top priority for the Grand Council Treaty #3.

The Purposes and Principles of a Treaty 3 Education Law

Following a brief hiatus of political action in the 2000s, the development of a written national education law again gathered momentum in 2007 at the annual Elders' gathering in Kenora, Ontario. There the assembled Elders determined the five purposes of a written education law for the Anishinaabe Nation in Treaty #3:

1. to preserve the Anishinaabe in the student;
2. to protect the language and cultural identity of the student;
3. to provide an education that enables the student to become a functional citizen in the Anishinaabe Nation and society at large;
4. to clarify relationships between the Grand Council and other governments in Canada; and
5. to harmonize administration of Anishinaabe law in education and administration of Crown government laws in education.[20]

These imperatives are to be understood in conjunction with Elder Fred Kelly's thesis that the central purpose of establishing a written education law is to "exercise the inherent jurisdiction in education of the Anishinaabe Nation in Treaty #3, now and for future generations," which is to say exercise our inherent right to self-determination and cultural sovereignty.[21]

For the Anishinaabe, the concept of sovereignty relates to a word in Anishinaabemowin known as dibendizowin, which translates loosely as "sacred freedom." As Elder Kelly goes on to explain, dibendizowin is the "sacred gift to the Anishinaabe Nation to do whatever is necessary to achieve all its legitimate ends that comes from the Creator and the Ancestors, including the inherent right to its system of governance; laws and institutions; citizenship; trade and commerce; and the right to enter into treaties with other nations."[22] Although the revitalization of any traditional law can enhance the distinctive social, economic, and political well-being of an Indigenous nation, education is especially important in the sense that the nation is making a conscious and targeted investment in the generations of tomorrow. Thus, by establishing an education law that facilitates the construction of a localized Anishinaabe education system, the students of the education system can benefit in multiple ways. Some of these benefits include the following:

(a) fully develop one's individual potential as distinct Anishinaabe members living in a modern era while also honouring one's heritage;

(b) engage in studies with high academic standards as well as technical studies and skilled trades, land-based learning for traditional knowledge, and institutional learning;

(c) become fluent in Anishinaabemowin and ensure cultural transmission of the oral history to the next generation;

(d) develop a connection to the land, aki, and gain a sense of responsibility to care for the land using traditional knowledge systems;

(e) engage in learning opportunities with Anishinaabe Elders, knowledge holders, and oral historians so that they can transmit their knowledge to the next generation of youth for maintaining the strength of the culture and language and the living civilization of the nation;

(f) understand the nature of Indigenous rights from an international perspective, know the inherent rights of the Anishinaabe Nation in Treaty #3, and be competent to speak to those rights publicly and transmit the knowledge to future generations;

(g) promote a sense of social responsibility and tolerance for the beliefs of others in a global community;

(h) understand the importance of contributing to the social, economic, political, and spiritual development of the Anishinaabe Nation in Treaty #3.[23]

In 2008, Treaty 3 Elders again met for an open discussion to provide direction and guidance for the initiation and development of a written law on education. At this gathering, the Elders established seven "Guiding Principles" to be observed in the development of a written education law. It should come as no surprise that, with the declining use of our language, the first guiding principle was related to Anishinaabemowin: language revitalization. In particular, the Elders were concerned about how younger generations were being ridiculed for their imprecise pronunciation of Anishinaabemowin words, which deterred youth from learning and speaking the language. The ridicule suffered by younger generations, however, has not been limited just to the way we talk but also to the way we look and the way we act. In *"Real" Indians and Others: Mixed Blood Urban Native Peoples and Indigenous Nationhood*, Bonita Lawrence describes an instance when "one woman mentioned how her mother would scold her in Cree whenever she grew her hair long—telling her that she looked like 'a big, thick Indian!'"[24] I too can recall a time when my aunt scornfully called me a "Real Anishinaabe!" for not knowing how to operate an outboard motor, with the implication that "real Anishinaabe" know nothing of modern technology. With regard to that example, I think that it is important to mention that my aunt's phrase was actually saturated with irony and thus a joke. Among my family, I am different in the sense that I grew up and still live in an urban environment, at the cost of not learning how to speak my language and having only episodic experiences of common cultural practices such as fishing, hunting, and trapping. As a result of my limited experience, I grew up with a general sense of detachment from the rest of my family. Most of my extended family, conversely, grew up and continue to live on or near the land where they were born and raised. Because of their upbringing on the land, almost all of my uncles, aunts, and cousins acquired and developed skills in fishing and hunting at an early age. Thus, as a fourteen-year-old, out on the land, I was expected to have the basic knowledge of firing up an outboard motor, taking us from place to place, and knowing where all the good fishing spots were. But, as I mentioned, I did not grow up that way, so I did not have such experience or knowledge yet. Therefore, as I was struggling to get us going, my aunt identified an opportunity to rip a joke at my expense. The irony was that, if I were a "real Anishinaabe," I would have known what the hell I was doing as opposed to being an obvious city slicker.

Unfortunately, for many Indigenous peoples, the ridicule and scorn that they experience from family members are often symptomatic and indicative of an internalization of colonization, as a result of their family members' own acute experiences of colonization, which then develops into intergenerational trauma. As Anishinaabe scholar Sheila Cote-Meek explains, these effects "have largely been passed from one generation to another as a direct result of unresolved historical trauma," and they "originate from the loss of lives, land and vital aspects of Native culture promulgated by the European conquest of the Americas."[25] Thus, to address this problem, it was decided at the 2008 Elders' gathering that a safe and supportive learning environment must be developed, one that reflects our Anishinaabe identity, values, and beliefs. The Elders determined, in accordance with the Seven Generations Education Institute, that "the first guiding principle for Anishinaabe education is to revitalize and maintain our way of speaking, our way of processing and expressing thought; our way of communicating with the creation, with the spirit, and with one another. It is to ensure the connection of our language to our worldview, language to culture, language to relatedness and identity, and . . . language to the natural environment."[26] As such, the Treaty 3 education law ensures that Anishinaabemowin will be the first language of the education system. In this system, Kinamaadiwin Inaakonigewin states that the "students will be encouraged to speak Anishinaabemowin as their first language," with the objective of every school and learning lodge being "to graduate students who are equally proficient in Anishinaabemowin and English."[27] To help accomplish this task, it was further decided that "the teaching staff and administrative staff of every school" and learning lodge will use Anishinaabemowin "to the greatest possible extent as their language of work," including as the language of instruction for course content.[28] Given these objectives, a section of the draft education law is dedicated specifically to the use and priority of our language.

The second guiding principle on education is Anishinaabe Inendamowin, which has been articulated as "our way of thinking, our beliefs, our way of perceiving and of formulating thought. It is the foundation for our Anishinaabe philosophy and worldview."[29] The basis of this principle is the intent to develop our students' ability to employ Anishinaabe ways of thinking so that their intellectual minds are informed and inspired by the spiritual intelligence of their hearts. According to the Seven Generations Education Institute—an Anishinaabe organization within Treaty 3 territory—this process involves developing a student's ability to operate within an Anishinaabe paradigm of seeing the whole of reality, "informed by all the senses (physical, emotional, mental, and spiritual) and maintain[ing] the interdependent, interconnected and holistic experience and integrity of the total environment."[30] In other words, Anishinaabe Inendamowin answers questions of an ontological nature. Within an educational context, Sandra Styres has pointed out that "developing an understanding of the contemporary and historical connections Indigenous people have to their places, and the ways Indigenous peoples have existed and continue to exist first and foremost in deeply intimate, spiritual, and respectful relationships to their lands, one another, and indeed all relations (animate and inanimate/human and non-human), is the key to success for all students as active and respectful participants, first in their own places, as well as in the wider global arena."[31] The principle of Anishinaabe Inendamowin is also important to the extent that it addresses Elders' concerns about Treaty 3 Anishinaabe youth who might be too embarrassed or ashamed to speak our language or learn our Anishinaabe ways of life. To rectify these negative thought processes, the Elders stated that "the youth need to be taught at a young age about our relationship with the land, water, creatures, plants, and one another through the clan system."[32] This restorative process would include ascribing traditional Anishinaabe names to youth and teaching them about ceremonies and rites of passage.

The third Anishinaabe guiding principle on education is Anishinaabe Gikendaasowin, which has been translated as "our knowledge and way of knowing." As an epistemological line of study, Anishinaabe Gikendaasowin teaches students about the knowledge of our origins, our way of life, and our worldview. Although it might seem that there is significant overlap in these principles, there are certain nuances that differentiate the metaphysics between epistemological and ontological lines of inquiry. Rauna Kuokkanen helps to explain the challenge of teaching these different processes: "In attempting to explain indigenous epistemes in language that is foreign to them, we risk violating their integrity, because they are not easily translatable into other systems, nor can they be reduced to simple categorizations."[33] One way in which these principles might be better understood, however, is through the application of an "Indigenous Holistic Framework," which could provide some guidance on how to address complex theoretical questions while honouring Indigenous epistemologies, ontologies, and axiologies.[34] That said, Aanishinaabe Gikendaasowin directs us to increase the highest sense of consciousness from a place of Anishinaabe identity, thinking, knowing, and way of being. The Elders have described this principle as everything that "we learn from the time of our birth, until the time when we pass to the other world."[35] Anishinaabe Gikendaasowin is also understood to be the process by which we share our knowledge: that is, through the oral tradition. Renate Eigenbrod and Renee Hulan have described the oral tradition as "distinct ways of knowing and the means by which knowledge is reproduced, preserved and conveyed from generation to generation."[36] As the Elders have said repeatedly, with every teaching there are certain protocols in place that dictate "what we learn, when we teach, and how and where."[37]

Anishinaabe Inaadiziwin is the fourth Anishinaabe guiding principle on education. It has been described as "our behaviour, our values and our way of living our life, and being Anishinaabe in the fullest sense. It is the development of the highest quality of Anishinaabe personhood, connected to the earth and in relationship to all of creation."[38] Significantly, Anishinaabe Inaadiziwin is considered to be the process by which a person develops creative and artistic expression. According to the Seven Generations Education Institute, Anishinaabe Inaadiziwin activates "the whole person in the learning experience—body, mind, heart and spirit—in such a way to generate the highest quality of experience and inspire the finest creativity of response and expression."[39]

The fifth guiding principle is Anishinaabe Izhichigewin, which relates to the form and content of the education process, both teaching and learning. Based upon my experience working with the Grand Council Treaty #3 in the development of the education law, I understand that Anishinaabe Izhichigewin is meant to strengthen the capacity of Anishinaabe students to learn the Anishinaabe way of doing things, in terms of helping students to develop the skills for effective Anishinaabe functioning in the world and making positive contributions to their communities.

Given the residential school system's injurious and sustained attacks on Indigenous languages and spirituality for such a long period of time, and accounting for the subsequent impacts on communities, as well as the dearth of Indigenous spiritual expression in the public school system, revitalizing Anishinaabe spirituality has been a major emphasis for Elders in Treaty 3 territory. Attending to this concern, the Elders developed two related but distinct guiding principles to be applied in the pursuit of education. The first and sixth in total is Anishinaabe Enawendiwin, which has been articulated as "our way of relating to each other and to all of Creation. It is an all-inclusive relationship that honours the interconnectedness of all our relations, and recognizes and honours the human place and responsibility within the family of Creation."[40] Scholars such as Marlene Brant Castellano and Margaret Kovach have argued that Indigenous ethics should not be limited to a defined set of rules; rather, "they are about knowing who you are, the values you hold, and your understanding of how you fit within a spiritual world."[41] That said, Anishinaabe Enawendiwin can be thought of as a cultivation of values that not only relate to the individual but also maintain the integrity of the entire community. It promotes the strengthening of relationships that are deeply personal, to be attended to with care and compassion in accordance with kinship law.

Similarly, Gidakiiminaan, the seventh and final guiding principle, explores our connection to and relationship with the land as well as the total experience of relating to the Earth and the environment. Treaty 3 Elders have said that Gidakiiminaan is distinguished as being "the primary shaper of Anishinaabe identity," which constitutes the "total relationship with Creation that informs our environmental ethic."[42] In that regard, Gina Starblanket and Heidi Stark explain that "Indigenous ways of relating with one another, animals, and the environment, and with past and future generations form the basis for projects of decolonization as they call into question the hegemony of Western thought."[43] This principle is perhaps best understood alongside another important Indigenous concept: all our relations or relationality, which I have discussed. Finally, Gidakiiminaan is also meant to ensure that educators provide an environment of teaching and learning situated on the land, within the natural environment.

Taken and applied together, the seven Anishinaabe guiding principles of education form the foundation of Kinamaadiwin Inaakonigewin, the Treaty 3 education law. The law is designed to facilitate the governance and administration of an education system that will provide a learning experience both relevant and responsible to the members of the Anishinaabe Nation in Treaty #3 in preparing for life both on and off the territory.

Kinamaadiwin Inaakonigewin recognizes that the youth of our nation are the most precious and therefore the most valuable of all resources, so it is intended to protect and perpetuate Anishinaabe cultural and linguistic transmission for future generations. Kinamaadiwin Inaakonigewin further serves to promote intragovernmental coordination within the Anishinaabe Nation in Treaty #3 as well as with the provincial and federal governments of Canada. According to Elder Fred Kelly, the law also recognizes that each Anishinaabe community within Treaty 3 territory "has its own cultural, historical and constitutional meaning and significance within the Nation" and affirms the autonomy of individual communities to govern themselves in accordance with their local and specific needs and interests.[44] These objectives are in line with what Linda Goulet and Keith Goulet have argued in *Teaching Each Other: Nehinuw Concepts and Indigenous Pedagogies*, in which they write that hierarchical, paternalistic relationships of the colonial past must be "replaced by interactive, more equitable social relationships that serve to create learning environments conducive to the success of Indigenous students."[45] The legislative and institutional structure of the law is thus designed to be consistent with the principles of governance adhered to by the Grand Council Treaty #3; it is a non-hierarchical structure, with an *egalitarian* constitution or disposition, unlike Western or colonial forms of governance.

According to notes from a 2008 Treaty 3 Chiefs' Assembly, the Chiefs provided direction on other considerations to be made in the development of the written education law, such as "the meaning, purpose, and mission of Anishinaabe education; the provision of Anishinaabemowin and culturally relevant education; jurisdiction over . . . and provision for access to: Early Childhood Education, Elementary Education, Secondary Education, Post-Secondary Education, and Special Education; and administrative considerations such as: Educational Authority; Planning, Policy and Regulations; Curriculum Development; Teaching Methodology; Standards, Quality and Accreditation; Counselling; Facilities; and Finance, Personnel and Administration."[46] The Chiefs also stated that the written law should clarify the relationship between national and community laws, with regard to providing protection of and support for local community autonomy as well as infringement by other jurisdictions. Given the experiences of the Anishinaabe Nation in Treaty #3, as well as other Indigenous nations in Canada that have been subjected to unilateral decisions by the federal government, particularly decisions that relate to education, it is not surprising that the Chiefs were mindful of and attentive to the importance of supporting local autonomy and jurisdiction. As such, the Chiefs unanimously agreed that the written law ought to "provide that the Nation and any of its communities may enter into an agreement with any other government for services that it may want or to harmonize the administration of its jurisdiction."[47] Finally, financing the education system was also discussed at the assembly, where it was decided that the written law should state that Canada is to provide the resources for all aspects of education according to the promises made during the Treaty 3 negotiations. Based upon these directives, the Grand Council Treaty #3 was then tasked with establishing a Technical Working Group for the drafting phase of the written education law, Kinamaadiwin Inaakonigewin.

Following the Chiefs in Assembly gathering, an initial Technical Working Group was indeed established to draft a written law on education in 2008. However, faced with mounting financial difficulties because of more cutbacks by the federal government, the members of the Technical Working Group struggled to collaborate effectively and were therefore unable to complete their task. A written education law thus remained only a dream for several more years. It was not until 2015, with a Liberal federal government in power, that fortunes began to change. The Liberals' pro-Indigenous platform during the election brought a record number of Indigenous voters to the polls, which undoubtedly helped Justin Trudeau to get elected as prime minister of Canada. During the campaign, and even after the election, Trudeau made concrete promises to fulfill the Truth and Reconciliation Commission's Calls to Action, implement the UNDRIP, and lift the 2 percent funding cap on Indigenous education.[48]

First Nations Lifelong Learning Table

While Indigenous nations, including the Anishinaabe Nation in Treaty #3, continue to wait for the substantive elements of the federal government's electoral promises to be fulfilled, a framework for a First Nations Lifelong Learning Table was negotiated in 2016. The framework was supposed to provide the Anishinaabe Nation in Treaty #3 with additional funds to supplement existing education programs in its communities. Described as a "bilateral process" between the Ministry of Education, the Indigenous Education Office, and the Chiefs of Ontario, the First Nations Lifelong Learning Table "aims to support mechanisms in which First Nations and the Province work together as full partners in the design, development and implementation of First Nations education programs for First Nation learners in the provincial education system."[49] Over a three-year period, the program was designed to enhance a vast series of education programs and services, based upon five "mutual priorities": relationships; languages and culture; curriculum; information, access, and accountability; and policy development.

Early reports from the Grand Council Treaty #3, however, have demonstrated that barriers continue to impede effective partnerships between Anishinaabe communities in Treaty 3 territory and provincial school boards. These barriers include insufficient representation on school boards and committees; a lack of communication and collaboration between school boards and community education directors; unclear roles and responsibilities of school board staff and members; and a need to share resources while also providing teachers and staff with culturally relevant professional development opportunities. Regarding the priority areas of languages and culture and policy development, community education directors reported that the recruitment and retention of Anishinaabe language and knowledge holders must be a top priority and that the unique skill sets of these subject matter experts must be recognized and valued by providing them with pay equal to that of other teachers within the provincial education system.[50] Although the issue of equal pay for Indigenous educators and staff has been a source of malcontent for Indigenous nations for a number of years, community education directors also said that Anishinaabe-"based approaches to language programs and language teacher certification must be adopted within the provincial education system."[51] On the issue of curriculum, it was reported that Treaty 3 communities were concerned about the lack of representation on curriculum development teams with the Ministry of Education. Additionally, Treaty 3 Elders said that Anishinaabe curriculum development needs to be led by our own people, "based on regional, territorial culture and knowledge," given that "certain things should only be discussed and/or taught by people who have the background, understanding and expertise."[52] Finally, with regard to the priority area of information, access, and accountability, it was also determined that provincial school boards need to share relevant data with Treaty 3 communities that might affect the success and well-being of Anishinaabe students within provincial schools.

The frustration expressed at the 2018 Treaty 3 education gathering seems to echo Glen Coulthard's criticism of the state's approach to reconciliation, such that the current politics of reconciliation is unable "to adequately transform the structure of dispossession that continues to frame Indigenous peoples' relationship with the state."[53] Coulthard goes on to explain that what sometimes gets represented in the media and by the state as Indigenous ressentiment is actually a manifestation of righteous resentment: "that is, our bitter indignation and persistent anger at being treated unjustly by a colonial state both historically and in the present. . . . It is actually a sign of our *critical consciousness*, of our sense of justice and injustice, and of our awareness of and unwillingness to *reconcile* ourselves with a structural and symbolic violence that is still very much present in our lives."[54] Despite the rosy verbiage of *partnership* in its strategic plan, it appears that the First Nations Lifelong Learning Table is just another inadequately funded, short-sighted, state-sponsored initiative that falls short of its mark. "After all," Taiaiake Alfred writes, "the negotiation is between unequal partners; the terms of restitution are calculated not according to morality or rationality, but according to what the Settlers themselves determine they can afford or want to pay in return for their new post-colonial identity."[55]

The consensus at the 2018 Treaty 3 education gathering—which hosted community directors of education, Elders, education personnel from the Grand Council Treaty #3, as well as Grand Chief Francis Kavanaugh—was that the education programs and services of the Lifelong Learning Table—that is, the actual teaching and learning that take place within an ever-shape-shifting education system—are being asphyxiated on the exhaust of travel expenses and high administrative costs, notably senior management salaries.[56] Although there are often legitimate grounds for such expenditures, I would be remiss if I did not mention that all Indigenous nations bear a certain responsibility to be exceptionally judicious with their limited resources. During my time working with the Grand Council Treaty #3, I noticed an exorbitant amount of spending to host events in places such as Winnipeg. Although these were important nation-building exercises, one cannot overlook that tens of thousands of dollars could have been saved—and reallocated to education programming—just by hosting the events at a local venue in Kenora. Unfortunately, it is a problem all too familiar that plagues many institutions and communities and underlines the challenge of mobilizing people to participate in the development of national laws. A more pressing concern relates to the recruitment and retention of talented Indigenous professionals, especially in isolated communities in remote regions of northwestern Ontario. With regard to homegrown talent, most Indigenous people who achieve educational success and go on to earn credentials in education, law, or business administration most often leave their home communities in order to accept higher-paying jobs in cities. In trying to recruit off-reserve individuals to come to and work in the community, the reality is that the remuneration is high to persuade the best minds to leave a luxurious metropolis for a boil water advisory; compensation in these circumstances is a fundamental necessity for which existing budgets do not allow. Consequently, many Indigenous nations and communities are often forced to juggle staffing dollars and programming expenses with inadequate budgets, which means that either staffing or programming or both are likely to suffer in the administration of education services. To run successful Indigenous education programs, education and administrative professionals are needed, but they must also be equipped with sufficient resources to do their jobs. The fact is that, if any indigenized education program has any chance at success, then a significantly larger investment must be made to account for the costs of isolation associated with remote, rural bush living; it has to be an investment that eventually leads to a redistribution of wealth in which Indigenous communities are placed on an equal footing with non-Indigenous communities.

The legacy of the First Nations Lifelong Learning Table is still unclear; however, if history is any guide, then likely it will be one of many band-aid solutions soon forgotten.[57] Given this possibility, the Treaty 3 Chiefs gathered once again on the matter of education at the 2018 Fall Assembly, and again they resolved to draft a written education law. At this gathering, the Chiefs focused on administrative aspects of an Anishinaabe education system, seeking concrete answers to questions of how an Anishinaabe education system will be administered, how communities will be represented, and how those communities will receive their education programs and services. To help answer these questions, I had the honour of being invited to be part of another Technical Working Group and to "draw upon a consolidation of existing reports and previous bona fide consultations in addition to their expert advice to identify elements for inclusion in the drafting of the law and for use in community consultations."[58] Based upon the advice of Elders and other knowledge holders of the education law, over the next few months, I conducted an archival review of Treaty 3 education documents, and participated in several engagement sessions with community directors of education, one of which included my previously mentioned visit to Lac Courte Oreilles, Wisconsin, to observe the administration of an existing Anishinaabe education system. As a quick note, the Lac Courte Oreilles Ojibwe School is a Kindergarten to Grade 12 school initially established in 1975; it describes itself as a "comprehensive academic, culturally and community-based education system" specifically designed to meet the needs of the Lac Courte Oreilles community.[59]

Administrative Tasks and Responsibilities

In addition to the engagement session with community directors of education in Wisconsin, the Technical Working Group held a youth gathering in Fort Frances, Ontario, as well as Elders' gatherings in Winnipeg and Thunder Bay. One of the constant messages among all Treaty 3 education stakeholders was that Kinamaadiwin Inaakonigewin must explicitly assert legislative jurisdiction within the broad field of education. According to the Elders, it is a matter of sacred law that legislative, executive, and administrative jurisdiction "is vested in the members of the Anishinaabe Nation in Treaty #3 who are the rights holders and are represented through their leadership of the Ogichidaa [i.e., the Grand Chief] and the Grand Council Treaty #3," so it is stated as such in the draft Treaty 3 education law.[60] At another gathering, the community directors of education clawed back some local authority by saying that it is incumbent on the Grand Council Treaty #3 to "support Treaty #3 communities' local jurisdiction over education through kinamaadiwin inaakonigewin and follow its provisions and regulations."[61] I note quickly here that within Treaty 3 territory historically there has been an uneasy relationship between the communities and the central government, the Grand Council Treaty #3, based upon concerns about unilateral authority that communities have been subjected to through their experiences with the Indian Act. To alleviate these concerns, Elder Fred Kelly suggested that the Grand Council Treaty #3 "establish and authorize a Treaty #3 Education Commission to act on its behalf to implement the provisions of the written education law."[62] Under this arrangement, all matters of education are to be managed by the Treaty #3 Education Commission, which is then responsible to the members of the Anishinaabe Nation in Treaty #3, as represented by the Grand Council Treaty #3. Elder Kelly's idea is very similar to one endorsed by the Standing Senate Committee on Aboriginal Peoples back in 2011. Stated in that committee's report, "Reforming First Nations Education: From Crisis to Hope," is that "we strongly support and encourage the efforts of First Nations to establish educational authorities, separate from band councils and accountable to the parents and community members, and believe they need a legislative basis from which to operate."[63] It stands to reason that, if the Senate recognizes that a Treaty #3 Education Commission needs a legislative basis from which to operate, then the Treaty 3 education law, Kinamaadiwin Inaakonigewin, could be that basis. To reiterate, the Treaty #3 Education Commission would effectively administer and better communicate the elements of our education law with external forms of government, in conjunction with the consensus of its constituent communities.

From the Elders' perspective, the initial responsibility of the Treaty #3 Education Commission would be the formulation of policies, procedures, and regulations to guide the application of the written education law. This would include the establishment of a "Treaty 3 education plan, code of conduct, curriculum, and education standards for the benefit of the Anishinaabe Nation in Treaty #3 and its communities" and would be articulated as such in the draft form of Kinamaadiwin Inaakonigewin.[64] From an administrative standpoint, the community directors of education said that the Treaty #3 Education Commission should also be responsible for the design of education programs and resource materials, enrolment criteria, assessment and appeal procedures, and other services such as transportation, counselling, student housing, and means for parental engagement through an independent Community Education Council.[65] With regard to education programming, there was consensus among all Treaty 3 stakeholders that Anishinaabe knowledge should be a part of "every course in the school curriculum."[66]

According to Marie Battiste, the source of Indigenous knowledge "lies within the changing ecosystem, from which Indigenous peoples develop their awareness and their strategies of living within that ecology."[67] In other words, Indigenous knowledge is *local*. Thus, Treaty 3 Anishinaabe knowledge is unique to its territory, located in the heart of the Canadian Shield, which *The Canadian Encyclopedia* helpfully explains: "While at times a barrier to settlement, the Shield has also yielded great resources, including minerals, coniferous forests and the capacity for hydroelectric developments."[68] For the Anishinaabe in Treaty 3, the rugged terrain has not been "a barrier to settlement," demonstrated by the fact that we have occupied the territory for thousands of years and effectively have mastered *bush life*, in the rich tradition of the hunting and gathering mode of production.[69] This way of life has produced knowledge that is unique and local to its territory. Over many generations, as Battiste goes on to explain, "the knowledge manifests itself in many other social forms and processes: stories, symbolic and creative manifestations, technologies, ways of being and learning, traditions, and ceremonies."[70]

To that point, it was agreed further at the 2018 Treaty 3 education gathering that Anishinaabe spirituality would be "part of the curriculum, along with ceremonies practised in the school system, with a place offered to other faith traditions as well," and it is stated as such in the draft version of Kinamaadiwin Inaakonigewin.[71] This is an important resolution, especially given that, within most education systems today, Indigenous ceremonies are almost completely absent. Indigenous spiritualities, ceremonies, and cultural practices are not just hollow activities; they serve real and legitimate purposes. Perhaps no purpose is more important than understanding one's place on the land, aki. To help explain this perspective, I turn to Vine Deloria Jr. in *God Is Red: A Native View of Religion*:

> The task of the tribal religion, if such a religion can be said to have a task, is to determine the proper relationship that the people of the tribe must have with other living things and to develop the self-discipline within the tribal community so that man acts harmoniously with other creatures. The world that he experiences is dominated by the presence of power, the manifestation of life energies, the whole life-flow of a creation. Recognition that the human beings hold an important place in such a creation is tempered by the thought that they are dependent on everything in creation for their existence.[72]

That said, Treaty 3 leaders were also attentive and responsive to the fact that some Anishinaabe students will not be able to attend schools where Anishinaabe ceremonial and spiritual practices are offered. To advocate for students who attend schools within the provincial education system, the draft law states that an Anishinaabe school trustee should be appointed to the provincial school board to ensure that the educational, cultural, and spiritual needs of our youth are met.[73]

As the administrative structure of the Treaty #3 Education Commission continues to develop in accordance with the provisions set out in Kinamaadiwin Inaakonigewin, another important aspect of its jurisdiction will be finance. The draft law states that the Treaty #3 Education Commission will be responsible for negotiating and entering into contracts and agreements with funding agencies—primarily the provincial and federal governments of Canada—for its "capital programs, construction, operations, and maintenance."[74] This objective includes achieving recognition and affirmation of the federal government's obligations to fulfill the treaty right to education, as manifested through the negotiation of long-term agreements, settlements, and/or contracts. Although all "agreements and comprehensive transfer payments" from the federal and provincial governments will be negotiated with the approval of the Grand Council Treaty #3, the key priority of this endeavour will be to ensure that funding is equitable and consists of "multi-year payments with mutually agreed upon accountability standards that are clear, consistent, and comparable across Canada."[75]

Additional budget considerations in the administration of an Anishinaabe education system include the costs of regional and community-based infrastructure for second- and third-level education services such as professional development opportunities for teachers and administrators; curriculum research, development, and evaluation; the purchase of educational materials; establishment of policies and regulations; data collection and analysis; strategic planning; and special education needs. In regard to that point, a section of Kinamaadiwin Inaakonigewin will be reserved for "special needs and gifted students" whereby a special education policy framework is to be developed by the Treaty #3 Education Commission that makes "provision for schools, courses, or services for the blind, physically challenged, and gifted children" "within the cultural and linguistic context of the Anishinaabe Nation in Treaty #3."[76] It will also be incumbent on the Treaty #3 Education Commission to ensure that any revenue collected from the state includes compensatory funding that accounts for a history of failed education programs—that is, the residential school system—as well as incidental emergencies related to unforeseen events such as natural disasters to help offset the overall higher costs associated with remote bush living. That said, it is worth observing that the report of the Standing Senate Committee on Aboriginal Peoples recommended, back in 2011, that the minister of Aboriginal affairs and northern development Canada be given statutory authority to make payments from the Consolidated Revenue Fund to First Nations education authorities. In addition to providing better education services on reserves, the committee's recommendation was based primarily upon establishing a methodology for making payments to Indigenous organizations—to be done in consultation with Indigenous organizations—and that this methodology "would consider key cost drivers such as demographics and remoteness; and that the formula for establishing payments include, among other things, First Nations language preservation and revitalization programs."[77] Unfortunately, the significance of the Senate committee's report was muted when the proposed First Nations Education Act was derailed in 2014. Indeed, as Jody Wilson-Raybould points out in her political memoir *Indian in the Cabinet: Speaking Truth to Power*, once the First Nations Education Act failed to pass, the federal government soon "abandoned the vision of a broad and comprehensive framework for recognition and implementation of rights. It is not talked about much anymore, and they do not frame their work that way because they are not doing it and do not really know how."[78] Nevertheless, in spite of that setback, the draft law also states that the Treaty #3 Education Commission would be expected to apply for grants from charitable foundations and other external sources for projects related to education, such as the establishment of endowment funds, as well as scholarships and bursaries for its students.[79] Another source of revenue for the education system could come from research grants through the development of partnerships with postsecondary institutions. To meet these objectives, and comply with internal policies related to transparency and accountability, the Treaty #3 Education Commission would be expected to prepare an annual budget to be approved by the Grand Council Treaty #3 and passed by resolution from the Chiefs in Assembly. This process would "include an annual report on the education plan with statistics and performance indicators" as well as reports on "the review of education standards and recommendations, a review of policies and recommendations, and a review of staffing."[80] As neat and tidy as all that might sound, history has shown that it is much more complicated in practice, for these processes of governance often take months to organize and convene.

Another important consideration in the development of any Indigenous education system is community participation, particularly as it relates to the involvement of parents, guardians, and Elders. The lack of community participation in educational activities has been a steadfast complaint by Indigenous leaders that goes as far back as the "Indian Control of Indian Education" opus in 1970. Harold Cardinal, a key figure in the development of that work, wrote again in 1977, stating that "parents must regain the right to make decisions about the lives of their children; their education, the values they grow up with, their preparation for life. We are talking about the right to make the decisions that will allow our communities to flourish, the simple right to earn a living in the way we feel will best reflect our identity and our society."[81] More recently, Leanne Simpson has argued that parental involvement in education policy development is vital in terms of "figuring out the kinds of citizens we want to create, the kinds of communities we want to live in, and the kinds of leaders we want to create, then tailoring our parenting and our schooling to meet the needs of our nations."[82] To that point, Simpson adds that, "if we are truly interested in decolonizing, then we must critically evaluate how we are parenting and educating the next generation because it is one of the few areas of our lives we can assert a certain degree of control and it is critical to the decolonizing project."[83] In response to these assertions, Kinamaadiwin Inaakonigewin states that "parents, guardians, and community members may form a Community Education Council, to bring their recommendations" to the Treaty #3 Education Commission.[84] As such, a representative of the Community Education Council, as chosen by its constituents, would be eligible to occupy a seat on the board of the Treaty #3 Education Commission, with an active role in the development and evaluation of education standards and curriculum for the respective education system. In addition to providing guidance on policy development, Kinamaadiwin Inaakonigewin states that the Community Education Council would also be involved in the hands-on learning of Treaty 3 students by providing instruction on "land-based learning, oral history, cultural and spiritual knowledge, and cultural mapping of the territory," as well as serving as a mediator in instances of student misconduct prior to the cases being advanced to the Treaty #3 Education Commission for disciplinary action.[85] As Linda Goulet and Keith Goulet explain, these are important tenets of the education law since "giving voice to our language and our people in the curriculum," and in the administration of education, helps to foster "a sense of balanced ownership" between the school and the community.[86]

In general, the Community Education Council would serve as a measure of checks and balances in the administration of Kinamaadiwin Inaakonigewin complemented by the existence of a dispute resolution clause, whereby a "special hearing committee" would be established to adjudicate complaints. The administration of the written education law would be supplemented by the drafting of regulations and procedures specifically related to any amendments that might need to be made to the law. The regulations are to be drafted by the Treaty #3 Education Commission and brought to the Grand Council Treaty #3 for approval, where they would then have the "force of law."[87] Some of the regulations to be considered under this section of the law include, but are not limited to, the duties of the director of the Treaty #3 Education Commission; the establishment of professional staff qualifications, training, and certification of teachers, counsellors, therapists, and other professional staff employed by the Treaty #3 Education Commission; the organization, administration, and supervision of all constituent schools under the law; the establishment of education and curriculum standards; counselling services; fiscal management policies; as well as school administration guidelines that could include an attendance policy, social programming for students and their families, the calendar year, special needs and gifted students policies, home schooling, and a student code of conduct.[88]

The Treaty 3 Law-Making Process

In outlining the conversations that have taken place, as well as the purposes of a written Anishinaabe education law, along with its "guiding principles," I have tried to show the progress made in the development of a written Treaty 3 education law. The Treaty 3 law-making process generally follows an unofficial ten-step approach, which can be paraphrased as follows:

Step 1: The people of the Anishinaabe Nation determine the need for a law.

Step 2: The Chiefs in Assembly agree with the people.

Step 3: The Chiefs seek advice from Elders.

Step 4: Feast the process.

Step 5: Community consultation begins.

Step 6: A report is given to the Chiefs in Assembly.

Step 7: The Chiefs follow the direction provided by the people.

Step 8: Ceremonies take place.

Step 9: There is a final Elders feast.

Step 10: The National Assembly grants approval.[89]

According to the Grand Council Treaty #3, Anishinaabe traditional law, Kete Inaakonigewin, recognizes that our relationships with all people and the land are based upon harmony and balance. They involve having respect for the diversity and autonomy of all peoples as well as recognizing the importance of consensus building to manage disputes and holistic approaches to problem solving. As such, Kete Inaakonigewin requires the people's consent in matters affecting our traditional lands and resources and all matters affecting our self-determination as a nation, including education. These principles are consistent with the articles of the United Nations Declaration on the Rights of Indigenous Peoples and other international instruments that confirm the rights of Indigenous governments stating that "free, prior, and informed consent" must be obtained "before adopting and implementing legislative or administrative measures that may affect them."[90] That said, on 16 May 2007, at the National Assembly of the Anishinaabe Nation in Treaty #3, the principles of consultation and consensus were satisfied in resounding fashion when one Elder exclaimed that "it is acknowledged that a written law on education has been discussed for some time. Indeed, the communities have said: 'Get on with it!'"[91] After that, a feast was held. From that moment, it could be said, the first five steps of the Treaty 3 law-making process were satisfied.

In the months following this historic occasion, which have since dragged into years, a "Draft Record of Decision" emerged from the 2008 Treaty 3 Chiefs in Assembly with regard to the Treaty 3 written education law. According to the Draft Record of Decision, Kinamaadiwin Inaakonigewin "shall be subject to, and consistent with, all aspects of Kagagiwe Inaakonigewin and Anishinaabe Inaakonigewin," which for greater clarity are our sacred and customary laws.[92] It further stipulates that, "*notwithstanding that the law may be written in another language, Anishinaabemowin shall be its official language.*"[93] This provision is significant in the sense that it attends to the issue, which I identified earlier, of translating Anishinaabe legal concepts into a foreign language while also making it accessible to non-language speakers, thus maintaining and even revitalizing our legal tradition. Moreover, this stipulation recognizes that English is the language of international diplomacy, and that there is a certain necessity to use it, even if only to communicate better with our neighbours. With step 6 of the Treaty 3 law-making process being a report to the Chiefs in Assembly, the Draft Record of Decision implies that a report was indeed made to them, whereby the Chiefs gave direction to the executive director, the administrative arm of the Grand Council Treaty #3, on how to draft a written law on education.

In March 2019, a draft of the written education law was completed by the Technical Working Group based upon the guidance provided by Elders, youth, parents, educators, and other relevant Treaty 3 stakeholders and submitted to the Grand Council Treaty #3. Unfortunately, in the following months, the onset of the COVID pandemic stalled the progress made to that point. As of the time of writing, the draft law remains in the possession of the Grand Council Treaty #3, but I have been informed that the administration wants to do another round of community engagement to ensure that the draft law will meet community expectations. According to step 7 of the Treaty 3 law-making process, the Chiefs will follow the direction provided by the people.[94] To initiate this phase, Diane Longboat recommends that a motion be made at a formal gathering to discuss the draft education law at a subsequent Chiefs in Assembly, at which time the Chiefs will vote on whether or not to "accept in principle the draft Education Law and begin the community consultation phase and public information sessions."[95] In due time, the Grand Council Treaty #3 will provide copies of the draft education law to the communities, notifying the members of its intention to pass a Treaty 3 education law based upon community approval. Once copies of the draft law have been distributed to the communities, the Grand Council Treaty #3 is to give community members at least thirty days notice of a general meeting to discuss the proposed education law. Following that meeting, community members will be given at least another thirty days to provide comments on the draft law, which can be submitted "in writing or orally by deposition" to a designated official of the Grand Council Treaty #3.[96] After the period of community review has elapsed, representatives of the Grand Council Treaty #3 will review the comments and decide on any amendments to the draft education law. If amendments are required, then the Grand Council Treaty #3 will make them and then reintroduce the amended draft law to the communities, following the same procedures as before, to give the communities sufficient time to review the amendments. Once it is determined that the people are in favour of the draft law, and that no other amendments are necessary, a vote can take place at a special meeting with the Treaty 3 Chiefs in Assembly to pass the education law. For it to pass, it is recommended that the education law obtain 75 percent support from the Chiefs in Assembly, at which time it can finally be said that step 7 of the Treaty 3 law-making process has been fulfilled.[97]

Once the draft education law has been accepted by the Treaty 3 Chiefs in Assembly, the Ogichidaa and the head of the education portfolio will refer the document to the Elders for direction on the next protocols required. It is stated in the Treaty 3 Record of Decision that, "upon receipt of the completed draft written law by the Elders, they will advise on the protocols for its validation and consecration in ceremony."[98] This traditional and highly ritualized practice involving the Elders constitutes step 8 of the Treaty 3 law-making process. While in ceremony—which, for greater clarity, traditionally involves sweat lodge and shaking tent ceremonies—the Elders in Assembly will scrutinize the draft law and ensure that it is consistent with sacred and traditional laws. During this time, the Elders can also advise on revision or reconsideration of the written law based upon their respective knowledge. Following the written law's validation and consecration in traditional ceremony, the Elders will transmit it to the Ogichidaa, "who will acknowledge its receipt in the name of the Anishinaabe Nation in Treaty #3 and certify a true copy."[99] When the education law is approved, the Grand Council Treaty #3 will pass a resolution, by way of a National Chiefs Assembly, to proclaim the effective date of the law. At that time, all members of the Treaty 3 National Assembly will sign the resolution, and a traditional feast and celebration of the written law will follow. In complying with these directives and protocols, the Treaty 3 law-making process can be said to be complete, with the last two steps being a final Elders' feast and National Assembly approval. Notwithstanding the approval of the written law, it is important to note that "the law takes effect locally when an individual constituent nation assents" to the provisions of the law, so as to maintain harmony and respect for an individual nation's inherent right to autonomy, self-determination, and independent sovereignty.[100]

Summary

In the time period since our travails with the residential school system, and more recently with the public education system, much energy and vision have gone into revitalizing our traditional education law so that we, as Indigenous peoples, can begin to establish and administer our own education systems. The Anishinaabe, as Leanne Simpson writes in *Dancing on Our Turtle's Back*, are entering the period of the Seventh Fire. During this time, she says, it is the responsibility of this generation of Anishinaabe to "pick up the pieces of our lifeways, collectivize them and build a political and cultural renaissance and resurgence. It is also foretold that if this is done in a good way, it has the power to transform settler society such that respectful political relationships can be re-established, based on the Indigenous principles of peace, justice, and righteousness as embodied in mino bimaadiziwin."[101] To do this, the written laws that we create, Ozhibiige Inaakonigewin, must be consistent with our customary values and beliefs, especially with our sacred and traditional laws, but they must also reflect the conditions of our present society, both locally and abroad. By establishing purpose and guiding principles that follow a traditional law-making process, a foundation has been laid for a written law in education, Kinamaadiwin Inaakonigewin. It is a foundation further reinforced by the *consent* and *consensus* of its people, which have the Anishinaabe Nation in Treaty #3 on the cusp of achieving peace, justice, and righteousness, as described by Simpson. Yet there is still much more work to be done before our self-determination is actualized. Beyond carrying out the last steps of the law-making process, an institutional entity must be formed—that is, the Treaty #3 Education Commission—and headed by a leader from among our people who has both the knowledge and the ability to transform our vision into reality. Moreover, a vast series of policies and regulations needs to be established that not only supplements the written education law but also gives form and content to the incumbent Treaty 3 education system. In the next chapter, I will address these outstanding issues with an examination of administrative concerns such as the implementation of an education plan and other policy and regulatory matters such as the development of curriculum and education standards. This analysis will include insights learned about the treaty relationship and further discuss why Kinamaadiwin Inaakonigewin must be recognized and affirmed by the Canadian state.

Chapter 4

RECONCILIATION AS RECOGNITION *AND* AFFIRMATION

As I have argued throughout this book, the hardships that Indigenous peoples and nations have endured as a result of colonization have made it necessary to revitalize our legal traditions. Fortunately, as we have entered a new era of Indigenous and settler relations, the government of Canada has taken important first steps toward reconciling its relationship with Indigenous nations—to the extent that it has apologized for its role in the Indian residential school system, drafted and passed new UNDRIP legislation, and committed itself to fulfill the Truth and Reconciliation Commission's ninety-four Calls to Action—but the government has much more work to do to fulfill its mandate. Although important, these initial steps toward reconciliation are largely focused on one issue: the residential school system. If the government of Canada is genuinely committed to the process of reconciliation, then it must expand its mandate to address the injustice of the Indian Act and, perhaps most importantly, the severely neglected treaty relationship. After many decades of abuse and mistrust, there is no quick and easy fix to any of these issues, but nothing, in my estimation, could better signify the government's goodwill and intent than to recognize and affirm Indigenous nations' traditional laws. As John Borrows has recently said, in doing so "we would discover that the resurgence of Indigenous law would help reconcile us to one another and bind ourselves in healthier relationships with the earth."[1] The all-important caveat, however, is that the government of Canada must not only *recognize* but also *affirm* Indigenous laws through concrete, observable actions. In this chapter, I will illuminate further what these processes of recognition and affirmation look like when applied in the context of Kinamaadiwin Inaakonigewin, the Treaty 3 education law.

On Struggle and Resolution

Recognition, in a Hegelian sense, is earned and won through struggle and confrontation. According to Hegel, when a consciousness—which could represent an individual or a national consciousness—meets another consciousness, an inevitable struggle ensues at some point to assert order in any given social dynamic. The struggle might not necessarily be a physical confrontation, a battle of brawn per se; it could be a battle of wits, a confrontation of intellects, or an ideological or legal dispute. Through this struggle, one consciousness recognizes the other consciousness, and order is achieved.[2] Indigenous peoples in Canada certainly have experienced their share of struggle as a result of deceit and coercion manifested by state policies only beginning to be recognized by the broader society. In more practical terms, deceit has been and continues to be experienced by Indigenous peoples through the state's refusal to honour its treaty obligations, and the residential school system epitomizes the coercion employed by the state to suffocate Indigenous consciousness. Our struggle, as Indigenous peoples, is a testament to the virtue of our consciousness and will ultimately serve as the catalyst by which our inherent right to self-determination is eventually recognized. In other words, the struggle will continue until our consciousness is recognized and affirmed. It is our *truth*, Fanon says, "what hastens the dislocation of the colonial regime, what fosters the emergence of the nation. Truth is what protects the 'natives' and undoes the foreigners."[3] Thus, Indigenous peoples must continue to speak our truths of injustice, oppression, redemption, and reconciliation. For our voices to be heard, however, we must speak our truth in a way recognized and understood by Western society—that is, through the written word.

Recognition, however, means nothing without affirmation. It is like pillow talk without follow-through. As Harold Cardinal says, "if claims regarding treaties or aboriginal rights are not settled using our definitions of nation, identity, and religious right, there will be a continuing sense of injustice and grievance among Indians, which will destroy the settlement."[4] For justice to be realized, then, state affirmation must come bearing gifts of political, legal, and economic action that support Indigenous initiatives, particularly those in the field of education. Some Indigenous scholars, however, have challenged this assertion on the basis that there is no willingness by Canadians or the state to change the status quo and therefore have decided to turn their backs on Canada. In *As We Have Always Done: Indigenous Freedom through Radical Resistance*, for example, Leanne Simpson writes that "very few Canadians will directly proclaim they are in favor of the position of Indigenous peoples in Canada, but a very large number of Canadians will do everything they can to preserve the social, cultural, and economic systems of the country, even though this system is predicated on violence and dispossession of Indigenous lands and bodies. Therefore, we do not need the help of Canadians."[5]

Although I understand and empathize with Simpson's position, since the government of Canada has given Indigenous peoples little reason to believe that it will change its ways, I also share a concern with Aaron Mills, about the effectiveness of a "turn away" strategy because of its anti-relational nature; as he says, it "cannot be squared with Anishinaabe constitutionalism."[6] To that point, I would add that such a position fundamentally contradicts the "spirit and intent" of the treaties, predicated on the notion of "peace, friendship, and respect" *as long as the sun shines and the rivers flow*. That said, one must also acknowledge that different social, economic, and political contexts might require different strategies and approaches to achieve Indigenous cultural resurgence and reconciliation. For example, Anishinaabe scholar Gail Guthrie Valaskakis has written about the "walleye warriors" who resolutely practised their treaty right to fish season after season—even while slogans such as "save a pickerel, spear an Indian" abounded—until that right was eventually and formally recognized by the American government.[7] Thus, for Leanne Simpson, who theorizes cultural resurgence in the context of the Michi Saagig Nishnaabeg territory (completely occupied by eastern Ontario settler townships as a result of fraudulent land surrenders stemming from the Williams treaties), a turn away strategy might be the only viable option to have their treaty rights recognized and affirmed.

It has been said that affirmation, as a form of restitution in the process of reconciliation, involves "the return of what was stolen, accepting reparations (either land, material, or monetary recompense) for what cannot be returned, and forging a new socio-political relationship based on the Settler state's admission of wrongdoing and acceptance of the responsibility and obligation to engage Indigenous peoples in a restitution-reconciliation peace-building process."[8] Without this, I suspect that Canada will experience an uptick—in both frequency and scale—of Indigenous protest and civil disobedience, the likes of which were observed in Tyendinaga in 2020.[9] In Glen Coulthard's view, however, this is exactly what *needs* to happen. Coulthard says that, in order to remove colonial, racist, patriarchal, legal, and political obstacles, Indigenous peoples must "continue to assert our presence on all of our territories, coupled with an escalation of confrontations with the forces of colonization through the forms of direct action that are currently being undertaken by communities like Elsipogtog" and Tyendinaga.[10] Coulthard goes on to explain that rail and road blockades and other sites of reoccupation—Oka and Ipperwash immediately come to mind—should be considered expressions of "direct action" for the following reasons: "First, the practices are directly undertaken by the subjects of colonial oppression themselves and seek to produce an immediate power effect; second, they are undertaken in a way that indicates a loosening of internalized colonialism, which is itself a precondition for any meaningful change; and third, they are prefigurative in the sense that they build the skills and social relationships (including those with the land) that are required within and among Indigenous communities to construct alternatives to the colonial relationship in the long run."[11]

Taiaiake Alfred further argues that these forms of direct action are the basis of a contention by Indigenous peoples that "demands accountability for the underlying power relationship and the state's domination of our existence. It refuses to be drawn into maintaining the colonial system, and takes a firm stand (intellectually, politically, and physically) in defence of the principles, institutions, and lands that form the core of indigenous nations."[12] From this perspective, Albert Memmi's astute words in *The Colonizer and the Colonized* are prescient: "Far from being surprised at the revolts of colonized peoples, we should be, on the contrary, surprised that they are not more frequent and more violent."[13] Yet, as important as Indigenous forms of resistance are to tyrannical government policies, a full-scale revolution is not a realistic option for Indigenous peoples given their drastic minority status in Canada as well as the fact that the use of violence runs counter to many Indigenous philosophies. With this in mind, it is important to make clear that Indigenous peoples' expressions of direct action—in the forms of blockades, reoccupations, marches, hunger strikes, and even writing our own laws—are meant not to usurp state authority but to attain recognition and affirmation that our communities are suffering and that a collective shift in ideological values is needed to address properly the suffering experienced by Indigenous peoples.

The Butterfly Effect and Idle No More

I once organized a protest movement called March 4 Justice. This is my story. Back in 2012, when I was an ambitious graduate student working on my master's degree, and learning about the history of Indigenous peoples in Canada, as well as their present circumstances, and theories on how to create social change, I became very interested in the Indian Act. As you will recall, the Indian Act is a piece of Canadian legislation that has been used and continues to be employed as a tool of social and cultural oppression. In the past, it was used to ban traditional ceremonies such as the potlatch and sundance, as well as to implement enfranchisement laws, which stripped Indigenous people of their Indian status for serving in the army, getting a postsecondary degree, or marrying non-Indigenous people. At one point, it also banned Indigenous people from leaving their reserves unless they obtained a "pass permit" from the local "Indian agent." Perhaps most importantly, the Indian Act was also the means by which the government enforced Indigenous children's attendance at residential schools. And, as I mentioned earlier, although it has been amended many times over the years, the Indian Act continues to dictate the regulations for registration of Indian status as well as the rules of governance within Indigenous communities. The more I learned about the Indian Act, the more convinced I became that someone should do something about this oppressive piece of legislation.

As the story goes, in January 2012, the government of Canada convened in a highly anticipated parliamentary session to discuss which changes, if any, should be made to the Indian Act. Unfortunately, the only outcome of the debate was that a "progress report" would be presented in a year's time.[14] As someone who expected, perhaps naively, a more substantive resolution to the issue, I was angry with the lack of urgency displayed. So, in an effort to draw more attention to the issue, I took it upon myself to do something and decided to organize a protest movement in which I pledged to march across Canada from Vancouver to Ottawa with a copy of the Indian Act chained to my waist. To publicize the movement, I engaged different media outlets, but none were really interested apart from APTN National News, which ran a two-minute segment of my story on the program. Despite the lack of media interest, I started the march on 23 April 2012.

As I made my way across Canada, I spoke to many people and visited many communities. One of my more significant speaking engagements was at the Truth and Reconciliation Commission's national event in June 2012 in Saskatoon in front of about 300 people or so.[15] In all of my speaking engagements, whether with local media or Indigenous communities, my messages were usually the same. One such message was that, if there is going to be federal legislation about Indigenous peoples in Canada, *and there should be*, then that legislation needs to be written *by* Indigenous people *for* Indigenous people. The other message that I often had for people was that, if you desire social change in your community, then you cannot be idle and wait for that change to happen. You must go out and seek such change yourself. All social change begins at the individual level.

Fast-forward a few months to November 2012 when four women— namely, Sheelah McLean, Sylvia McAdam, Jessica Gordon, and Nina Wilson (who happened to be in the same master's program as me at the time)—organized a teach-in event for the public in Saskatoon under the banner Idle No More. The teach-in event was held in response to the government's introduction of Bill C-45, which aimed to overhaul the Navigable Waters Protection Act. Although I cannot be sure whether the organizers of Idle No More had heard my message, it was nevertheless very encouraging that people's social consciousness had been awakened and that they were now actively seeking the types of social change that they wanted to see in their communities. That said, the next key event around that time was an Assembly of First Nations General Assembly in Ottawa in December. In the lead up to that event, I was again asked to speak about my experience with March 4 Justice and share my views about the Indian Act, and again I issued a call for action at that event.

The following day several Chiefs—including Anishinabek Nation Grand Council Chief Patrick Madahbee, Serpent River First Nation Chief Isadore Day, Onion Lake Cree Nation Chief Wallace Fox, and Assembly of Manitoba Chiefs Grand Chief Derek Nepinak—seemingly answered that call, went to Parliament Hill, and tried to force their way into the House of Commons to tell then-prime minister Stephen Harper that time was up and that they intended to take direct action to address their grievances.[16] Following the entry of the Chiefs onto Parliament Hill, the

Idle No More movement picked up momentum and organized dozens more protests across Canada before and after the Christmas season, most of which consisted of flash mobs in which protesters participated in round dances in shopping malls. There was also a blockade on the CN main rail line between Toronto and Montreal that lasted three hours. As a result of those protests, the Idle No More movement gained international attention, to the point that solidarity protests were held in other countries, approximately thirty of which were in the United States, followed by other demonstrations in Stockholm, London, Berlin, Auckland, and Cairo.

The rapid spread of the Idle No More movement ultimately elicited a response from Harper, who announced that he would host a meeting with Indigenous leaders planned for 11 January 2013. On the day of the meeting, the leaders of Idle No More organized another protest on Parliament Hill that drew approximately 3,000 people and brought some remarkable images and sound bites from national media outlets to the public.[17] The protest was also significant in the sense that it demonstrated for the first time that Indigenous peoples were united on a cause and demanded that their voices be heard. Although John Duncan, the minister of Aboriginal affairs at the time, said that high-level dialogue would continue, the meeting between Harper and AFN leaders failed to yield any meaningful results. Nevertheless, I hope that by sharing this story I have shown that even the smallest of currents can sometimes cause massive social waves.

Polishing the Silver

When Indigenous people protest the injustices perpetrated against us and our communities, we draw attention to the fact that we are in crisis mode. We require political and economic support from a state whose financial resources and wealth come in large measure from tax revenues gained by underwriting the extraction of natural resources on Indigenous lands. As Harold Cardinal and others have said repeatedly, Indigenous nations and the Canadian state "must discover that not only are they not adversaries, they are in fact partners, more than partners—brothers and sisters—who have similar problems to face, the first of which is the creation of a better environment for the future."[18] In this context, it is imperative that the state recognizes and affirms that there is a kinship relationship with Indigenous peoples as well as with the land and that unilateral policy decisions will not work. To that end, Anishinaabe scholar Dale Turner recommends the development of a "critical Indigenous philosophy" that not only unpacks the colonial framework but also asserts indigeneity within the dominant culture and defends the legal and political integrity of Indigenous communities.[19]

There are many lessons to be drawn from previous and ongoing political engagements between Indigenous peoples and the Canadian state. One such lesson is in fact universal: violence begets more violence. We must find a way to return to moral principles of kinship and peace and goodwill (discussed in Chapter 2) as stated in the treaties.[20] These principles invoke the spirit and intent of treaties and other agreements such as the Covenant Chain, notably one of the original agreements between Indigenous nations and the Crown. In *Linking Arms Together: American Indian Treaty Visions of Law and Peace, 1600–1800*, Robert Williams Jr. uncovers a quotation from a 1796 treaty council that describes how the treaty relationship should be observed and acted on with reference to the Covenant Chain: "Brothers: We pray you to take this matter into good consideration, and do by us as you would wish to be done by Brothers, this is what we wish for; that every brother might have their rights throughout this continent, and all to be of one mind, and to live together in peace and love, as becometh brothers; and to have a chain of friendship made between you and us, too strong ever to be broke, and polished and brightened so pure as never to rust. This is our sincere wishes."[21]

The notion of polishing the silver—or, to put it differently, renewing the relationship—is as old as the art of diplomacy itself and in fact a fundamental element of any diplomatic negotiation. The failure to renew treaties from the Confederation era is nothing short of negligent. In the context of Treaty 3, specifically, if we consider what was spoken—as well as written—at the negotiations by Treaty Commissioner Alexander Morris himself, then it seems to be evident that an enduring, healthy relationship is predicated on principles of peace and goodwill. By his own account in *The Treaties of Canada*, just prior to signing the treaty, Morris said that "I hope we are going to understand one another today. And that I can go back and report that I left my Indian friends contented, and that I have put into their hands the means of providing for themselves and their families at home. . . . *[W]e are anxious to show you that we have a great desire to understand you—that we wish to do the utmost in our power to make you contented so that the white and the red man will always be friends.*"[22]

The phrase "I have put into their hands the means of providing for themselves" is of particular interest here since it connotes an element of self-determination. When Morris talked about leaving his "Indian friends contented," and giving us "the means of providing" for ourselves, we Anishinaabe understood that we would have a choice in terms of how we exercise our rights, particularly our right to education. Apart from that, biographer Robert Talbot notes that, upon concluding the treaty negotiation, "Morris took Mawedopenais's hand and promised that he would keep his word, believing that the treaty he was signing would 'bind the red man and the white together as friends forever.'"[23] Again we see that the promises were meant to be honoured, in the interest of being friends, "always" and "forever," principles that can be accomplished only through regular maintenance and renewal.

On the interpretation of socio-political discourse, which would include diplomatic processes such as the treaties and the Covenant Chain, Michel Foucault argues in *The Archaeology of Knowledge and the Discourse on Language* that "these systems of formation must not be taken as blocks of immobility, static forms that are imposed on discourse from the outside, and that define once and for all its characteristics and possibilities."[24] Rather, they should be viewed as living entities that must be nourished, and treated with respect, since they help to define and articulate the spirit and intent of the relationship set forth. The statements made during these diplomatic processes must obviously be considered within the contexts in which they were made but also allow for modification with the passage of time. According to Foucault, "the statement, then, must not be treated as an event that occurred in a particular time and place, and that the most one can do is recall it—and celebrate it from afar off—in an act of memory. . . . [The statement] is endowed with a certain modifiable heaviness, a weight relative to the field in which it is placed, a constancy that allows for various uses, a temporal permanence that does not have the inertia of a mere trace or mark, and which does not sleep on its own past."[25] In other words, the treaty must be allowed to be modified constantly to give relevance to its temporal permanence. As Michael Coyle points out, in entering into a relationship expected to endure indefinitely, "*the historical treaty partners would be prepared, in the face of significant changes in circumstances over time, to negotiate, in good faith, a new consensus as to how their treaty understandings should be renewed to address both sides' contemporary needs and interests in relation to the treaty lands.*"[26] In other words, a formal process must be established to renew the terms of the treaty, the likes of which are typical—if not mandatory—in standard collective bargaining agreements today. This is a process of renewal similar to what James Tully has described as a "mediated peace," guided by the three conventions of justice: mutual recognition, continuity, and consent. According to Tully, "if this view of constitutionalism came to be accepted, the allegedly irreconcilable conflicts of the present would not have to be the tragic history of our future."[27] That said, in my view, it makes sense to renew the terms every ten years so that treaty obligations become major political platforms, and are in constant view of the public, thereby facilitating a transparent and accountable political environment. Moreover, renewing the terms of the treaty every ten years would give enough time to implement new policies and assess their impacts while also bridging the needs of one generation with the next.

A second lesson, as I discussed in Chapter 1, relates to ideological differences about the land. When treaties were negotiated between Indigenous nations and the Crown, a major point for Indigenous leaders was ensuring that their people would be able not only to maintain their traditional way of life, as well as teach that way to their children, but also to have the choice to participate in broader society and the market economy if they so wanted. As Michael Asch points out in *On Being Here to Stay: Treaties and Aboriginal Rights in Canada*, the Crown promised "to provide assistance in times of need so that they would be 'free from hunger,' to ensure that they would be as 'wealthy' as the Settlers, and, perhaps most important of all, to make certain that their economic security would not require that they be required by the Crown to change their way of life."[28] At the same time, however, the Crown also sought to preserve its interest in the land by stipulating its desire to take up industrial activities whenever doing so was suitable. Curiously, these different ideologies with fundamentally opposed interests meet in the hunting and fishing clauses of the Numbered Treaties: "Her Majesty further agrees with Her said Indians that they, *the said Indians, shall have right to pursue their avocations of hunting and fishing throughout the tract surrendered as hereinbefore described*, subject to such regulations as may from time to time be made by Her Government of Her Dominion of Canada, and saving and *excepting such tracts as may, from time to time, be required or taken up for settlement, mining, lumbering or other purposes by Her said Government of the Dominion of Canada*, or by any of the subjects thereof duly authorized therefor by the said Government."[29]

That the Crown exercised its right to pursue its mining, lumbering, and hydro avocations, and that these practices in effect interfered—indeed compromised—Indigenous nations' ability to sustain our traditional ways of life, are primary reasons that there has been so much dispute and discord in the treaty relationship. As Gina Starblanket and Heidi Stark have pointed out, "settler movements towards development, technological advancement, progress, and innovation have a strong association with the discontinuity or loss of Indigenous traditions."[30] Moreover, the omnipresence of corporate development and its pervasive impact on Indigenous lands has forced many Indigenous communities into a state of economic dependence, such that an unhealthy reliance on the revenues and jobs created by resource extraction agencies has been cultivated within localized Indigenous consciousness. These circumstances have led Indigenous scholars such as Dale Turner to suggest that Indigenous leaders and intellectuals bear a responsibility to participate in three distinct activities: "(a) they must take up, deconstruct, and continue to resist colonialism and its effects on indigenous peoples; (b) they must protect and defend indigeneity; and (c) they must engage the legal and political discourses of the state in an effective way."[31]

With that in mind, Glen Coulthard discusses the concept of "grounded normativity," inspired and informed by our collective struggle over land use. According to Coulthard, the struggle is

> not only *for* land in the material sense, but also deeply *informed* by what the land *as a system of reciprocal relations and obligations* can teach us about living our lives in relation to one another and the natural world in nondominating and nonexploitative terms—and less around our emergent status as "rightless proletarians." I call this place-based foundation of Indigenous decolonial thought and practice *grounded normativity*, by which I mean the modalities of Indigenous land—connected practices and longstanding experiential knowledge that inform and structure our ethical engagements with the world and our relationships with human and nonhuman others over time.[32]

Coulthard's concept of grounded normativity and the teachings that it provides seem to point to a potential solution to our collective worries: *indigenized education*, a system of education founded upon traditional

Indigenous philosophies of relationship, land stewardship, balance, peace, and harmony. Indeed, in this age of environmental crisis because of deforestation, resource extraction, and industrial development, Indigenous knowledge of the land, and how we care for it, has never been more important to the survival of our species and ultimately the world. As James Tully says, "there are important lessons from a sustainable human-with-nature relationship for a sustainable human-with-human relationship because all human-with-human relationships (social systems) are embedded in and dependent on human-with-nature relationships."[33] As a critical construct, grounded normativity has many elements in line with the principles that I outlined in the previous chapter on Kinamaadiwin Inaakonigewin, the Treaty 3 written education law. It can be said that by developing and implementing Kinamaadiwin Inaakonigewin in a good way—that is, by recognizing and affirming that Indigenous peoples have a right to govern their own education systems—we, as Canadians *and* Indigenous peoples, would take important steps, together, toward repairing our frayed relationship. This process would be akin to repolishing the silver on the Covenant Chain, which means honouring the treaties and ultimately recommitting to coexist peacefully with one another. Finally, with regard to indigenized education, Leanne Simpson makes the critical point that "Indigenous education is not Indigenous or education from within our intellectual practices unless it comes through the land, unless it occurs in an Indigenous context using Indigenous processes."[34] To put it differently, *indigenized education* means that Indigenous peoples must be in control of Indigenous education using Indigenous processes. For the Anishinaabe Nation in Treaty #3, Kinamaadiwin Inaakonigewin is the framework within which that can happen. In light of these extensive considerations, in the rest of this chapter I will chart a path on which these objectives and the overall goal of reconciliation can be traced and followed.

On Transitioning from Canadian Law to Indigenous Law

In the previous chapter, I provided some historical context for the Anishinaabe Nation in Treaty #3 to develop our own written law in education. Briefly stated, existing education programs designed by the state and the funding provided to such programs are inadequate. Although significant progress has been made in the Treaty 3 law-making process, including the drafting of a proposed education law, a lot remains to be done before the law can be ratified and an Anishinaabe education system established.

As I indicated in Chapter 3, one of the primary tasks will be to establish a Treaty #3 Education Commission to administer the programs and services of the corresponding education system. In addition to assessing the educational needs and demands of each constituent community, as well as acquiring the requisite financial support from funding agencies to do its work, the Treaty #3 Education Commission will have to produce a number of policies and regulations related to its administrative agenda. Once the law is ratified, the Grand Council Treaty #3 will have to select a head of education to provide leadership and direction in the administration of the Treaty #3 Education Commission. As the head of the education portfolio, this person will be responsible for designing policies, plans, and programs that serve the educational goals of the Anishinaabe Nation of Treaty #3 as well as addressing the specific—that is, local—educational needs of each constituent community. This process will include establishing a board of directors for the Treaty #3 Education Commission composed of Treaty 3 Elders, parents who are active members on the Community Education Council, community directors of education, and various representatives of the state (both internal and external).

In consideration of the initial tasks and responsibilities of implementing an Indigenous education law, Diane Longboat—the Indigenous legal scholar who designed a template for such laws—suggests that a two-year period of transition be allowed from when a written education law is ratified to its full implementation.[35] During this period, Longboat says, it will be the responsibility of the institutional administration—i.e., Treaty #3 Education Commission—to seek formal recognition and affirmation from the state that its federal and provincial laws related to education "will cease to apply" in the communities where the law is to be implemented.[36] This process is consistent with what John Borrows has written about in *Law's Indigenous Ethics*: "Anishinaabe law calls for the reversal of federal and provincial laws directed towards diminishing reserves and assimilating Indigenous peoples."[37] Until such recognition and affirmation can be achieved, however, the existing education programs and services of each community will continue to be administered under the authority of its local government, with support from the Grand Council Treaty #3. That is also to say that all contracts for education personnel as well as all funding agreements will continue to be in force until they have either been renegotiated or terminated under mutually agreeable terms. According to Longboat, an Indigenous education law "does not abrogate the rights of its members based on inherent or Treaty rights or their rights established in the federal laws of Canada," nor does the law "diminish the Honour of the Crown, the trust responsibility of the government of Canada or its duty to provide funds for the education of the First Nation members."[38] Finally, notwithstanding the state's cooperation on these objectives, the period of transition is also important in the sense that it allows for the completion of all policies and regulations related to the written education law. Following the completion of these tasks, Kinamaadiwin Inaakonigewin—as defined by the Grand Council Treaty #3 and its representative body, the Treaty #3 Education Commission—will supersede "any other Act passed federally or provincially or territorially, or any regulations of any institution, agency or body with respect to management, finances, programs, certification of standards and all matters regarding First Nation education."[39] If that seems to be out of step with what the federal government might be willing to do, consider that the report of the Standing Senate Committee on Aboriginal Peoples recommended that federal legislation "should explicitly recognize First Nations authority over education, as well as provide a legal under-pinning for First Nations second and third level education authorities."[40]

Education Plan and Standards

Given that Indigenous nations and communities in Canada historically have struggled to launch successful education programs as a result of chronic underfunding, this undoubtedly will be a challenge that the Anishinaabe Nation in Treaty #3 must be prepared for. To ensure a smooth period of transition, the Treaty #3 Education Commission will have the monumental task of striking a delicate balance between developing an education plan that not only meets the needs of the people whom it is intended to serve but also is palatable to its primary funding agency, the Canadian government. As Harold Cardinal has said, "to be successful, any development proposal must first have the support of the group or individual it is designed to help, and second, the support of whoever or whatever is financing it."[41] The education plan will have to be as detailed as possible, such that it clearly articulates the social, environmental, economic, political, spiritual, and cultural objectives of the education system, with a view toward the strategy for both intermediate and long-term sustainability. In relation to that point, the draft version of Kinamaadiwin Inaakonigewin contains a clause that allows the education plan to be modified on a cyclical basis so as best to represent the educational needs of the Anishinaabe Nation in Treaty #3 for each generation of learners as well as to incorporate the most recent "social and economic trends of Canadian society with a view to impacts on the Anishinaabe Nation of Treaty #3 and the need for skilled labour, workers in the professions, technology professionals, and general labour."[42]

Apart from assessing annual costs for education programming and service delivery, which would include construction and renovation projects, Kinamaadiwin Inaakonigewin states that the education plan must also weigh the "housing, sanitation, nutrition, and . . . general health and social needs that affect [the] educational success" of Treaty 3 youth.[43] At the fundamental level, the education plan is an exercise of the Anishinaabe Nation in Treaty #3's basic human rights in accordance with the UNDRIP as well as a manifestation of the treaty right to education. This point is in line with a policy paper written by the Assembly of First Nations entitled "Tradition and Education: Towards a Vision of Our Future, a Declaration of First Nations Jurisdiction over Education," which asserts that "education for First Nations people is a matter of an inherent aboriginal right. The federal government has a legal obligation through various treaties to provide adequate resources and services for education. The federal government is obligated to provide resources for quality education programs, facilities, transportation, equipment, and materials to meet the needs as determined by First Nations."[44] In other words, if long-standing treaty disputes and the denial of basic human rights accorded to Indigenous peoples are the causes of so much conflict—particularly related to education—then supporting an education plan designed by Indigenous peoples for Indigenous peoples is one tangible way in which the state can redeem itself from its heinous history.

In addition to the education plan, the Treaty #3 Education Commission will have to establish education standards for the Treaty 3 Anishinaabe education system. Kinamaadiwin Inaakonigewin states that the education standards of the Treaty 3 Anishinaabe education system must be accountable to our language, culture, history, spirituality, and traditional knowledge systems.[45] The standards are to be developed in accordance with the nation's sacred law, Kagagiwe Inaakonigewin, under the supervision and counsel of Elders, educators, administrators, community members, and parents. Accordingly, once the standards have been developed by the

Treaty #3 Education Commission, they are to be submitted and eventually approved through a formal resolution by the Grand Council Treaty #3 at a National Chiefs Assembly.

As I mentioned in Chapters 2 and 3, one of the major and potentially contentious aspects of getting Kinamaadiwin Inaakonigewin recognized and affirmed involves achieving the harmonization of intragovernmental education laws. The challenge is presented as one in which provincial governments in Canada have zealously defended their legal jurisdiction over education. Ever since the signing of Treaty 9, in which the Crown first insisted that the government of Ontario be included in treaty negotiations, Canada has made a point of saying that Indigenous governance structures and laws are subject to existing federal and provincial laws.[46] A typical justification for this view is that Indigenous education systems lack academic rigour. As such, virtually all agreements negotiated by Indigenous nations and the state since the Numbered Treaties contain a "transferability clause" essentially stating that any education program undertaken by an Indigenous nation must conform to provincial standards. With Kinamaadiwin Inaakonigewin, the Anishinaabe Nation in Treaty #3 is essentially flipping the script by insisting, in its own terms, that the education standards of the Treaty 3 education system must "meet or exceed those of the provinces and territories . . . [and] preserve Anishinaabemowin along with cultural and spiritual traditions and enable students to develop to their maximum potential."[47] Treaty 3 leaders have identified this clause as important not only to obtain Crown support but also to ensure that students can transfer to an adjacent education system if circumstances require it. Some scholars, however, have challenged the notion of transferability on the ground that its necessity constitutes an infringement of Indigenous educational sovereignty. As one example, Métis scholar Laura Forsythe argues that "the transferability clause regarding content and assessment along with set standards for certification and accreditation do not provide the nation with the autonomy required for true Indigenous educational sovereignty, which demands cultural and language education free from external interference."[48] Notwithstanding Forsythe's astute analysis of the Tla'amin Final Agreement Act of 2016, I think that the term "sovereignty" as constructed here merits closer attention.

If sovereignty is understood or recognized only as absolute authority or autonomy, I would question first whether *any* nation has such omniscient power or authority. Beyond that, I wonder whether it is even helpful to think of sovereignty in such a way that might require a secession from Canada. In this post-9/11 era of international diplomacy, any challenge to state sovereignty is always defended to the extreme from external threats as well as internal ones—and Indigenous forms of direct action sometimes have been labelled "domestic terrorism"[49]—so for this reason I believe that Indigenous nations that wish to exercise their right to self-determination—especially as it relates to education—should do so with tact to have their needs met or be prepared for blowback from the state. As former minister of justice and regional chief of the Assembly of First Nations Jody Wilson-Raybould points out, a secession from Canada is not only unworkable but also probably undesirable. For her, sovereignty entails "structuring proper nation-to-nation relationships between Crown governments and Indigenous governments that recognize Indigenous Nationhood, title, rights, jurisdictions, and laws."[50] Sovereignty can and should be imagined in a number of ways that do not necessarily conform to an absolute stereotype. It could be argued further that each nation is inextricably linked, or related, and thereby accountable to others, regardless of any claim to national sovereignty. Indeed, the idea that we are all related, including non-human beings, is the philosophy upon which relationality was conceived, hence *all* our relations. As such, it might be more appropriate to view sovereignty as a "shared" concept, as described by the RCAP commissioners: "Shared sovereignty, in our view, is a hallmark of the Canadian federation and a central feature of the three-cornered relations that link Aboriginal governments, provincial governments and the federal government. These governments are sovereign within their respective spheres and hold their powers by virtue of their constitutional status rather than by delegation. Nevertheless, many of their powers are shared in practice and may be exercised by more than one order of government."[51]

In his chapter "Rooted Constitutionalism: Growing Political Community," Anishinaabe scholar Aaron Mills offers a beautiful analogy of a forest as a theoretical representation of shared sovereignty. In the analogy, each nation or order of government represents a different species of tree within a forest. With regard to the Anishinaabe, Mills envisions our constitutional order as such:

> Creation stories set out a people's way of being in and (if rooted) of the earth. They give us our ideas of what a person is, what freedom is, and thus what community is. The trunk is

the constitutional order that manifests these understandings as political community. It's our framework for living together called into being by the story we tell. I mean as peoples, which may have nothing to do with founding documents. Our branches are our legal tradition(s): the assemblage of processes and institutions we use to generate, sustain, alter, and destroy norms. The leaves are our provisionally settled norms. They experience the highest degree of change within the set of relationships that constitute a normative order. Some will fall off, never to return. Others will return after renewal. All come from, all recur with, earth.[52]

With this in mind, I believe that the transferability of education standards across other jurisdictions serves only to benefit those Anishinaabe students who wish to continue their education at another institution, postsecondary or otherwise, and has no bearing on the breadth or scope of any Indigenous nation's sovereignty. Regardless of how one might construe the term "sovereignty," the main point is that Indigenous nations possess the inherent right to determine for themselves what their education systems will be and how they will govern them.

One issue that came up frequently during the course of my research for this book was related to the provision of programs and services for special needs and gifted students. Parents, educators, administrators, and Elders agreed unanimously that services must be available for early detection and diagnosis of physical, mental, and spiritual (dis)abilities, along with appropriate learning schedules. Similarly, it was decided further that enriched learning opportunities should be available for exceptional or gifted students to maximize their potential. Therefore, in response to these concerns, the draft form of Kinamaadiwin Inaakonigewin states that "the Treaty #3 Education Commission may provide the establishment and operation of special schools, courses, and learning services suited to the special education needs of the students within the cultural and linguistic context of the Anishinaabe Nation in Treaty #3."[53] With regard to evaluating student performance, it is also stated that the education standards of the Anishinaabe education system will take into account linguistic achievement as well as other culture-added values such as "emotional literacy, development of character according to rites of passage, [and] civic duty for nation building" as indicators of educational success.[54] To develop these skills, language instruction is to be offered at all grade levels with an emphasis on teaching cultural and spiritual knowledge. This includes teaching the history and modern governance structure of the Anishinaabe Nation of Treaty #3, its relationships with external governments, treaties and inherent rights, as well as sovereignty and self-governing status.

It bears repeating that one of the main reasons that Indigenous nations want to establish and administer our own education systems is the failure of the dominant public education system to represent adequately our distinctive cultures and contributions to history. Another reason is to address how the public education system marginalizes and assimilates our youth, which, as I have mentioned, has led to adverse social conditions in many Indigenous communities across Canada. Thus, to address and mitigate social issues such as addiction, teen pregnancy, and domestic violence, Kinamaadiwin Inaakonigewin states that course content in the Anishinaabe education system will comprise health and nutrition instruction and teaching on noxious substances, addictions, safe sex and parenting, "and the effect[s] on the individual, family, and nation with a view to discussing traditional healthy foods and lifestyles."[55] In *Colonized Classrooms: Racism, Trauma and Resistance in Post-Secondary Education*, Anishinaabe scholar Sheila Cote-Meek explains that these objectives require the development of a holistic pedagogy that includes a number of strategies, such as

> creating space in the academic programming for students to speak and/or write about any relevant issues that arise in the class that affect them personally; supporting the rekindling of the student's spirit; exposing the ways in which power relations diminish women who are survivors of violence; creating an environment where abuse and violence are made visible and not tolerated; treating students respectfully and worthily; teaching to and supporting students' strengths; and supporting culture-based initiatives and traditional spiritual practices that build cultural pride and understanding of oppression and increase a student's self worth.[56]

Moreover, with the land and environmental sustainability being key aspects of Anishinaabe knowledge, the Anishinaabe education system can be a leading institution in the fight against climate change and environmental destruction. In conversations with Treaty 3 Elders and educators, it was decided that this can be achieved best by developing course content at all grade levels on the historical, political, cultural, and socio-economic elements of the land base and natural resources. As such, Kinamaadiwin Inaakonigewin states that Treaty 3 courses should chart "the historical development of the land base, the legal status of the land tenure, cultural knowledge of the land, modern management practices of lands and resources, social and economic impacts of natural resource extraction, careers in land management, ecology, Indigenous environmental studies, and the sciences."[57] In reclaiming authority over the education of our youth in this way, the Anishinaabe Nation in Treaty #3 is exercising its inherent right to self-determination and cultural resurgence. As Anishinaabe scholar Lindsay Borrows points out, "when First Nations communities control their civic life, there is a strong correlation of lower rates of suicide. Self-determination makes a difference. It can actually save lives."[58] In other words, self-determination is associated with healthy living.

With regard to teaching, parents and Elders have said consistently that the number or ratio of Anishinaabe teachers should reflect the composition of the student body. This assertion is therefore stipulated in the draft version of Kinamaadiwin Inaakonigewin.[59] Such policies are consistent with and respond to what other Indigenous leaders have called for, including Harold Cardinal, who has written that "Native teachers and counsellors who have an intimate understanding of Indian traditions, psychology, way of life and language are best able to create the learning environment suited to the habits and interests of the Indian child."[60] More recently, Linda Goulet and Keith Goulet have asserted that "students should not have to leave their Indigenous identities behind to be successful in school. It is incumbent upon teachers to find and incorporate Indigenous knowledge and understandings (epistemologies) and to use Indigenous practices and methods to support learning and fully develop students' potential."[61] To reiterate, an Anishinaabe education system must be employed by Anishinaabe teachers, administrators, and staff; it is a local occupation.[62] Upon achieving these education standards, Anishinaabe students will be able to relate more easily to their teachers and course content and develop strong relationships that sustain and enhance their educational experiences.

During the Treaty 3 education gatherings that I attended, Elders often commented that their experiences with the public education system were cold and sterile and that the student-teacher relationships were severe and authoritarian. That method of teaching and learning runs counter to Anishinaabe ways of knowing and being. As Linda Goulet and Keith Goulet have reported, "teachers emphasized that relationships were the key to effective teaching—that is, relationships between the teacher and students, among the students, and class, with the learning environment (the how, or the process, of learning), and to the construction of knowledge (the what, or content) in the classroom."[63] This observation is based upon the knowledge that each person—whether a teacher or a student—offers an intrinsic value and contribution to the well-being of others. As Māori scholar Jill Bevan-Brown explains further, "this sentiment is echoed in the course mantra of 'learning with, from and about each other' and exemplified in interaction with children, families, and community."[64] Moreover, the development of strong teacher-student relationships has been shown to improve student attendance at school.[65] This insight is particularly important given that attendance at school—tied directly to educational achievement—has been and continues to be an issue for many Indigenous students. With that in mind, one of the top priorities for Treaty 3 educators will be the cultivation of an environment of respect and trust, predicated on Anishinaabe values of teaching and learning, that makes students feel welcomed and respected so that they want to be there and participate in class to the best of their ability.

Curriculum and Pedagogy

The last aspect of Kinamaadiwin Inaakonigewin that I would like to discuss relates to Treaty 3 curriculum and pedagogy. The draft law defines curriculum as "a systematic, planned program of culturally responsive study with goals, objectives, content, pedagogy, assessment tools and schedules, evaluation, and reporting across the grade levels."[66] Indigenous education scholars such as Sheila Cote-Meek have argued that a culturally responsive curriculum should consider how Indigenous peoples have been oppressed and marginalized in the dominant society through ongoing forms of colonial violence, but it should also question how systems of domination are established and reinforced in sites such as the classroom through the positionality of educators and their pedagogical practices.[67] Dwayne Donald explains that, if a traditional story "is 'infused' or 'incorporated' into curricula as just a story, and without the necessary care and attention given the ideologies, mythologies, and ways of becoming real human beings it describes, nothing good will grow from it."[68] Under these circumstances, Donald argues, "the fundamental curriculum my-thologies of individualism, progress, and anthropocentrism maintain their hegemonic influence as universalized common sense, and the story is marginalized based on those cultural assumptions."[69] To put it differently, storytelling, as a form of Indigenous pedagogy, needs to be recognized and respected as a valid form of knowledge transmission, along with the relational values that such traditional stories teach. It is a key feature of many Indigenous intellectual traditions that has been practised from generation to generation since time immemorial. With that in mind, the continuance of Indigenous storytelling could be considered an act of cultural resurgence that challenges other systems of domination.

As master storytellers and gatekeepers of vast sums of knowledge, Elders are essential in the development and application of a cultur-ally responsive education curriculum. This point cannot be emphasized enough. Their expertise as language and cultural knowledge holders is critical in the teaching and learning of Anishinaabe traditional practices. One such practice is *akinoomaage*. According to renowned Anishinaabe Elder Basil Johnston, that word means "learning by observation" and is formed from two roots: *aki* and *noomaage*. More specifically, *aki* means "land," and *noomaage* means "to point towards and take direction from," conveying the idea that teaching and learning occur by observing the land as well as the non-human entities (i.e., animals) around us.[70] To help envision what this land-based pedagogical practice would look like in an educational setting, Glen Coulthard offers the following account from a Dene perspective: "This could take the form of "walking the land" in an effort to refamiliarize ourselves with the landscapes and places that give our histories, languages, and cultures shape and content; to revitalizing and engaging in land-based harvesting practices like hunting, fishing, and gather[ing], and/or cultural production activities like hide-tanning and carving, all of which also serve to assert our sovereign presence on our territories in ways that can be profoundly educational and empowering; to the reoccupation of sacred places for the purposes of relearning and practicing our ceremonial activities."[71]

In other words, *akinoomaage* represents yet another act or expression of Anishinaabe self-determination and cultural resurgence by virtue of just teaching and practising our local land-based traditions. *Akinoomaage* can also be interpreted as an occupation of "Indigenous space." According to Patricia Johnston, such space refers to "the recognition, theory, and practice of worldviews that draw from knowledge bases that encompass the ways in which Indigenous Peoples think about their world and articulate their relationships within their world."[72] Thus, in accordance with these insights, Kinamaadiwin Inaakonigewin states that "the worldview of the Anishinaabe Nation of Treaty #3, from traditional times to the present-day cultural traditions, will be reflected in all aspects of the curriculum in the schools and learning lodges of the nation to provide context to all parts of the curriculum."[73] As John Borrows points out, "Indigenous laws are best revitalized when they are rooted in a peoples' longer-term relationship with the earth, and . . . [when] the application of Indigenous law is drawn from these enduring connections."[74]

A recent development in Indigenous education in Canada has been the advancement of land-based and treaty curriculums developed by numerous Indigenous academics, educators, and government administrators. Most recently, Bimose Tribal Council, a Treaty 3 organization that provides education and technical services in an advisory capacity, has developed primary- and secondary-level treaty curriculums for the Anishinaabe schools that it serves in Treaty 3 territory.[75] The treaty curriculum offers four core strands for teaching and learning about treaties: treaty relationships, spirit and intent of treaties, historical context of treaties, and treaty rights and provisions. From Bimose's perspective, "by examining these issues, as well as other critical concepts such as interpretation and implementation, through a historical context, learners of Manitou Mazinaa'igan Gakendaasowin will gain a comprehensive understanding of the treaty relationship, and what it means to be Anishinaabe."[76] This is a huge development in treaty education from my days in grade school when students were awarded full marks if they simply remembered the jarring maxim "wined them, dined them, and signed them." In another initiative, Bimose Tribal Council is developing a land-based curriculum. It will be designed to teach students about traditional Anishinaabe land-based practices such as fishing, hunting, and harvesting both to promote environmental sustainability in the face of ongoing resource extraction and to maintain and strengthen Anishinaabe linguistic, spiritual, and legal traditions. These goals are squarely in line with the principles of Kinamaadiwin Inaakonigewin.[77]

The inclusion of Anishinaabe texts is another way in which a prospective curriculum can be made to reflect Anishinaabe culture. I can testify that I failed Grade 10 English because I struggled to relate to the course content, which had a heavy emphasis on Shakespeare. Although the study of Shakespeare is important, given his stature in world literature, I am suggesting here that more space could be created for other writers, such as the celebrated Cree playwright Tomson Highway.[78] The same could be said of Harper Lee's *To Kill a Mockingbird*, another staple text in the dominant education system. Lee's themes of racial prejudice and oppression could be explored locally, as they are in Beatrice Culleton Mosionier's classic *In Search of April Raintree*.[79] That Indigenous texts continue to be excluded from the public education system points to a problem of "hyperseparation" in literary study, which Rauna Kuokkanen explains that: "Indigenous literatures are not regarded as 'proper' compared to European literatures, with their centuries-old aesthetic and literary traditions. Because of differences in structure, format, story line, mode of expression, and even purpose, indigenous literary conventions are often looked down on as 'folklore,' 'myths,' and 'legends,' or even worse, as 'primitive,' 'childlike,' 'overpopulated,' or 'having no clear plot.' All of these terms denote inferiority."[80]

To that point, it is imperative that teachers receive the necessary cultural training to understand that classical humanism, as represented in Western texts, plays the same role as the oral tradition does in Anishinaabe and other Indigenous cultures. Such training is stipulated as mandatory in Kinamaadiwin Inaakonigewin.[81] Moreover, expanding our understanding of other literature in this way could open the possibility for students to be introduced to other great writers and storytellers deserving of some of the attention currently given to Shakespeare and Austen. From an Anishinaabe pedagogical perspective, it would make sense, first, to teach Anishinaabe students about their own "classics" from the oral tradition—such as Nanabush stories—as told by Elders. Nanabush is a central figure in the Anishinaabe oral tradition known as a shape-shifter or trickster who can be either hero or villain from one story to the next. Nanabush is present in a number of "creation stories," as well as comedies and tragedies, and often represented as a teacher of moral virtue.[82] Second, students could become better acquainted with contemporary Anishinaabe literature, with Louise Erdrich and Winona LaDuke being the most prominent examples. From there, students could learn about Indigenous literature in a Canadian context (Jeannette Armstrong comes to mind), then international literature (Harper Lee), and finally Western literature, preferably that with some relevance to Anishinaabe students. Prioritizing Anishinaabe literature in

this way can strengthen not only students' cultural identity but also their
critical consciousness while also supporting their academic success. As
Frank Deer has written, "the perspective, the exploration of the people,
histories, narratives, and values, is as essential to Indigenous identity development as any activity, artifact, or other referent reflected in a student
outcome."[83] That is, if the texts that we were assigned in my Grade 10
English class had been more relevant culturally, then it is very likely that
I would have been much more engaged in the course—not to mention
better informed about the history and culture of my people—which undoubtedly would have resulted in a better academic achievement. That
could be true of any student at any grade level.

The catalogue of potential Indigenous educational resources also includes Indigenous music, film, and other art forms (beading, painting,
dance, etc.). In utilizing these pedagogical tools, Anishinaabe students
would have the benefit of learning traditional drum songs, beading techniques, powwow dances, and regalia designs. Although powwows and
other ceremonies have creative and artistic elements such as song and
dance, the raison d'être of these traditional practices is spiritual, which
distinguishes them from performance art such as opera and ballet. As Vine
Deloria Jr. points out in *God Is Red*, however, "authorization to perform
ceremonies comes from higher spiritual powers and not by certification
through an institution or any formal organization."[84] For this reason, as
important as it is for Indigenous youth to learn about these aspects of
their cultural heritage, the implementation of traditional ceremonies and
practices as part of an academic curriculum must be done with extreme
care so that they do not become spectacles to be exploited or, worse, lose
their intrinsic spiritual purposes. "The issue," Emma LaRocque points
out, "is how these concepts get stereotyped and how they get played out
in real-life circumstances, such as in government policies, legislation,
education, or health, or in our textbooks and theatres."[85] To LaRocque's
point, if a headdress—which holds a tremendous amount of spiritual,
cultural, and political esteem—is worn outside its intended purpose,
then the sanctity of the sacred item will be tarnished and marred. Yet
Leanne Simpson suggests that, if Indigenous spiritual, cultural, artistic,
and land-based practices are implemented with care and respect, then they
have the potential "to disrupt and interrogate forms of settler colonialism
and advance the project of resurgence and Indigenous nation building."[86]
That said, in the process of teaching students about their cultural heritage,

teachers and administrators must also bear in mind the harmful effects of colonization on gender roles in Indigenous communities. This is particularly pertinent in regard to the exclusion of women in drum groups as well as restrictions on female participation in ceremonies such as the sweat lodge and sundance. Finally, with regard to other Indigenous forms of knowledge and artistic media such as painting, students can learn about traditional techniques such as petroglyphs as a form of writing as well as more conventional painting methods made famous by Norval Morrisseau. The possibilities with which Indigenous forms of knowledge and aesthetic practice can be applied as educational resources are almost endless; they are as rich in tradition and offer as deep insight into the human and social condition—as well as our shared relationship with the land—as any settler-colonial form of art. For these reasons, they form a core component of Kinamaadiwin Inaakonigewin.[87]

Summary

The struggle for Indigenous self-determination is only beginning to be understood properly in Canada. For many decades, treaties have been neglected and forgotten, civil rights have been abused and broken, and hopes and dreams have been crushed by the weight of law. In spite of these adversities, Indigenous peoples have remained vigilant: rehearsing their stories, remembering their ceremonies, and revitalizing their laws. In this regard, the Anishinaabe Nation in Treaty #3 has composed a written education law for the administration of a local Anishinaabe education system. Such acts of cultural resurgence, as well as other forms of non-violent direct action, are the means with which to facilitate the state's recognition of Indigenous consciousness and self-determination. Recognition without affirmed action, however, is mere lip service. Although the government of Canada has committed recently to honour its treaty promises, as well as to fulfill the Truth and Reconciliation Commission's Calls to Action, it still has important work to do. Until the state's actions speak louder than its words, the struggle for Indigenous self-determination will only continue to escalate. One way in which the state can affirm its position on reconciliation is by recognizing and affirming Kinamaadiwin Inaakonigewin, the Treaty 3 education law. This process would include a formal negotiation to find funding solutions with the aim to bring historical treaty promises into modern forms, thus honouring the original spirit and intent of the treaties.

Although an extended history of cultural and political subordination has displaced Indigenous understandings of the treaty relationship, recent progress in terms of human and civil rights issues has stoked whatever embers of hope have remained into flames now illuminating a path to reconciliation. That path has always been there; it was established by sacred and traditional laws maintained and reinforced through the knowledge and wisdom of our Elders and ancestral knowledge keepers. But a light that illuminates a path toward reconciliation is useful only to the extent that it is used effectively. It is one thing to see or recognize a path, made visible through the development of enlightened principles and laws drawn from the history of relevant case laws, national commissions, international declarations, and, most importantly, our people's voices. It is quite another thing to feel or touch that path, and affirm its being, by walking on it in a good way as our ancestors did. The way to do that is to put our tobacco down, give thanks to the Creator, and always bear in mind that we walk both for those who walked before us and for those who will walk in our footsteps long after us.

Chapter 5

REFLECTIONS

The success of an Anishinaabe education system depends not so much on the laws and regulations that we create as on our ability to apply them effectively. This can be accomplished only with the resources needed to administer programs and services. If we are truly in a new era of Indigenous-settler relations in Canada, one in which reconciliation is indeed a matter of state and public concern, then the mistakes of the past must not be repeated. By this, I mean that we must learn from failures like those in 1970 in which the state "accepts our policy paper publicly with great fanfare, says it marks a milestone, but they don't do a damned thing about providing the necessary new money."[1] Government lip service is good only to the extent that the government's actions are equal to or the same as its words. And, as Jacques Derrida has said, "one should accredit, guarantee, and legitimate the discourse. . . . Otherwise, one pays with words . . . by which one understands the words in this case are simulacra, money without value—devalued or counterfeit."[2] In other words, those who break their word also break their honour. So, if the state says that it wants to make treaties right, that it will implement the new UNDRIP legislation in a good way, and that it will answer the Truth and Reconciliation Commission's Calls to Action, and it has said so, then there is an obligation to affirm these words with appropriate actions.[3] At the most basic, material level, this means providing adequate funding for quality education programs and services for Anishinaabe youth and communities. It is an obligation recognized by the Supreme Court of Canada, which has said that "*the Crown must be assumed to intend to fulfill its promises.*"[4] I fear that, if the state fails to do so, then there will be significant repercussions in the form of increased protest and civil disobedience, which could lead eventually to violent confrontations.

If we accept that the purpose of Aboriginal and treaty rights is for "the reconciliation of the pre-existence of aboriginal societies with the sovereignty of the Crown," then the Crown has a constitutional obligation to fulfill its treaty promises.[5] As Michael Asch points out in *On Being Here to Stay*, reconciliation "requires the establishment of proper principles to govern the continuing treaty relationship and to complete treaties that are incomplete because of the absence of consensus," and justice "requires the fulfillment of the agreed terms of the treaties as recorded in the treaty text and *supplemented* by oral evidence."[6] As I discussed in Chapter 2, oral evidence includes testimony from treaty Elders who have long asserted that our people were promised Crown protection and assistance to develop and prosper. These promises are understood in general terms, with regard to a continuing and comprehensive Crown responsibility, as well as in specific terms with reference to the economic assistance required in implementing the treaty right to education.

Although it can be acknowledged that the state has a limited budget to finance Indigenous education programs and services under its existing structure, it is unreasonable to stand by idly and allow Indigenous communities to suffer for it. A recent report by former Toronto Dominion economist Don Drummond says that "the funding gap between First Nations schools vs. other schools across Canada averages around 30 percent," and that is completely unacceptable.[7] Again, if reconciliation is to be considered a genuine political platform, then the state must be willing to step outside its comfort zone. One potential solution, as suggested by Canadian legal scholar Julie Jai, is to create "a jointly appointed Crown–First Nation dispute resolution body" "to oversee the renewal of historic treaties."[8] According to Jai, such a process of resolution offers the opportunity to "encourage negotiations between the parties, bring the historic treaty rights into a modern form that recognizes the ongoing treaty relationship and the need for static provisions to evolve, and more accurately reflect the spirit and intent of the treaty."[9] Interestingly, in 2005, a Treaty Relations Commission of Manitoba was established as a partnership between the Assembly of Manitoba Chiefs and Canada with a mandate to "strengthen, rebuild and enhance the Treaty relationship and mutual respect between First Nations and Manitobans as envisaged by the Treaty Parties."[10] Although this would seem to be an appropriate forum with which to resolve treaty issues, strangely it does not adjudicate on such matters. If anything, it further demonstrates the immense challenge of operating within state-sponsored institutions.

Be that as it may, as Indigenous people, we must face the challenge before us directly; it is not as if our problems with the Canadian state will just disappear magically if we turn our back against it. Although there are many good reasons to view the project of reconciliation with skepticism and contempt, we must rise above our feelings of doubt and hopelessness to do what is best for our children and our children's children. We can do that by picking up the weapon of our oppressor, the pen, and level the battlefield by writing our own laws and making them recognize and affirm the righteousness of our self-determination. Yet, as Canadians, we have a collective responsibility to do what is right for all of our fellow citizens. If Aboriginal and treaty rights continue to be marginalized, then it signals the failure of the Constitution and its justice system. As Dale Turner has pointed out, "Canadian society prides itself on being a progressive democratic society; this demands that Aboriginal peoples be included in the dialogue over the meaning of their rights. It does not guarantee that Aboriginal understandings will dictate the meaning and content of Aboriginal rights; what it does is broaden the intellectual landscape from which the normative language of rights can evolve."[11] That is, Canadians must accept that Indigenous peoples have unique rights as a result of our history on the land and embrace the concepts of peace and goodwill stated in the treaties. With regard to the treaty right to education, the Standing Senate Committee on Aboriginal Peoples has stated clearly that Indigenous education is a matter of local jurisdiction:

> Only when First Nations are able to take full responsibility for education, including developing curricula, defining educational standards and certifying teachers, will the quality of on-reserve education improve and the future of First Nations students be secure. The process of renewal and reform of First Nations education will undoubtedly be challenging. It will require all parties to work collectively to bring about systemic change. It will demand sustained political commitment at the highest levels of the federal government and challenge First Nations leaders to come together to establish educational systems that are, first and foremost, accountable to their communities.[12]

In the final analysis, if an Anishinaabe education system can be considered a worthy representation of the treaty right to education, as well as a reflection of the articles of the United Nations Declaration on the Rights of Indigenous Peoples, and fulfills the Truth and Reconciliation Commission's Calls to Action on education, then the state must recognize and affirm the authority of Kinamaadiwin Inaakonigewin, the Treaty 3 written education law, and all other Indigenous education laws that follow. This process requires cooperation and commitment from the state to negotiate, in good faith, potential funding solutions through respectful and constructive dialogue to finance Indigenous education initiatives. One solution to create revenue for this venture could include the creation of a new "reconciliation tax," specifically designated for reconciling the relationship between Indigenous nations and Canada. Another idea is to provide Indigenous nations with a share of revenue already gathered from the taxation of land-based industries. Such strategies would not only generate the revenue required to develop and implement the education system but also symbolize all Canadians' contributions to the treaty relationship. This is the type of commitment and investment in Indigenous education required to facilitate and achieve the broader goals of reconciliation in Canada. By making Indigenous education a priority with demonstrated, definitive action, the state will signal to Indigenous nations and the rest of the country that it truly has the needs and interests of all of its citizens at heart. Only then will reconciliation between the Crown and Indigenous nations become a reality.

In closing, I wish to put my tobacco down and again offer a prayer and thanks to Elder Fred Kelly for sharing his love and wisdom with me, as well as my community of Lac Des Mille Lacs for supporting me throughout the writing of this book, and to the Grand Council Treaty #3 for giving me the immense honour and privilege to participate in the greatest act of cultural resurgence that I can possibly imagine, the revitalization of our traditional education law: Kinamaadiwin Inaakonigewin.

Chi-Miigwech.

ACKNOWLEDGEMENTS

The research and writing of this book would not have been possible without the love and support of the following people and organizations. I therefore wish to give thanks to them.

To my community, Lac Des Mille Lacs First Nation. In particular, I would like to thank Chief Judy Whitecloud and Mark Berkan, who have supported my academic endeavours since 2008, when I first returned to school. I am indebted to you and forever committed to giving the learning that I received back to the community. Miigwech.

To the Grand Council Treaty #3. I am deeply humbled by the honour and privilege given to me to participate in such an important nation-building exercise as the revitalization of our traditional education law. I stand willing and able to complete this work that we started together. Miigwech.

To Treaty #3 Elder Fred Kelly. In just a few years, you have become a father figure to me. Your love as well as your wealth of knowledge have been instrumental to the completion of this book. Miigwech.

To my family, my loving and beautiful wife, Maria, and our three sons, Levi, Oscar, and Ben. Maria, I recognize that you have made tremendous sacrifices throughout this process for my betterment and that of our family so that I could finish this book. I am forever grateful to you and love you and our children with all my heart. Miigwech.

To my mother, Diane Baskatawang. Without you, I wouldn't exist. You are my reason for life. I love you. Miigwech.

To my advisory committee. Dr. Peter Kulchyski, you are the first person who supported this project. I have learned so much from you and am forever grateful for your tutelage of and belief in me. Drs. Aimée Craft and Frank Deer, thank you for being a part of this journey with me. Your comments and feedback on this book have made it immeasurably better. Miigwech.

I would also like to extend heartfelt gratitude to Dr. James Daschuk, who graciously wrote a most eloquent foreword to this book. Your resounding voice has added great strength and validation to the points made herein. Miigwech.

To my colleagues and friends. In particular, Mrs. Belinda WanderingSpirit, thank you for always being there for me, for being someone to talk to and share ideas with. You lifted me up when I was down and rejoiced when I succeeded. That means the world to me. Miigwech.

Finally, to everyone at the University of Manitoba Press, with special thanks to Jill McConkey, for taking a chance on me and my work. Your expertise and attention to detail have helped to make this book the best it could be. Miigwech.

APPENDIX A: KINAMAADIWIN INAAKONIGEWIN

Whereas:

The Creator, Kizhe Manito, provided the Anishinaabe Nation in Treaty #3 with rules for teaching and learning, and these rules were passed down to our ancestors from generation to generation, so that our people, the Anishinaabe, could live a good life, mino-bimaadziwin;

These sacred gifts and trusts bestowed upon us by the Creator and our ancestors include our sovereignty and nationhood and inherent jurisdiction and governance;

As such, our sacred law, Kagagiwe Inaakonigewin, bestows:

Legislative jurisdiction upon the Anishinaabe Nation in Treaty #3 as the sole and exclusive prerogative of the people as a democratic nation and in accordance with their procedures; and

Executive jurisdiction as delegated authority to the Grand Council Treaty #3, the traditional government of the Anishinaabe Nation in Treaty #3, under the will of the people; and

Administrative jurisdiction to officials and employees of the government to carry out our laws and policies;

It is our belief that our children are sacred gifts from the Creator, Kizhe Manito, and raising and teaching them are the exclusive responsibility of the family, the community, and the nation;

The Anishinaabe Nation in Treaty #3 believes that lifelong learning is a right of self-determination that pertains to our people and the land, aki. We exercise this right through the use of our Anishinaabe language, Anishinaabemowin, as well as through our culture and the traditional ways of our ancestors that continue to be practised in our communities and taught to our children;

Reaffirming that education is an inherent treaty right that was guaranteed in the Northwest Angle Treaty of October 3rd, 1873, which states:

> "And further, Her Majesty AGREES TO MAINTAIN SCHOOLS for instruction in such reserves hereby made as to Her Government of Her Dominion of Canada may seem advisable WHENEVER THE INDIANS OF THE RESERVE SHALL DESIRE IT"; and

> During the treaty negotiations, the Crown's official representative, Alexander Morris, said:

> "I will also establish schools whenever any band asks for them, so that your children may have the learning of the white man."

Let it be known that the Anishinaabe Nation in Treaty #3 has never relinquished claims to sovereignty or sovereign lands and has a continuing inherent right to autonomy in internal affairs, a right of self-determination, and a right to self-government;

The government of Canada has a fiduciary obligation to act in the best interest of the Anishinaabe Nation in Treaty #3, and this obligation has been further entrenched and protected by Section 35(1) of the Canadian Constitution Act of 1982 as well as corresponding case laws, which state in part:

> "Treaties should be liberally construed and ambiguities or doubtful expressions should be resolved in favour of the aboriginal signatories"; and

> "In searching for the common intention of the parties, the integrity and honour of the Crown is presumed"; and

> "In determining the signatories' respective understanding and intentions, the court must be sensitive to the unique cultural and linguistic differences between the parties"; and

> "Treaty rights of aboriginal peoples must not be interpreted in a static or rigid way. They are not frozen at the date of signature. The interpreting court must update treaty rights to provide for their modern exercise. This involves determining what modern practices are reasonably incidental to the core treaty right in its modern context."

In accordance with Articles 13 and 14 of the United Nations Declaration on the Rights of Indigenous Peoples, the Anishinaabe Nation in Treaty #3 declares its right to:

> "revitalize, use, develop and transmit to future generations our histories, languages, oral traditions, philosophies, writing systems and literatures"; and

> "establish and control our own educational systems and institutions that provide education in Anishinaabemowin, which is delivered in a manner appropriate to our distinct cultural methods of teaching and learning."

Therefore:

The Anishinaabe Nation in Treaty #3, with the approval of Elders and citizens, and through validation in traditional ceremony, and with ratification by the National Assembly, proclaims this law:

Name:

1.0 This law is called Kinamaadiwin Inaakonigewin.

Interpretation:

2.0 The official language of this law is Anishinaabemowin.

2.1 This law is to be interpreted in accordance with:

Kagagiwe Inaakonigewin (sacred/supreme law); and

Kete Inaakonigewin (traditional law); and

Anishinaabe Inaakonigewin (customary law).

2.2 For greater certainty, in this law:

"aki" means land;

"Anishinaabe" means the Anishinaabe people of Treaty 3;

"Anishinaabemowin" is the traditional language of the Anishinaabe;

"community" refers to any one of the twenty-eight (28) Anishinaabe communities located in Treaty 3 territory;

"counselling" means career preparation, applications to postsecondary-level studies, scholarships and bursaries, personal counselling, academic counselling, social and mental health counselling;

"curriculum" means a planned and ongoing systematic learning program provided for students as an accredited program of studies;

"education plan" means an annual plan that establishes priorities for the school and determines how the staff will address the priorities;

"education standards" means the acceptable level of performance that an educational institution will meet in order to provide high-quality education programs, curriculums, and services;

"Elders" are respected wisdom keepers, political statesmen, ceremonial leaders, with traditional Anishinaabe knowledge systems needed in the education system to act as teachers, planners, speakers;

"inaakonigewin" means law;

"kete" means ancient or traditional;

"kinamaadiwin" means education;

"mino-biimaadziwin" means the good life;

"ogichidaa" means the Grand Chief of Treaty #3;

"schools" are defined as having students within an education institution governed by the Treaty #3 Education Commission attending an accredited learning program duly authorized by Kinamaadiwin Inaakonigewin and the Grand Council Treaty #3;

"school facilities" include the standard established for floor space with gymnasium, cafeteria, library with information technology, science labs, sports fields, suited to the needs of the Anishinaabe Nation in Treaty #3, the geographical terrain and location;

"special needs student" means a student who has a challenge of a cognitive, physical, sensory, emotional, or behavioural nature, has a learning disability, or has special gifts or talents;

"teacher" means a professionally accredited person holding a valid teacher's certificate; a member in good standing with the Elementary Teachers Federation of Ontario and the Ontario Secondary Schools Teachers Federation; teachers in schools under the Treaty #3 Education Commission must also hold a valid certificate in cultural competency on the history, language, and culture from the Treaty #3 Education Commission;

"Treaty #3 Education Commission" is a legislated body under Kinamaadiwin Inaakonigewin with responsibility to govern the education system of the Anishinaabe Nation in Treaty #3.

Purpose:

3.0   To exercise the inherent jurisdiction in education of the Anishinaabe Nation in Treaty #3, now and for future generations.

3.1   To enhance the distinctive political, economic, and cultural heritage of the Anishinaabe Nation in Treaty #3 through education as a pillar of sovereignty and self-determination and through a targeted investment in the human capital of our nation.

3.2   (a) To preserve the Anishinaabe in the student;

       (b) to protect the language and cultural identity of the student;

       (c) to provide an education that enables the student to become a functional citizen in the Anishinaabe Nation and society at large;

       (d) to clarify relationships between the Grand Council and other governments in Canada;

       (e) to harmonize administration of Anishinaabe law in education and administration of Crown government laws in education.

3.3   The education system of the Anishinaabe Nation in Treaty #3 will enable students to:

       (a) fully develop one's individual potential as distinct Anishinaabe members living in a modern era while also honouring one's heritage;

       (b) engage in studies with high academic standards as well as technical studies and skilled trades, land-based learning for traditional knowledge, and institutional learning;

       (c) become fluent in Anishinaabemowin and ensure cultural transmission of the oral history to the next generation;

       (d) develop a connection to the land, aki, and a sense of responsibility to care for the land using traditional knowledge systems;

       (e) engage in learning opportunities with Anishinaabe Elders, knowledge holders, and oral historians so that they can transmit their knowledge to the next generation of youth for maintaining the strength of the culture and language and the living civilization of the nation;

       (g) understand the nature of Indigenous rights from an international perspective, know the inherent rights of the Anishinaabe

Nation in Treaty #3, and be competent to speak to those rights publicly and transmit the knowledge to future generations;

(h) promote a sense of social responsibility and tolerance for the beliefs of others in a global community;

(i) understand the importance of contributing to the social, economic, political, and spiritual development of the Anishinaabe Nation in Treaty #3.

Guiding Principles:

4.0 This law declares and gives effect to the following principles:

(a) Anishinaabemowin (language): Revitalize and maintain our way of speaking; our way of processing and expressing thought; our way of communicating with the creation, with the spirit, and with one another. It is to ensure the connection of our language to our worldview, language to culture, language to relatedness/identity, and language to the natural environment.

(b) Anishinaabe Inendamowin (thinking): Develop the learner's ability to source and employ Anishinaabe ways of thinking that use the totality of the mind in its intellectual, intuitive, and spiritual capacities—a way of knowing in which the intelligence of the mind is inspired and informed from the intelligence of the heart.

(c) Anishinaabe Gikendaasowin (knowing): Instill and advance in learners our ways of knowing, our knowledge of our origins, ways of life, ways of being, ways of doing things, and our worldview. It directs us to increase in the learner the highest consciousness and ability at all levels of sensing, knowing, and experiencing, from a place of Anishinaabe identity, thinking, knowledge base, and way of being.

(d) Anishinaabe Inaadiziwin (being): Develop in the learner the fullest capacity of the Anishinaabe way of being that is the total response of the total person with and within the total environment. It is to activate the whole person in the learning experience—body, mind, heart, and spirit—in such a way as to generate the highest quality of experience and inspire the finest creativity of response and expression.

(e) Anishinaabe Izhichigewin (doing): Strengthen the capacity inherent in the learner of the Anishinaabe way of doing things and develop the abilities and skills for effective Anishinaabe functioning in the world and for quality of living and contributing to the quality of the community. The processes and styles of teaching and learning will be consistent with the values and directives of this principle.

(f) Anishinaabe Enawendiwin (relations): Provide a learning process and an environment that is in keeping with our all-encompassing way of relating to the world, which is respectful of the individual and responsive to the integrity of the collective whole—a relationship that is personal, caring, responsive, sharing, and built upon our identity with and connection to the land and family of creation.

(g) Gidakiiminaan (connecting to the land): Ensure learners' connections to and relationships with the land and creation, and provide an environment of teaching and learning that is situated on the land and within the natural and cultural environments—and that encourages operating within and being sensitive to the essential principles of the environmental ethic of Gidakiiminaan.

4.1 Kinamaadiwin Inaakonigewin will protect and perpetuate the members of the Anishinaabe Nation in Treaty #3 as the most valuable of all resources in their homelands to ensure cultural and linguistic transmission over the generations.

4.2 Kinamaadiwin Inaakonigewin is designed to provide a learning experience of excellence for the members of the Anishinaabe Nation in Treaty #3 as a preparation for life, both on and off the territory.

4.3 Kinamaadiwin Inaakonigewin will promote intragovernmental coordination within the Anishinaabe Nation in Treaty #3.

4.4 Kinamaadiwin Inaakonigewin will provide opportunities for improvement of education through the development of local solutions to local issues.

4.5 All policies or resolutions in education are subject to Kinamaadiwin Inaakonigewin, and those inconsistent with the law will be revised or repealed.

4.6   Regulations will accompany Kinamaadiwin Inaakonigewin to ensure the effective implementation of the law and financial transparency for accountability purposes.

Duty to Consult and Accommodate, International Standards of Free, Prior, and Informed Consent

5.0   Kete Inaakonigewin has governed external relations with other peoples and is based upon harmony and balance between human beings and the natural world, respect for the diversity and autonomy of all peoples, the value of consensus building to manage disputes, and holistic approaches to problem solving.

5.1   Kete Inaakonigewin requires that our consent is needed in matters affecting our traditional lands, resources, and self-determination as a nation.

5.2   The UNDRIP sets out government obligations in instruments of international law to consult with Indigenous nations, including explicit requirements for governments to seek our free, prior, and informed consent to certain proposed government decisions or actions (UNDRIP, General Assembly Resolution 61/296, October 2, 2007).

5.3   Federal and provincial governments will consult with the Anishinaabe Nation in Treaty #3 for any proposed change to education policy, legislation, or standards that may affect our nation's education system regarding programs, standardized assessments, teacher certification, graduation requirements, curriculum, facilities, accreditation, transferability of students to other jurisdictions, transportation, labour laws, equity programming, evaluation, services, and other areas to be specified in the regulations.

5.4   The Anishinaabe Nation in Treaty #3 will define consultation standards to which it holds external governments and agencies accountable for doing business within the boundaries of its jurisdiction.

5.5   The Crown owes the Anishinaabe Nation in Treaty #3 the duty of consultation to arrive at a solution to accommodate the nation's rights and interests and provide funding to ensure that the Anishinaabe Nation in Treaty #3 can adequately participate in the consultation process to ensure free, prior, and informed consent.

5.6 Governments, corporations, agencies, boards, and organizations must be made aware of the Anishinaabe Nation in Treaty #3's laws and policies on consultation in order to respect and implement our fundamental rights as a people and nation.

Administration
Role of the Grand Council Treaty #3:

6.0 Kagagiwe Inaakonigewin establishes sovereignty over Treaty 3 territory and occupies the field of jurisdictional issues affecting the people of the Anishinaabe Nation in Treaty #3.

6.1 Jurisdiction over education is vested in the members of the Anishinaabe Nation in Treaty #3, who are the rights holders and are represented through their leadership of the ogichidaa and the Grand Council Treaty #3.

6.2 The Grand Council Treaty #3 shall support Treaty 3 communities' jurisdiction over education through Kinamaadiwin Inaakonigewin and follow its provisions and regulations.

6.3 The Grand Council Treaty #3 will establish and authorize a Treaty #3 Education Commission to act on its behalf to implement the provisions of Kinamaadiwin Inaakonigewin.

6.4 On behalf of the Treaty #3 Education Commission, the Grand Council Treaty #3 holds the chair of the Treaty #3 Education Commission through the education portfolio holder of the Grand Council Treaty #3.

Role of the Treaty #3 Education Commission:

7.0 To implement Kinamaadiwin Inaakonigewin.

7.1 To formulate policies, procedures, and regulations to guide the implementation of Kinamaadiwin Inaakonigewin, including the establishment of a Treaty #3 Education plan, code of conduct, curriculum, and education standards for the benefit of the Anishinaabe Nation in Treaty #3 and its communities.

7.2 To ensure that the language in education agreements that describe the provision of education services and programs is consistent with the language for jurisdiction as expressed in Kinamaadiwin Inaakonigewin of the Anishinaabe Nation in Treaty #3.

7.3   To design education programs, assessments, services, appeals proce-
      dures, and enrolment criteria; approve education resource materials
      and other supplies; establish a code of conduct for students, atten-
      dance policies, counselling, and transportation schedules, routes,
      and buses; provide a system of traffic controls on roads if necessary;
      provide housing for students and supervision of students within
      such housing; manage volunteers and parental engagement through
      a Community Education Council.

7.4   To ensure that Indigenous knowledge is part of every course in
      the school curriculum and defined broadly to include the beliefs,
      practices, values, and attitudes implicit in the integrated Indigenous
      worldview of the Anishinaabe Nation both past and present.

7.5   To make spirituality part of the curriculum, along with ceremonies
      practised in the school system, with a place offered to other faith
      traditions as well, as defined in Kinamaadiwin Inaakonigewin of
      the Anishinaabe Nation in Treaty #3.

7.6   To provide counselling services.

7.7   To maintain records, evaluations of personnel, minutes of meetings,
      and student information.

7.8   To undertake evaluations.

7.9   To conduct research, development, and publishing.

7.10 To coordinate the central purchasing of educational materials and
      cost sharing with neighbouring Indigenous governments.

7.11 To be responsible for finance and administration, performance and
      productivity.

7.12 To enter into contracts or agreements.

7.13 To administer grants from foundations and other external sources
      for projects related to education under the auspices of the Treaty
      #3 Education Commission.

7.14 To raise, invest, or borrow money and guarantee the repayment.

7.15 To establish endowment funds and award scholarships and bursa-
      ries.

7.16 To prepare financial reports for the Grand Council Treaty #3 to be
      submitted annually with projections for the coming school year.

7.17 To provide reports to the Grand Council Treaty #3, including an
      annual report on the education plan with statistics and performance

indicators; a review of education standards and recommendations; a review of policies and recommendations; and a review of staffing.

7.18 To establish committees for curriculum, teacher classification, and education standards to ensure that the design and content meet or exceed those of the province in content, pedagogy, assessment, and quality.

7.19 To establish a Community Education Council of parents and community members.

7.20 To evaluate and recognize the activities of an education program undertaken by a student outside the Treaty #3 Education system.

7.21 To conduct inspections of schools.

7.22 To oversee capital programs, construction, operations, and maintenance.

7.23 To prepare standards for hiring, evaluation, and dismissal of teachers, counsellors, specialists, technical support workers, therapists, principals, directors of education, and administrative staff specified in the regulations.

7.24 To engage in dispute resolution through an ombudsman employed by the Grand Council Treaty #3 and to serve all programs of the government as an arbitrator.

7.25 To appoint an Anishinaabe school trustee to the provincial school board to represent the educational needs of Anishinaabe students in the provincial system of education.

7.26 To mount events that celebrate the linguistic, cultural, and spiritual life of the Anishinaabe Nation in Treaty #3.

7.27 To establish financial regulations and policies for transparency and accountability.

Education Plan:

8.0 The education plan is prepared by the director of education for the Treaty #3 Education Commission in regard to seeking authorization from the Grand Council Treaty #3.

8.1 The education plan is a five-year strategic plan and a ten-year strategic plan that reflects the Anishinaabe Nation in Treaty #3's spiritual, social, cultural, health, education, economic, and environmental objectives and the long-term development goals of the Grand Council Treaty #3 for sustainability and self-determination.

8.2   The education plan is integrated with housing, sanitation, nutrition, and general health and social needs that affect educational success within the Anishinaabe Nation in Treaty #3.

8.3   The education plan feeds into the long-term strategy of the Anishinaabe Nation in Treaty #3 for its staffing requirements in programs, services, and institutions for nation-building purposes.

8.4   The education plan incorporates social and economic trends of Canadian society with a view to impacts on the Anishinaabe Nation in Treaty #3 and the need for skilled labour, workers in the professions, technology professionals, and general labour.

8.5   The education plan includes an annual school success plan that provides the goals for the education system, key indicators, and performance measures based upon the value system of the Grand Council Treaty #3 and the Treaty #3 Education Commission.

8.6   The education plan estimates annual costs for education programming and service delivery, construction, and renovation requirements.

8.7   The education plan provides a one-year summary of that coming year's goals, objectives, performance indicators, and measurable key elements to be submitted to the Grand Council Treaty #3 for approval as the annual education plan for that particular year.

8.8   The education plan includes a report on attendance of students and counselling offered to truant students and their families with options on next steps.

8.9   An annual operational report will be based upon the last school year measured against the goals set out in the annual education plan, and the report will be submitted for approval to the Grand Council Treaty #3.

8.10 Operational reports will be prepared, especially concerning emergency measures.

Anishinaabemowin:

9.0   Fluency in Anishinaabemowin is prescribed in the curriculum of the schools under the jurisdiction of the Grand Council Treaty #3 and with support from the Treaty #3 Education Commission.

9.1   Anishinaabemowin is deemed to be the first language of the school system.

9.2   Students will be encouraged to speak Anishinaabemowin as their first language.

9.3   Every school, learning lodge, and curriculum in use shall teach Anishinaabemowin.

9.4   The objective of every school and learning lodge will be to graduate students who are equally proficient in Anishinaabemowin and English.

9.5   The teaching staff and administrative staff of every school and learning lodge will use Anishinaabemowin to the greatest possible extent as their language of work.

9.6   The languages of instruction are Anishinaabemowin and English as determined by the Treaty #3 Education Commission according to the wishes of the community.

9.7   The Treaty #3 Education Commission will negotiate with post-secondary institutions so that proficiency in Anishinaabemowin is considered as fulfilling the requirement for having a second language for admission to their programs.

Curriculum:

10.0 The Treaty #3 Education Commission will be responsible for ensuring that the curriculum in schools, learning lodges, alternative education programs, institutes, and college and university courses is consistent with the goals of the Grand Council Treaty #3.

10.1 Curriculum means a systematic, planned program of culturally responsive study with goals, objectives, content, pedagogy, assessment tools and schedules, evaluation, and reporting across the grade levels.

10.2 The school program will contain core subject areas to meet or exceed the education standards of the province.

10.3   Supplemental electives will be offered to deepen the students' understanding of the core areas of study.

10.4   Integrated learning modules will also be available to show students how their core subjects are fundamental to careers and applicable in the modern world.

10.5   In every grade, a spiral curriculum will be offered in Anishinaabemowin fluency in the early years and primary grades, with a view to reading and writing beginning in Grades 4–8 and continuing through senior grade levels; traditional cultural knowledge systems will be woven through all grades and learning programs under the jurisdiction of the Treaty #3 Education Commission.

10.6   Anishinaabemowin will be used as the first language in the school system, with a view to proficiency in this language as being equal to proficiency in English on graduation.

10.7   Teachers and administrative staff at each school will use Anishinaabemowin as their language of work to the greatest possible extent consistent with the benefits to the students and their families and with the efficient working of the school.

10.8   A Council of Elders will approve the historical, traditional, cultural, and linguistic curriculum and include the complex worldview of values, attitudes, beliefs, and behaviours significant to the tradition of the Anishinaabe Nation in Treaty #3.

10.9   The worldview of the Anishinaabe Nation in Treaty #3, from traditional times to the present-day cultural traditions, will be reflected in all aspects of the curriculum in the schools and learning lodges of the nation to provide context to all parts of the curriculum.

10.10   Traditional ceremonies will be practised in the schools and learning lodges under the direction of the Treaty #3 Education Commission and the Council of Elders.

Education Standards:

11.0   Education standards will apply to all Treaty #3 Education Commission programs and services and facilities.

11.1   Education standards refer to levels of performance of students or requirements demanded by the education institution for successful completion of programs of study.

11.2   Education standards will meet or exceed those of the provinces and territories, preserve Anishinaabemowin along with cultural and spiritual traditions, and enable students to develop to their maximum potential.

11.3   Education standards will recognize and include the importance of language, culture, history, spirituality, and traditional knowledge systems of the Anishinaabe Nation in Treaty #3.

11.4   The Treaty #3 Education Commission will establish education standards for every grade level and be the final arbiter of whether a student has achieved the expected outcomes for graduation.

11.5   Transferability of students across jurisdictions is a primary concern, and every effort will be made to meet or exceed the education standards of other jurisdictions.

11.6   Equity in education services, programs, and facilities with the standards of the province will be established over a specified period of time as the Treaty #3 Education Commission evolves its education plan with sufficient federal funding commitments.

11.7   Student performance measures with key indicators will include linguistic and "culture-added values" as indicators of educational success as well as social and emotional literacy, development of character according to rites of passage, and civic duty for nation building.

11.8   The percentage of Anishinaabe teachers should reflect the student composition in the classroom.

11.9   Sports and recreational programs and physical education are essential parts of the school program to promote optimal physical health and build character and camaraderie among peers.

11.10 Special needs students will have timely assessments, diagnoses, and placements, and their needs will be part of the education standards.

11.11 Enriched learning opportunities for gifted children will be part of the school program and embedded in the education standards.

11.12 Culturally responsive education standards will govern all schools and education programming under the jurisdiction of the Grand Council Treaty #3 and managed under the Treaty #3 Education Commission.

11.13 Assessment standards will include tests, standardized testing, reporting, data collection and use, monitoring, and evaluation that meet the culturally responsive education standards of the Treaty #3 Education Commission.

11.14 Parental involvement in designing education standards will be established through the Community Education Council to ensure that all parents and guardians have a voice in determining the kind of education offered to their children.

11.15 Education standards will involve language instruction in all grade levels, courses, and course content including an orthography.

11.16 Education standards will also comprise health and nutrition instruction and teaching on noxious substances, addictions, and their effects on the individual, family, and nation, with a view to discussing traditional healthy foods and lifestyles.

11.17 Education standards will consist of studies in parenting and family life for all grade levels, courses, and course content that describe Anishinaabe family life in the community, parenting, cultural practices, and the need for parental involvement in the school.

11.18 Education standards will include courses and course content for all grade levels that provide knowledge on the historical, political, cultural, environmental, and socio-economic elements of the land base and natural resources. The courses will include the historical development of the land base, the legal status of the land tenure, cultural knowledge of the land, modern management practices of lands and resources, social and economic impacts of natural resource extraction, careers in land management, ecology, Anishinaabe environmental studies, and the sciences.

Special Needs and Gifted Students:

12.0 A special education policy framework will be developed by the Treaty #3 Education Commission.

12.1 The Treaty #3 Education Commission may provide the establishment and operation of special schools, courses, and learning services suited to the special educational needs of the students within the cultural and linguistic context of the Anishinaabe Nation in Treaty #3.

12.2   The Treaty #3 Education Commission may make provision for
       schools, courses, or services for the blind, physically challenged,
       and gifted children.

Community Education Council:

13.0   Parents, guardians, and community members may form a coun-
       cil to bring their recommendations to the Treaty #3 Education
       Commission, director of education, principal, school administra-
       tion, and professional staff at the school.

13.1   The Community Education Council will be involved in the devel-
       opment of education standards, policies, programs, extracurricular
       activities, planning, standards of evaluation, policies on school
       governance, improved communication, and the annual report on
       the state of education in the education system for the Anishinaabe
       Nation in Treaty #3.

13.2   Parents and community members will have one seat on the Treaty
       #3 Education Commission.

13.3   The Community Education Council offers additional resources
       to assist the school in informal learning for students, particularly
       land-based learning, oral history, cultural and spiritual knowledge,
       and cultural mapping of the territory.

13.4   The Community Education Council will consult with the principal
       to advise on regulated Early Childhood Education programming
       and maternal infant care, parenting programs, and K–12 program-
       ming to bring the community voice forward in policies, programs,
       and services at the elementary and secondary school levels.

13.5   The principal, teachers, and school professional staff, along with
       community members and the local Elders Council in consultation
       with the Community Education Council, will develop a culturally
       appropriate policy on behaviour based upon cultural values of the
       Anishinaabe Nation for the discipline of students to manage positive
       relationships and resolve conflicts.

13.6   Failure to meet one's responsibilities as a student will be mediated
       by the Community Education Council prior to advancing to the
       Treaty #3 Education Commission.

13.7   Parental involvement is encouraged in all aspects of the school's func-
       tions and especially through the Community Education Council.

13.8   The principal will seek ways to involve parents in school functions and ensure monthly communication with parents through newsletters sent home with students.

13.9   The Treaty #3 Education Commission will communicate to the Community Education Council any amendments to Kinamaadiwin Inaakonigewin.

13.10 The Treaty #3 Education Commission will provide in-service training for parents and community members on priority education issues.

Dispute Resolution:

14.0   When disputes occur between the Grand Council Treaty #3 and the Treaty #3 Education Commission, a process to set a special hearing and a special hearing committee will begin.

14.1   A special hearing committee shall be struck with one member each from the Grand Council Treaty #3 and the Treaty #3 Education Commission, a member from a neighbouring Anishinaabe community appointed by a tribal council providing second-level services to the Treaty #3 Education Commission, two persons appointed by the regional political First Nations organization of which the Grand Council Treaty #3 is a member (and these persons cannot be members of the Anishinaabe community where the complaint was lodged), and the chair of the committee, who will be the director of education for the regional political organization or a designate such as the Ontario Native Education Counselling Association or other First Nations organization.

14.2   A complaint will be received by the Grand Chief of the regional political organization of which the Grand Council Treaty #3 is a member, who will set a special hearing within forty-five days of receiving the complaint and establish the special hearing committee.

14.3   The special hearing committee shall make a report to the regional political organization within ninety days of the hearing, and the decision of the Grand Chief and the executive committee will be final.

Finances of the Anishinaabe Nation in Treaty #3 Education Comprehensive Transfer Payments: Crown Funding Agencies:

15.0   There will be recognition of the inherent right and the treaty right obligation of the Crown and the government of Canada to provide funds for the education of Anishinaabe learners of Treaty 3 through long-term agreements, settlements, and contracts between the government of Canada and the Grand Council Treaty #3.

15.1   The Treaty #3 Education Commission will be granted the authority to pursue funding from external and multiple sources through agreements to fulfill education obligations under Kinamaadiwin Inaakonigewin in order to meet the objectives of the education plan.

15.2   Education funds will be confirmed by agreement with the government of Canada and/or its provincial representatives to the Grand Council Treaty #3 and transferred to the education account under the control of the Treaty #3 Education Commission.

15.3   Funds will be used according to the terms of the funding agreement and agreed upon plans and budgets established in the agreement with the Treaty #3 Education Commission and the funding agencies.

15.4   Agreements or comprehensive transfer payments from the federal or provincial government, including equalizing payments, will be negotiated with the Grand Council Treaty #3.

15.5   The Treaty #3 Education Commission will prepare an annual budget for approval by the Grand Council Treaty #3 to be passed by resolution.

15.6   Upon the approval of the Grand Council Treaty #3, the Treaty #3 Education Commission may request by resolution a budget that allows expenditures to exceed revenues.

15.7   Funding shall be deemed to be equitable, multi-year payments with mutually agreed upon accountability standards that are clear, consistent, and comparable across Canada.

15.8   The Grand Council Treaty #3 will appoint negotiators to seek equitable contracts, agreements, and comprehensive long-term funding.

Budget Preparation:

16.0   The Treaty #3 Education Commission will prepare its own budget and ensure that the Grand Council Treaty #3 has approved it in due process.

16.1   Guidelines for the preparation of budgets regarding format, dates, and procedures will be published by the Treaty #3 Education Commission.

16.2   Costs will include community capacity building to strengthen jurisdiction and develop resources for implementation.

16.3   Funding includes the costs of regional and community-based infrastructure for second- and third-level services.

16.4   Compensatory funding will be provided to address long-term disadvantages, emergencies, underfunding, remote geographical locations, and increased costs because of shifting weather patterns of floods, winds, and so on.

16.5   Funds remaining at the end of the fiscal year may be retained or spent by the Treaty #3 Education Commission at its discretion on educational priorities, providing that the terms of the agreement for the funds are met.

16.6   Surplus funds may be placed in a trust fund account if not used immediately at the end of the school year.

16.7   Financial due diligence will be followed to avoid a deficit.

16.8   A deficit must be planned and approved by the Grand Council Treaty #3.

16.9   Any lobbying campaign required to meet the budgetary needs of the Treaty #3 Education Commission will be recommended to the Grand Council Treaty #3 for action.

Regulations of and Amendments to Kinamaadiwin Inaakonigewin:

17.0   Regulations drafted by the Treaty #3 Education Commission will be brought to the Grand Council Treaty #3 for approval.

17.1   Every regulation has the force of law.

17.2   Regulations further describe sections of this law and define the sections clearly.

17.3   For the duties of the director of education.

17.4   For the professional development of teachers.

17.5   For establishing professional staff qualifications, training, competency guidelines, and certification.

17.6   For organizing, administering, and supervising all schools under the law.

17.7   For classifying students and programs of study from early learning to Grade 12 and postsecondary.

17.8   For establishing curriculum and instruction standards.

17.9   For counselling services for students and their families.

17.10   For acquisition, financing, maintenance of school buildings, and construction.

17.11   For school administration guidelines, including attendance policy, truancy, social programming for students and their families, the calendar year, special needs students policy, home schooling, and the student code of conduct.

17.12   For fiscal management policies and funding formulas.

17.13   For establishing procedures to guide actions or goals of Kinamaadiwin Inaakonigewin when the law is insufficient.

Please note that the draft version of this law as presented here was developed in accordance with, and contains elements of Diane Longboat's "First Nations Education Law for First Nation Governments Template." The law has not yet been approved or ratified by the Grand Council Treaty #3 or its community members and is therefore subject to change. It is presented here for informational purposes only.

APPENDIX B: TREATY 3

Treaty 3 between Her Majesty the Queen and the Saulteaux Tribe of the Ojibbeway Indians at the Northwest Angle on the Lake of the Woods with Adhesions

(REPRINTED 1966)
(REPRINTED 1978)
LAYOUT IS NOT EXACTLY LIKE ORIGINAL
TRANSCRIBED FROM:
ROGER DUHAMEL, F.R.S.C.
QUEEN'S PRINTER AND CONTROLLER OF STATIONERY
OTTAWA, 1966
Cat. No. Ci 72-0366
ISBN 0-662-91350-7

Order in Council Setting up Commission for Treaty 3

The Committee have had under consideration the memorandum dated 19th April, 1871, from the Hon. the Secretary of State for the provinces submitting with reference to his report of the 17th of the same month that the Indians mentioned in the last paragraph of that report and with whom it will be necessary first to deal occupy the country from the water shed of Lake Superior to the north west angle of the Lake of the Woods and from the American border to the height of land from which the streams flow towards Hudson's Bay.

That they are composed of Saulteaux and Lac Seul Indians of the Ojibbeway Nation, and number about twenty-five hundred men, women and children, and, retaining what they desire in reserves at certain localities where they fish for sturgeon, would, it is thought be willing to surrender for a certain annual payment their lands to the Crown. That the American Indians to the south of them surrendered their lands to the Government of the United States for an annual payment which has been stated to him (but not on authority) to amount to ten dollars per head for each man, woman and child of which six dollars is paid in goods and four in money. That to treat with these Indians with advantage he recommends that Mr. Simon J. Dawson of the Department of Public Works and Mr. Robert Pither of the Hudson's Bay Company's service be associated with Mr. Wemyss M. Simpson—and further that the presents which were promised the Indians last year and a similar quantity for the present year should be collected at Fort Francis not later than the middle of June also that four additional suits of Chiefs' clothes and flags should be added to those now in store at Fort Francis—and further that a small house and store for provisions should be constructed at Rainy River at the site and of the dimensions which Mr. Simpson may deem best—that the assistance of the Department of Public Works will be necessary should his report be adopted in carrying into effect the recommendations therein made as to provisions, clothes and construction of buildings.

He likewise submits that it will be necessary that the sum of Six Thousand dollars in silver should be at Fort Francis subject to the Order of the above named Commissioners on the fifteenth day of June next— And further recommends that in the instructions to be given to them they should be directed to make the best arrangements in their power but authorized if need be to give as much as twelve dollars a family for each family not exceeding five—with such small Sum in addition where the family exceeds five as the Commissioners may find necessary—Such Subsidy to be made partly in goods and provisions and partly in money or wholly in goods and provisions should the Commissioners so decide for the surrender of the lands described in the earlier part of this report.

The Committee concur in the foregoing recommendations and submit the same for Your Excellency's approval.

Signed: Charles Tupper
25 April/71

Treaty No. 3
ARTICLES OF A TREATY made and concluded this third day of October, in the year of Our Lord one thousand eight hundred and seventy-three, between Her Most Gracious Majesty the Queen of Great Britain and Ireland, by Her Commissioners, the Honourable Alexander Morris, Lieutenant-Governor of the Province of Manitoba and the North-west Territories; Joseph Alfred Norbert Provencher and Simon James Dawson,

of the one part, and the Saulteaux Tribe of the Ojibway Indians, inhabitants of the country within the limits hereinafter defined and described, by their Chiefs chosen and named as hereinafter mentioned, of the other part.

Whereas the Indians inhabiting the said country have, pursuant to an appointment made by the said Commissioners, been convened at a meeting at the north-west angle of the Lake of the Woods to deliberate upon certain matters of interest to Her Most Gracious Majesty, of the one part, and the said Indians of the other.

And whereas the said Indians have been notified and informed by Her Majesty's said Commissioners that it is the desire of Her Majesty to open up for settlement, immigration and such other purpose as to Her Majesty may seem meet, a tract of country bounded and described as hereinafter mentioned, and to obtain the consent thereto of Her Indian subjects inhabiting the said tract, and to make a treaty and arrange with them so that there may be peace and good will between them and Her Majesty and that they may know and be assured of what allowance they are to count upon and receive from Her Majesty's bounty and benevolence.

And whereas the Indians of the said tract, duly convened in council as aforesaid, and being requested by Her Majesty's said Commissioners to name certain Chiefs and Headmen, who should be authorized on their behalf to conduct such negotiations and sign any treaty to be founded thereon, and to become responsible to Her Majesty for their faithful performance by their respective bands of such obligations as shall be assumed by them, the said Indians have thereupon named the following persons for that purpose, that is to say:—

KEK-TA-PAY-PI-NAIS (Rainy River.)
KITCHI-GAY-KAKE (Rainy River.)
NOTE-NA-QUA-HUNG (North-West Angle.)
NAWE-DO-PE-NESS (Rainy River.)
POW-WA-SANG (North-West Angle.)
CANDA-COM-IGO-WE-NINIE (North-West Angle.)
PAPA-SKO-GIN (Rainy River.)
MAY-NO-WAH-TAW-WAYS-KIONG (North-West Angle.)
KITCHI-NE-KA-LE-HAN (Rainy River.)
SAH-KATCH-EWAY (Lake Seul.)

MUPA-DAY-WAH-SIN (Kettle Falls.)

ME-PIE-SIES (Rainy Lake, Fort Frances.)

OOS-CON-NA-GEITH (Rainy Lake.)

WAH-SHIS-KOUCE (Eagle Lake.)

KAH-KEE-Y-ASH (Flower Lake.)

GO-BAY (Rainy Lake.)

KA-MO-TI-ASH (White Fish Lake.)

NEE-SHO-TAL (Rainy River.)

KEE-JE-GO-KAY (Rainy River.)

SHA-SHA-GANCE (Shoal Lake.)

SHAH-WIN-NA-BI-NAIS (Shoal Lake.)

AY-ASH-A-WATH (Buffalo Point.)

PAY-AH-BEE-WASH (White Fish Bay.)

KAH-TAY-TAY-PA-E-CUTCH (Lake of the Woods.)

And thereupon, in open council, the different bands having presented their Chiefs to the said Commissioners as the Chiefs and Headmen for the purposes aforesaid of the respective bands of Indians inhabiting the said district hereinafter described:

And whereas the said Commissioners then and there received and acknowledged the persons so presented as Chiefs and Headmen for the purpose aforesaid of the respective bands of Indians inhabiting the said district hereinafter described;

And whereas the said Commissioners have proceeded to negotiate a treaty with the said Indians, and the same has been finally agreed upon and concluded, as follows, that is to say:—

The Saulteaux Tribe of the Ojibbeway Indians and all other Indians inhabiting the district hereinafter described and defined, do hereby cede, release, surrender and yield up to the Government of the Dominion of Canada for Her Majesty the Queen and Her successors forever, all their rights, titles and privileges whatsoever, to the lands included within the following limits, that is to say:—

Commencing at a point on the Pigeon River route where the international boundary line between the Territories of Great Britain and the United States intersects the height of land separating the waters running to Lake Superior from those flowing to Lake Winnipeg; thence northerly, westerly and easterly along the height of land aforesaid, following its sinuosities, whatever their course may be, to the point at which the said height of land meets the summit of the watershed from which the streams flow to Lake Nepigon; thence northerly and westerly, or whatever may be its course, along the ridge separating the waters of the Nepigon and the Winnipeg to the height of land dividing the waters of the Albany and the Winnipeg; thence westerly and north-westerly along the height of land dividing the waters flowing to Hudson's Bay by the Albany or other rivers from those running to English River and the Winnipeg to a point on the said height of land bearing north forty-five degrees east from Fort Alexander, at the mouth of the Winnipeg; thence south forty-five degrees west to Fort Alexander, at the mouth of the Winnipeg; thence southerly along the eastern bank of the Winnipeg to the mouth of White Mouth River; thence southerly by the line described as in that part forming the eastern boundary of the tract surrendered by the Chippewa and Swampy Cree tribes of Indians to Her Majesty on the third of August, one thousand eight hundred and seventy-one, namely, by White Mouth River to White Mouth Lake, and thence on a line having the general bearing of White Mouth River to the forty-ninth parallel of north latitude; thence by the forty-ninth parallel of north latitude to the Lake of the Woods, and from thence by the international boundary line to the place beginning.

The tract comprised within the lines above described, embracing an area of fifty-five thousand square miles, be the same more or less. To have and to hold the same to Her Majesty the Queen, and Her successors forever.

And Her Majesty the Queen hereby agrees and undertakes to lay aside reserves for farming lands, due respect being had to lands at present culti-vated by the said Indians, and also to lay aside and reserve for the benefit of the said Indians, to be administered and dealt with for them by Her Majesty's Government of the Dominion of Canada, in such a manner as shall seem best, other reserves of land in the said territory hereby ceded, which said reserves shall be selected and set aside where it shall be deemed most convenient and advantageous for each band or bands of Indians, by the officers of the said Government appointed for that purpose, and such selection shall be so made after conference with the Indians; provided, however, that such reserves, whether for farming or other purposes, shall in no wise exceed in all one square mile for each family of five, or in that proportion for larger or smaller families; and such selections shall be made if possible during the course of next summer, or as soon thereafter as may be found practicable, it being understood, however, that if at the time of any such selection of any reserve, as aforesaid, there are any settlers within the bounds of the lands reserved by any band, Her Majesty reserves the right to deal with such settlers as She shall deem just so as not to diminish the extent of land allotted to Indians; and provided also that the aforesaid reserves of lands, or any interest or right therein or appurtenant thereto, may be sold, leased or otherwise disposed of by the said Government for the use and benefit of the said Indians, with the consent of the Indians entitled thereto first had and obtained.

And with a view to show the satisfaction of Her Majesty with the behaviour and good conduct of Her Indians She hereby, through Her Commissioners, makes them a present of twelve dollars for each man, woman and child belonging to the bands here represented, in extinguishment of all claims heretofore preferred.

And further, Her Majesty agrees to maintain schools for instruction in such reserves hereby made as to Her Government of Her Dominion of Canada may seem advisable whenever the Indians of the reserve shall desire it.

Her Majesty further agrees with Her said Indians that within the boundary of Indian reserves, until otherwise determined by Her Government of the Dominion of Canada, no intoxicating liquor shall be allowed to be introduced or sold, and all laws now in force or hereafter to be enacted to preserve Her Indian subjects inhabiting the reserves or living elsewhere within Her North-west Territories, from the evil influences of the use of intoxicating liquors, shall be strictly enforced.

Her Majesty further agrees with Her said Indians that they, the said Indians, shall have right to pursue their avocations of hunting and fishing throughout the tract surrendered as hereinbefore described, subject to such regulations as may from time to time be made by Her Government of Her Dominion of Canada, and saving and excepting such tracts as may, from time to time, be required or taken up for settlement, mining, lumbering or other purposes by Her said Government of the Dominion of Canada, or by any of the subjects thereof duly authorized therefor by the said Government.

It is further agreed between Her Majesty and Her said Indians that such sections of the reserves above indicated as may at any time be required for Public Works or buildings of what nature soever may be appropriated for that purpose by Her Majesty's Government of the Dominion of Canada, due compensation being made for the value of any improvements thereon.

And further, that Her Majesty's Commissioners shall, as soon as possible after the execution of this treaty, cause to be taken an accurate census of all the Indians inhabiting the tract above described, distributing them in families, and shall in every year ensuing the date hereof, at some period in each year to be duly notified to the Indians, and at a place or places to be appointed for that purpose within the territory ceded, pay to each Indian person the sum of five dollars per head yearly.

It is further agreed between Her Majesty and the said Indians that the sum of fifteen hundred dollars per annum shall be yearly and every year expended by Her Majesty in the purchase of ammunition and twine for nets for the use of the said Indians.

It is further agreed between Her Majesty and the said Indians that the following articles shall be supplied to any band of the said Indians who are now actually cultivating the soil or who shall hereafter commence to cultivate the land, that is to say: two hoes for every family actually cultivating, also one spade per family as aforesaid, one plough for every ten families as aforesaid, five harrows for every twenty families as aforesaid, one scythe for every family as aforesaid, and also one axe and one cross-cut saw, one hand-saw, one pit-saw, the necessary files, one grind-stone, one auger for each band, and also for each Chief for the use of his band one chest of ordinary carpenter's tools; also for each band enough of wheat, barley, potatoes and oats to plant the land actually broken up for cultivation by such band; also for each band one yoke of oxen, one bull and four cows; all the aforesaid articles to be given once for all for the encouragement of the practice of agriculture among the Indians.

It is further agreed between Her Majesty and the said Indians that each Chief duly recognized as such shall receive an annual salary of twenty-five dollars per annum, and each subordinate officer, not exceeding three for each band, shall receive fifteen dollars per annum; and each such Chief and subordinate officer as aforesaid shall also receive once in every three years a suitable suit of clothing; and each Chief shall receive, in recognition of the closing of the treaty, a suitable flag and medal.

And the undersigned Chiefs, on their own behalf and on behalf of all other Indians inhabiting the tract within ceded, do hereby solemnly promise and engage to strictly observe this treaty, and also to conduct and behave themselves as good and loyal subjects of Her Majesty the Queen. They promise and engage that they will in all respects obey and abide by the law, that they will maintain peace and good order between each other, and also between themselves and other tribes of Indians, and between themselves and others of Her Majesty's subjects, whether Indians or whites, now inhabiting or hereafter to inhabit any part of the said ceded tract, and that they will not molest the person or property of any inhabitants of such ceded tract, or the property of Her Majesty the Queen, or interfere with or trouble any person passing or travelling through the said tract, or any part thereof; and that they will aid and assist the officers of Her Majesty in bringing to justice and punishment any Indian offending against the stipulations of this treaty, or infringing the laws in force in the country so ceded.

IN WITNESS WHEREOF, Her Majesty's said Commissioners and the said Indian Chiefs have hereunto subscribed and set their hands at the North-West Angle of the Lake of the Woods this day and year herein first above named.

Signed by the Chiefs within named, in presence of the following witnesses, the same having been first read and explained by the Honorable James McKay:

JAMES McKAY,
MOLYNEUX St. JOHN,
ROBERT PITHER,
CHRISTINE V. K. MORRIS,
CHARLES NOLIN,
A. McDONALD, Capt.,
Comg. Escort to Lieut. Governor,
JAS. F. GRAHAM,
JOSEPH NOLIN,
A. McLEOD,

GEORGE McPHERSON, Sr.,
SEDLEY BLANCHARD,
W. FRED. BUCHANAN,
FRANK G. BECHER,
ALFRED CODD, M.D.,
G. S. CORBAULT,
PIERRE LEVIELLER,
NICHOLAS CHATELAINE,
ALEX. MORRIS L.G.,
J. A. N. PROVENCHER, Ind. Comr.,
S. J. DAWSON,

KEE-TA-KAY-PI-NAIS,
his x mark
KITCHI-GAY-KAKE,
his x mark
NO-TE-NA-QUA-HUNG,
his x mark
MAWE-DO-PE-NAIS,
his x mark
POW-WA-SANG,
his x mark
CANDA-COM-IGO-WI-NINE,
his x mark
MAY-NO-WAH-TAW-WAYS-KUNG,
his x mark
KITCHI-NE-KA-BE-HAN,
his x mark
SAH-KATCH-EWAY,
his x mark
MUKA-DAY-WAH-SIN,
his x mark
ME-KIE-SIES,
his x mark
OOS-CON-NA-GEISH,
his x mark
WAH-SHIS-KOUCE,
his x mark

KAH-KEE-Y-ASH,
his x mark
GO-BAY,
his x mark
KA-ME-TI-ASH,
his x mark
NEE-SHO-TAL,
his x mark
KEE-JEE-GO-KAY,
his x mark
SHA-SHA-GAUCE,
his x mark
SHAW-WIN-NA-BI-NAIS,
his x mark
AY-ASH-A-WASH,
his x mark
PAY-AH-BEE-WASH,
his x mark
KAH-TAY-TAY-PA-O-CUTCH,
his x mark

Indian Subscription to Treaty no 3
We, having had communication of the treaty, a certified copy whereof is hereto annexed, but not having been present at the councils held at the North West Angle of the Lake of the Woods between Her Majesty's Commissioners, and the several Indian Chiefs and others therein named, at which the articles of the said treaty were agreed upon, hereby for ourselves and the several bands of Indians which we represent, in consideration of the provisions of the said treaty being extended to us and the said bands which we represent, transfer, surrender and relinquish to Her Majesty the Queen, Her heirs and successors, to and for the use of Her Government of Her Dominion of Canada, all our right, title and privilege whatsoever, which we, the said Chiefs and the said bands which we represent have, hold or enjoy, of, in and to the territory described and fully set out in the said articles of treaty, and every part thereof. To have and to hold the same unto and to the use of Her said Majesty the Queen, Her heirs and successors forever.

And we hereby agree to accept the several provisions, payments and reserves of the said treaty, as therein stated, and solemnly promise and engage to abide by, carry out and fulfil all the stipulations, obligations and conditions therein contained, on the part of the said Chiefs and Indians therein named, to be observed and performed; and in all things to conform to the articles of the said treaty as if we ourselves and the bands which we represent had been originally contracting parties thereto, and had been present and attached our signatures to the said treaty.

IN WITNESS WHEREOF, Her Majesty's said Commissioners and the said Indian Chiefs have hereunto subscribed and set their hands, this thirteenth day of October, in the year of Our Lord one thousand eight hundred and seventy-three.

Signed by S. J. Dawson, Esquire, one of Her Majesty's said Commissioners, for and on behalf and with the authority and consent of the Honorable Alexander Morris, Lieutenant Governor of Manitoba and the North-West Territories, and J. A. N. Provencher, Esq., the remaining two Commissioners, and himself and by the Chiefs within named, on behalf of themselves and the several bands which they represent, the same and the annexed certified copy of articles of treaty having been first read and explained in presence of the following witnesses:

THOS. A. P. TOWERS,
JOHN AITKEN,
A. J. McDONALD,
UNZZAKI,
his x mark
JAS. LOGANOSH,
his x mark
PINLLSISE,
his x mark.

For and on behalf of the Commissioners, the Honorable Alexander Morris, Lieut. Governor of Manitoba and the NorthWest Territories, Joseph Albert Norbert Provencher, Esquire, and the undersigned

S. J. DAWSON,
Commissioner,
PAY-BA-MA-CHAS,

his x mark
RE-BA-QUIN,
his x mark
ME-TAS-SO-QUE-NE-SKANK,
his x mark

To S. J. Dawson, Esquire, Indian Commissioner, &c., &c., &c.

SIR, We hereby authorize you to treat with the various bands belonging to the Salteaux Tribe of the Ojibbeway Indians inhabiting the North-West Territories of the Dominion of Canada not included in the foregoing certified copy of articles of treaty, upon the same conditions and stipulations as are therein agreed upon, and to sign and execute for us and in our name and on our behalf the foregoing agreement annexed to the foregoing treaty.

NORTH-WEST ANGLE, LAKE OF THE WOODS,
October 4th, A.D. 1873.
ALEX. MORRIS,
Lieutenant-Governor.
J. A. N. PROVENCHER,
Indian Commissioner.

Adhesion by Halfbreeds of Rainy River and Lake (A.)

This Memorandum of Agreement made and entered into this twelfth day of September one thousand eight hundred and seventy-five, between Nicholas Chatelaine, Indian interpreter at Fort Francis and the Rainy River and acting herein solely in the latter capacity for and as representing the said Half-breeds, on the one part, and John Stoughton Dennis, Surveyor General of Dominion Lands, as representing Her Majesty the Queen through the Government of the Dominion, of the other part, Witnesseth as follows:

Whereas the Half-breeds above described, by virtue of their Indian blood, claim a certain interest or title in the lands or territories in the vicinity of Rainy Lake and the Rainy River, for the commutation or surrender of which claims they ask compensation from the Government.

And whereas, having fully and deliberately discussed and considered the matter, the said Half-breeds have elected to join in the treaty made between the Indians and Her Majesty, at the North-West Angle of the Lake of the Woods, on the third day of October, 1873, and have expressed a desire thereto, and to become subject to the terms and conditions thereof in all respects saving as hereinafter set forth.

It is now hereby agreed upon by and between the said parties hereto (this agreement, however, to be subject in all respects to approval and confirmation by the Government, without which the same shall be considered as void and of no effect), as follows, that is to say: The Half-breeds, through Nicholas Chatelaine, their Chief above named, as representing them herein, agree as follows, that is to say:—

That they hereby fully and voluntarily surrender to Her Majesty the Queen to be held by Her Majesty and Her successors for ever, any and all claim, right, title or interest which they, by virtue of their Indian blood, have or possess in the lands or territories above described, and solemnly promise to observe all the terms and conditions of the said treaty (a copy whereof, duly certified by the Honourable the Secretary of State of the Dominion has been this day placed in the hands of the said Nicholas Chatelaine).

In consideration of which Her Majesty agrees as follows, that is to say:

That the said Half-breeds, keeping and observing on their part the terms and conditions of the said treaty shall receive compensation in the way of reserves of land, payments, annuities and presents, in manner similar to that set forth in the several respects for the Indians in the said treaty; it being understood, however, that any sum expended annually by Her Majesty in the purchase of ammunition and twine for nets for the use of the said Half-breeds shall not be taken out of the fifteen hundred dollars set apart by the treaty for the purchase annually of those articles for the Indians, but shall be in addition thereto, and shall be a pro rata amount in the proportion of the number of Half-breeds parties hereto to the number of Indians embraced in the treaty; and it being further understood that the said Half-breeds shall be entitled to all the benefits of the said treaty as from the date thereof, as regards payments and annuities, in the same manner as if they had been present and had become parties to the same at the time of the making thereof.

And whereas the said Half-breeds desire the land set forth as tracts marked (A) and (B) on the rough diagram attached hereto, and marked with the initials of the parties aforementioned to this agreement, as their reserves (in all eighteen square miles), to which they would be entitled under the provisions of the treaty, the same is hereby agreed to on the part of the Government.

Should this agreement be approved by the Government, the reserves as above to be surveyed in due course.

Signed at Fort Francis, the day and date above mentioned, in presence of us as witnesses:

A. R. TILLIE,
CHAS. S. CROWE,
W. B. RICHARDSON,
L. KITTSON,
J. S. DENNIS, [L.S.]
NICHOLAS CHATELAINE, [L.S.]
his x mark

Adhesion of Lac Seul Indians to Treaty No. 3
LAC SEUL, 9th June, 1874.

We, the Chiefs and Councillors of Lac Seul, Seul, Trout and Sturgeon Lakes, subscribe and set our marks, that we and our followers will abide by the articles of the Treaty made and concluded with the Indians at the North West Angle of the Lake of the Woods, on the third day of October, in the year of Our Lord one thousand eight hundred and seventy-three, between Her Most Gracious Majesty the Queen of Great Britain and Ireland, by Her Commissioners, Hon. Alexander Morris, Lieutenant Governor of Manitoba and the North-West Territories, Joseph Albert N. Provencher, and Simon J. Dawson, of the one part, and the Saulteaux tribes of Ojibewas Indians, inhabitants of the country as defined by the Treaty aforesaid.

IN WITNESS WHEREOF, Her Majesty's Indian Agent and the Chiefs and Councillors have hereto set their hands at Lac Seul, on the 9th day of June, 1874.

(Signed) ACKEMENCE, Councillors,

his x mark
MAINEETAINEQUIRE,
his x mark
NAH-KEE-JECKWAHE,
his x mark

The whole Treaty explained by R.J.N. PITHER.

Witnesses:
(Signed) JAMES McKENZIE.
LOUIS KITTSON.
NICHOLAS CHATELAINE.
his x mark
R.J.N. PITHER, Indian Agent.
JOHN CROMARTY, Chief.
his x mark

Source: Canada, "Treaty Texts—Treaty No 3," https://www.rcaanc-cirnac.
gc.ca/eng/1100100028675/1581294028469.

APPENDIX C: THE PAYPOM TREATY

The following are the terms of the Treaty held at North West Angle the Third day of October, Eighteen Hundred and seventy three, viz:

1. The Government will give when Indians will be settled, Two hoes, one plough for every ten families Five harrows for every twenty families, one yoke of oxen, one bull and four cows for every band, one scythe and one axe for every family and enough of wheat, barley and oats for the land broken up; this is to encourage them at the beginning of their labour, once for all.

2. Fifteen hundred dollars every year in twine and munitions.

3. Twelve dollars for the first payment to every head of Indians and every subsequent year, Five Dollars. Twenty five Dollars to every chief every year. Councillor, first soldier and messenger Fifteen Dollars.

    The farming implements will be provided for during this winter to be given next year to those that are farming and to those who are anxious to imitate farmers, a set of carpenter tools will also be given.

    [. . .]

7. Coats will be given to the Chiefs and their head men every three years. With regard to the other Indians there is goods here to be given to them.

8. If their children are scattered come inside of two years and settle with you, they will have the same privilege as you have.

9. I will recommend to the authorities at Ottawa, assisted by the Indian Commissioner, the half breeds that are living with you to have the same privilege as you have.

10. The English Government never calls the Indians to assist them in their battles but he expects you to live in peace with red and white people.

11. Mr. Dawson said he would act as by the past about the Indians passage in his road. The Indians will be free as by the past for their hunting and rice harvest.

12. If some gold or silver mines be found in their reserves, it will be to the benefit of the Indians but if the Indians find any gold or silver mines out of their reserves they will be surely paid the finding of the mines.

13. The Commissioner and an agent will come to an understanding with the Indians about the reserve, and shall be surveyed by the Government. The Commissioners don't wish that the Indians leave their harvest immediately to step into their reserve.

14. About the Indian Commissioner, the Commission is pending on the authorities at Ottawa. I will write to Ottawa and refer Mr. Charles Nolin.

15. There will be no sale of liquor in this part of Canadian territory. It is the greatest pleasure for me to hear you and when we shake hands it must be for ever. It will be the duty of the English Government to deal with the Commissioners if they act wrong towards the Indians. I will give you a copy of the Agreement now and when I reach my residence I will send you a copy in parchment.

16. You will get rations during the time of the payment every year.

17. The Queen will have her policemen to preserve order and when there is crime and murder the guilty must be punished.

18. This Treaty will last as long as the sun will shine and water runs, that is to say forever.

Joseph Nolin
August Nolin

Elder Paypom explained how he obtained the document as follows:

> Linde was a photographer and a friend to the Indian people. One day, about forty or fifty years ago, he told me he had a paper and the Government wanted to buy it from him. He said they would give him $5,000.00 for it. But he wanted me to have it, "for your children" he said.
>
> That winter I saved all the money from my trapline. My family had a very hard winter that year because I saved that money,

but my wife never complained. She was a great woman, and she understood that the paper had on it the promises made to the people by the Government, and they were breaking those promises.

I saved my money and in the spring I gave it to Linde. He moved south, but he sent me a parcel in the mail. He sent it like a parcel of clothes so nobody would suspect it was the treaty.

The "Paypom Document" is an original set of notes made for Chief Powasson at the signing of the 1873 treaty between the Ojibway Indians and the Government of Canada at North West Angle on Lake of the Woods. The notes differ in many respects from the printed version of the treaty, delivered to the signatories by government officials sometime later. Recent treaty research indicates that the printed version might have been written a year before the 1873 North West Angle negotiations.

The notation below appears in pencil on the back of the original:

This copy was given to me in 1906 by Chief Powasson at Bukety—the Northwest Angle—Lake of the Woods.

(signed)
C.G. Linde

Source: This version of the Paypom Treaty can be found on the Anishinabek Nation website. See https://www.lostblogger.com/random/treaty-3-paypom-treaty/.

NOTES

Introduction

1   It is traditional practice of the Anishinaabe to introduce ourselves in such terms when speaking to others. It is how we let others know who we are, where we come from, and which clan we belong to. Having said that, the words here can be interpreted in English as follows:

Greetings.

My name is Blue Thunderbird.

I am from Lac Des Mille Lacs First Nation.

The caribou is my clan animal.

For further reference on the translation of Anishinaabemowin, see Ningewance, *Talking Gookum's Language*.

2   The terms "others" and "othering" are prevalent in postcolonial discourse—and employed *subversively* throughout this narrative—and most commonly understood as means "of establishing the binary separation of the colonizer and colonized and asserting the naturalness and primacy of the colonizing culture and world view." See Ashcroft, Griffiths, and Tiffin, *Postcolonial Studies*, 186.

3   See Coulthard, *Red Skin, White Masks*, 7.

4   On ideological apparatuses, see Althusser, *On the Reproduction of Capitalism*.

5   I have never lived "on reserve," but the territory around where my community is situated—that is, "Crown land"—is the traditional homeland of my family; I recognize that territory as my "home."

6   I invite the reader to check out Peter Kulchyski's article on "bush writing" for a refereed account of "bush" skills and knowledge. See Kulchyski, "Bush/Writing."

7   Section 289 provides that American Indians born in Canada cannot be denied admission into the United States if they possess at least 50 percent American Indian blood. By regulation, aliens eligible for INA 289 status may also become lawful permanent residents if they have maintained residence in the United States since their last time of entry.

8   See Appendix B.

9   See Starblanket and Stark, "Toward a Relational Paradigm," 188.

10   See Jai, "Bargains Made in Bad Times," 148.

11   Kelly, "Pimaatiziwin – Kizhewaatiziwin in Treaties."

Chapter 1: Colonization and Other Political Discontents

1   For more information on Canada's Indian residential school system, see Truth and Reconciliation Commission of Canada, *Final Report.*

2   See Bear Nicholas, "The Assault on Aboriginal Oral Traditions," 26.

3   Ibid., 18.

4   Ibid., 31.

5   See Indian Chiefs of Alberta, *Citizens Plus.*

6   See Alfred, *Peace, Power, and Righteousness*; Coulthard, *Red Skin, White Masks*; Simpson, *Dancing on Our Turtle's Back*; and Turner, *This Is Not a Peace Pipe.*

7   Deloria, *God Is Red,* 260.

8   See Blaut, *The Colonizer's Model of the World,* 28.

9   See Said, *Culture and Imperialism,* 8.

10   Saul, *A Fair Country,* 23.

11   See LaRocque, *When the Other Is Me,* 125–27.

12   Saul, *A Fair Country,* 23; see also Cairns, *Citizens Plus,* 64.

13   Said, *The Edward Said Reader,* 127.

14   Fanon, *The Wretched of the Earth,* 53.

15   LaRocque, *When the Other Is Me,* 43.

16   Simpson, *Dancing on Our Turtle's Back,* 70; see also Root, *Cannibal Culture.*

17   See Borrows, *Law's Indigenous Ethics,* 196.

18   For a dramatic, real-life account of a Windigo, see Fiddler and Stevens, *Killing the Shamen.*

19   Said, *The Edward Said Reader,* 78–79; emphasis added.

20   Memmi, *The Colonizer and the Colonized,* 71.

21   Ibid., 79.

22   Said, *The Edward Said Reader,* 133.

23   Ibid.

24   Blaut, *The Colonizer's Model of the World,* 19.

25   Kovach, "Indigenous Methodologies," 22.

26   Donald, "Homo Economicus and Forgetful Curriculum," 111.

27   See Battiste and Youngblood Henderson, *Protecting Indigenous Knowledge and Heritage,* 61.

28   Tully, "Reconciliation Here on Earth," 110.

29   Kuokkanen, *Reshaping the University,* 39.

30   See Marx, *Capital.*

31   Harvey, *The New Imperialism,* 145.

32   See Lipe, "Indigenous Knowledge Systems," 468; see also Berkes, *Sacred Ecology,* 3.

33   Root, *Cannibal Culture,* 159.

34   See Tuhiwai Smith, *Decolonizing Methodologies,* 165.

35   See Althusser, "Ideology and Ideological State Apparatuses."

36 Mills, "Rooted Constitutionalism," 147.

37 Freire, *Pedagogy of the Oppressed*, 73.

38 Ibid., 83.

39 Ibid., 72.

40 Goulet and Goulet, *Teaching Each Other*, 68.

41 See Deloria, *God Is Red*, 243.

42 See Maaka, "Education through Paideia," 11.

43 Cardinal, *The Rebirth of Canada's Indians*, 78.

44 Kulchyski, *Like the Sound of a Drum*, 4.

45 For further reading on the Indian Act, see Palmater, *Beyond Blood*.

46 Section 35(1) of the Indian Act reads thus: "Where by an Act of Parliament or a provincial legislature Her Majesty in right of a province, a municipal or local authority or a corporation is empowered to take or to use lands or any interest therein without the consent of the owner, the power may, with the consent of the Governor in Council and subject to any terms that may be prescribed by the Governor in Council, be exercised in relation to lands in a reserve or any interest therein."

47 See Appendix B.

48 United Nations, UNDRIP, Article 10.

49 Coulthard, *Red Skin, White Masks*, 100.

50 Alfred, *Wasáse*, 24.

51 Adams, *Prison of Grass*, 9.

52 Coulthard, *Red Skin, White Masks*, 16.

53 Ibid., 31.

54 Fanon, *The Wretched of the Earth*, 172.

55 Tuhiwai Smith, *Decolonizing Methodologies*, 74; see also LaRocque, *When the Other Is Me*, 127.

56 Root, *Cannibal Culture*, 38.

57 See Kulchyski, "Subversive Identities."

58 See Borrows, *Freedom and Indigenous Constitutionalism*, 181.

59 Fanon, *The Wretched of the Earth*, 178.

60 Memmi, *The Colonizer and the Colonized*, 114.

61 Absolon and Willett, "Putting Ourselves Forward," 113.

62 Deer, "Confronting Indigenous Identities," 241; see also Cote-Meek, *Colonized Classrooms*, 55; and Coulthard, *Red Skin, White Masks*.

63 King, *The Inconvenient Indian*, 72.

64 An organization called the League of Indians of Canada was established under the leadership of Fred O. Loft in 1919 to contest Duncan Campbell Scott's regime, but this organization ultimately dissolved after his death in 1934. See Kulchyski, "A Considerable Unrest."

65 See http://afn.ca.

66 Deer, "Confronting Indigenous Identities," 241.

67 LaRocque, *When the Other Is Me*, 25.

68 See Campbell, *Half-Breed*; Culleton Mosionier, *In Search of April Raintree*; and

Armstrong, *Slash*.

69 Coulthard, *Red Skin, White Masks*, 90.
70 Royal Commission on Aboriginal Peoples, *Final Report*.
71 Cote-Meek, *Colonized Classrooms*, 88.
72 Truth and Reconciliation Commission of Canada, *Final Report*.
73 See afn.ca.
74 Government of Canada, "Statement of Apology."
75 See Coulthard, *Red Skin, White Masks*, 155; Palmater, *Beyond Blood*, 26; and Simpson, *Dancing on Our Turtle's Back*, 22.
76 King, *The Inconvenient Indian*, 123.
77 Ibid., 124.
78 Simpson, *Dancing on Our Turtle's Back*, 22.
79 Battiste, *Decolonizing Education*, 170–74.
80 Ibid., 177.
81 Deer, "Confronting Indigenous Identities," 248.
82 Kuokkanen, *Reshaping the University*, 67.
83 See Goulet and Goulet, *Teaching Each Other*, 3.
84 Pidgeon, "Contested Spaces of Indigenization," 208.
85 Alfred, *Wasáse*, 59.
86 Root, *Cannibal Culture*, 79.
87 Wilson, *Research Is Ceremony*, 8.
88 LaRocque, *When the Other Is Me*, 21.
89 See Cote-Meek, *Colonized Classrooms*, 144.
90 United Nations, UNDRIP, Article 13(1).
91 Goulet and Goulet, *Teaching Each Other*, 74.
92 Grande, *Red Pedagogy*, 34.
93 Ibid.
94 Kuokkanen, *Reshaping the University*, 89.
95 The term "red pedagogy" comes from Grande, *Red Pedagogy*.
96 Tuhiwai Smith, *Decolonizing Methodologies*, 39.
97 Simpson, *Dancing on Our Turtle's Back*, 127.
98 Battiste, *Decolonizing Education*, 103.
99 Tully, "Reconciliation Here on Earth," 86.
100 Fanon, *The Wretched of the Earth*, 7.
101 Saul, *A Fair Country*, 36.
102 Acoose, *Iskwewak*, 51.
103 Vizenor, *Manifest Manners*, 70.
104 Borrows, *Law's Indigenous Ethics*, 66.
105 Ibid., 83.
106 Grande, *Red Pedagogy*, 26.
107 Starblanket and Stark, "Toward a Relational Paradigm," 199.
108 See Restoule and Nardozi, "Exploring Teacher Candidate Resistance," 320–26.
109 Kuokkanen, *Reshaping the University*, 71.

110 Wilson, *Research Is Ceremony*, 91.

111 See Styres, "Pathways for Remembering," 42.

112 Zinga, "Teaching as the Creation of Ethical Space," 284.

113 Goulet and Goulet, *Teaching Each Other*, 198.

114 Coulthard, *Red Skin, White Masks*, 52.

115 Restoule and Nardozi, "Exploring Teacher Candidate Resistance," 330.

116 Zinga, "Teaching as the Creation of Ethical Space," 285; see also Cote-Meek, *Colonized Classrooms*, 33.

117 Simpson, *Dancing on Our Turtle's Back*, 49.

118 Deer, "Confronting Indigenous Identities," 249; see also Cote-Meek, *Colonized Classrooms*, 157.

119 Johnston, "Is 'Space' the Final Frontier?," 484.

120 Ibid., 489.

121 Freire, *Pedagogy of the Oppressed*, 48.

122 See Kuokkanen, *Reshaping the University*, 56.

123 Simpson, *Dancing on Our Turtle's Back*, 87.

124 Ibid., 17.

Chapter 2: Indigenous Laws and the State

1 Borrows and Tully, "Introduction," 4.

2 Although some of what I say might have general application to Indigenous nations elsewhere in Canada, and around the world, in this chapter I focus on the specific context of the Anishinaabe Nation in Treaty 3 as it relates to our own educational needs and strategy for reconciliation with the Canadian state.

3 Kelly, "Eternal Law and Traditional Law."

4 Although this opinion is mine, it is substantiated by the fact that I am a member of the Anishinaabe Nation in Treaty 3 informed by the wisdom and guidance of national leaders and Elders. The use of the term "our" is a reflection of Emma LaRocque's great axiom, which I keep in mind as much as possible: "One's own voice is never totally one's self, in isolation from community. At the same time, one's self is not a communal replica of the collective." LaRocque, *When the Other Is Me*, 29.

5 Kelly, "Executive Summary and Elements."

6 Morris, *The Treaties of Canada*, 49.

7 A basic translation of mino-bimaadziwin is "the good life." Many Anishinaabe Elders and scholars identify mino-bimaadziwin as the raison d'être, or purpose of life, or reason for our existence on Earth. See Benton-Banai, *The Mishomis Book*; Borrows, *Recovering Canada*; Craft, *Breathing Life into the Stone Fort Treaty*; Doerfler, Sinclair, and Stark, *Centering Anishinaabeg Studies*; Johnston, *Ojibway Heritage*; Ningewance, *Talking Gookum's Language*; and Simpson, *Dancing on Our Turtle's Back*.

8 Derrida, *Of Grammatology*, 130.

9 Lévi-Strauss, *Tristes tropiques*, 298; emphasis added.

10 Derrida, *Of Grammatology*, 108.

11 Craft, *Breathing Life into the Stone Fort Treaty*, 70; see also Hamilton and Sinclair, *The Justice System and Aboriginal People*, 45.

12 Derrida, *Of Grammatology*, 109.

13 See Kulchyski, "Bush/Writing."

14 Derrida, *Given Time*, 6.

15 Kelly, "Implications of an Oral Constitution."

16 Grand Council Treaty 3, "The Creator Placed Us Here."

17 Longboat, "Historical Highlights," 3.

18 Kelly, "Implications of an Oral Constitution."

19 Hamilton and Sinclair, *The Justice System and Aboriginal People*, 22.

20 Kakeway, "Manito Aki Iinakonigaawin," 4.

21 Ibid.

22 See gct3.ca.

23 Ibid.

24 Coulthard, *Red Skin, White Masks*, 66.

25 For a more comprehensive account of the formation and history of these confederacies, see Clifton, McClurken, and Cornell, *People of the Three Fires*, in relation to the Three Fires Confederacy, and Johansen and Mann, *Encyclopedia of the Haudenosaunee (Iroquois Confederacy)*, on the Haudenosaunee Confederacy.

26 See Government of Canada website, https://www.rcaanc-cirnac.gc.ca/eng/1100100028589/1539608999656.

27 Simpson, *Mohawk Interruptus*, 32.

28 See Appendix B.

29 Kulchyski, *Like the Sound of a Drum*, 99.

30 Ibid.; emphasis added.

31 See Asch, *Aboriginal and Treaty Rights in Canada*; and Borrows, *Recovering Canada*.

32 See Craft, *Breathing Life into the Stone Fort Treaty*.

33 Cardinal, *The Rebirth of Canada's Indians*, 137.

34 Borrows and Coyle, *The Right Relationship*, 13.

35 Walters, "Rights and Remedies," 189; emphasis added.

36 Parmenter, "The Meaning of *Kaswentha*"; see also Alfred, *Peace, Power, and Righteousness*, 76.

37 Saul, *A Fair Country*, 65.

38 Derrida, *Given Time*, 111.

39 Miller, *Compact, Contract, Covenant*, 31.

40 Saul, *A Fair Country*, 69.

41 Royal Proclamation; emphasis added.

42 See Borrows, *Recovering Canada*.

43 Quoted in Miller, *Compact, Contract, Covenant*, 72.

44 Ibid., 73.

45 Ray, Miller, and Tough, *Bounty and Benevolence*, 33.

46 Craft, *Breathing Life into the Stone Fort Treaty*, 32.

47 The Red River Resistance, a flashpoint in Canadian history, has an important place in the nationhood of Métis peoples. For more on this history, see Peterson and Brown, *The New Peoples*; and St-Onge et al., *Contours of a People*.

48 See Craft, *Breathing Life into the Stone Fort Treaty*, 45.

49 Saul, *A Fair Country*, 66.

50 See Craft, *Breathing Life into the Stone Fort Treaty.*

51 Derrida, *Of Grammatology*, 150; emphasis added.

52 Coyle, "As Long as the Sun Shines," 41.

53 Morris, *The Treaties of Canada*, 31; emphasis added.

54 Asch, *On Being Here to Stay*, 88; see also Borrows, *Recovering Canada*; Craft, *Breathing Life into the Stone Fort Treaty*; and Krasowski and Wheeler, *No Surrender.*

55 Johnston, *Ojibway Heritage*, 25.

56 Wagamese, "'All My Relations' about Respect."

57 Craft, *Breathing Life into the Stone Fort Treaty*, 70.

58 Johnson, *Two Families*, 29.

59 Asch, *On Being Here to Stay*, 124; see also Williams, *Kayanerenkó:wa*, 2–3.

60 Borrows and Coyle, *The Right Relationship*, 3.

61 Coyle, "As Long as the Sun Shines," 50.

62 Cardinal, *The Rebirth of Canada's Indians*, 146.

63 Morris, *The Treaties of Canada*, 62.

64 See Appendix B.

65 Asch, "Confederation Treaties and Reconciliation," 44.

66 Morris, *The Treaties of Canada*, 71.

67 For the convenience of the reader, I have attached a transcribed copy of the Paypom Treaty as Appendix C to this book.

68 Morris, *The Treaties of Canada*, 58.

69 See Filice, "Treaty 3."

70 Quoted in Daugherty, "Treaty Research Report," 45.

71 Quoted in ibid., 47.

72 See Appendix C.

73 Ibid.

74 Morris, *The Treaties of Canada*, 11.

75 Palmater, *Beyond Blood*, 47.

76 See the Indian Act, s. 88.

77 Borrows and Coyle, *The Right Relationship*, 26.

78 Quoted in Talbot, *Negotiating the Numbered Treaties*, 118.

79 Ibid., 140.

80 Ibid., 160.

81 Daschuk, *Clearing the Plains*, 140.

82 Quoted in Asch, *On Being Here to Stay*, 145.

83 Ibid.

84 For a more comprehensive account of the government of Canada's starvation politics during this time, see Daschuk, *Clearing the Plains.*

85 *St. Catharines Milling and Lumber Co. v. R.*

86 See Craft, "Treaty Interpretation," 7, for the legal maxims upon which textual analysis is based.

87 Ibid.

88 See King, *The Inconvenient Indian*, 70–71.

89   See *Calder v. British Columbia.*

90   Constitution Act, 1982, s. 35.

91   *R. v. Sioui*; emphasis added.

92   *R. v. Marshall (No. 1).*

93   *Jones v. Meehan.*

94   LaRocque, *When the Other Is Me*, 38.

95   Craft, "Treaty Interpretation," 23.

96   Rotman, "Taking Aim at the Canons of Treaty Interpretation," 36; emphasis added.

97   *R. v. Badger.*

98   *Delgamuukw v. British Columbia.*

99   See Appendix B; emphasis added.

100 Notes from the Grand Council Treaty 3 Education Conference, 1989.

101 Cardinal, *The Rebirth of Canada's Indians*, 35.

102 See Stonechild, *The New Buffalo*, 115.

103 Battiste and Youngblood Henderson, *Protecting Indigenous Knowledge and Heritage*, 249.

104 *R. v. Marshall (No. 1).*

105 Government of Canada, "Statement of Apology."

106 For a comprehensive account of the residential school system in Canada, see Truth and Reconciliation Commission of Canada, *Final Report*; see also Miller, *Shingwauk's Vision*; Milloy, *A National Crime*; and Regan, *Unsettling the Settler Within.*

107 Quoted in Truth and Reconciliation Commission of Canada, *A Knock on the Door*, 32.

108 For a graphic representation of one student's journey home, see Downie, *Secret Path.*

109 J.R. Miller, *Shingwauk's Vision*, 6, writes that Chief Shingwauk of Garden River— near Sault Ste. Marie, Ontario—travelled to Toronto by canoe in 1871 to talk with Protestant clerics about establishing an education system in his community. During these conversations, Shingwauk is recorded as saying "I told the Blackcoats that before I died I should see a big teaching wigwam built at Garden River, where children from the Great Chippeway Lake would be received and clothed, and fed, and taught how to read and how to write; and also how to farm and build houses, and make clothing; so that by and bye [*sic*] they might go back and teach their own people."

110 See Stefanovich, "Pope Francis."

111 Truth and Reconciliation Commission, *Final Report*, Call to Action 10(vi).

112 See *R v. Marshall (No.1).*

113 Trudeau, speaking at the Assembly of First Nations General Assembly, December 2015.

114 See Kulchyski, *Aboriginal Rights Are Not Human Rights.*

115 See White Face, *Indigenous Nations' Rights in the Balance*, 3.

116 United Nations, UNDRIP, Article 4.

117 Ibid., Articles 5, 27.

118 Ibid., Article 37(1).

119 Ibid., Article 14(1).

120 Ibid., Article 18.

121 See Canadian Press, "Romeo Saganash's Indigenous Rights Bill."

122 AFN, Policy Statement on Bill C-262.

123 Barrera, "Trudeau Government Moving Forward on UNDRIP Legislation."

124 Quoted in Tasker, "Indigenous Groups Accuse Conservatives."

125 Quoted in Barrera, "Trudeau Government Moving Forward."

126 Quoted in ibid.

127 Quoted in Duncanson et al., "Federal UNDRIP Bill Becomes Law."

128 Truth and Reconciliation Commission, *Final Report*, Calls to Action 43 and 44.

129 Ibid., Call to Action 10.

130 Forsythe, "In Search of Indigenous Education Sovereignty," 86.

Chapter 3: Kinamaadiwin Inaakonigewin

1   I share this personal anecdote as an example of the intergenerational trauma that many Indigenous families have experienced as a result of failed government policies, particularly as they relate to education. For more info on intergenerational trauma, see Borrows, *Law's Indigenous Ethics*, 223; Cote-Meek, *Colonized Classrooms*; and Maaka, "Education through Paideia," 11.

2   Kulchyški, *Like the Sound of a Drum*, 177.

3   Simpson, *Dancing on Our Turtle's Back*, 146.

4   Kulchyski, *Like the Sound of a Drum*, 177.

5   See Adams, *Prison of Grass*, 153.

6   Wilson, *Research Is Ceremony*, 123.

7   See Ningewance, *Talking Gookum's Language*.

8   Hubbard, "Voices Heard in the Silence," 146.

9   Simpson, *Dancing on Our Turtle's Back*, 66.

10 Benton-Banai, *The Mishomis Book*, 89.

11 Ibid., 99; for more on Anishinaabe history, see Copway, *Traditional History and Characteristic Sketches*; and Warren, *History of the Ojibway People*.

12 The Anishinaabe Nation in Treaty #3 is the most prominent example of this phenomenon, less true for other treaty territories that contain multiple Indigenous nations.

13 See Appendix A, sec. 6.2.

14 Adams, *Prison of Grass*, 194.

15 Fanon, *The Wretched of the Earth*, 83; emphasis added.

16 Lawrence, *"Real" Indians and Others*, 114.

17 Hawthorn, *A Survey of the Contemporary Indians of Canada*, 12.

18 Kelly, "A Treaty-Based, Community-Driven Model," 65.

19 Ibid.

20 Treaty 3 Elders' Gathering, 2007.

21 Kelly, "Executive Summary and Elements."

22 Kelly, "Pimaatiziwin ~ Kizhewaatiziwin in Treaties."

23 See Appendix A, sec. 3.3.

24 Lawrence, *"Real" Indians and Others*, 110.

25 Cote-Meek, *Colonized Classrooms*, 30.

26 Seven Generations Education Institute, "Education Guiding Principles."

27   See Appendix A, sec. 9.4.

28   Ibid., sec. 9.5.

29   Seven Generations Education Institute, "Education Guiding Principles."

30   Ibid.

31   Styres, "Pathways for Remembering," 44.

32   Treaty 3 Elders' Gathering, 2008.

33   Kuokkanen, *Reshaping the University*, 60.

34   See Pidgeon, "Contested Spaces of Indigenization," 207.

35   Treaty 3 Elders' Gathering, 2008.

36   Eigenbrod and Hulan, *Aboriginal Oral Traditions*, 7.

37   Treaty 3 Elders' Gathering, 2008.

38   Seven Generations Education Institute, "Education Guiding Principles."

39   Ibid.

40   Ibid.

41   Kovach, *Indigenous Methodologies*, 146; see also Brant Castellano, "Ethics of Aboriginal Research."

42   Treaty 3 Elders' Gathering, 2008.

43   Starblanket and Stark, "Toward a Relational Paradigm," 194.

44   Kelly, "Executive Summary and Elements."

45   Goulet and Goulet, *Teaching Each Other*, 215.

46   Grand Council Treaty #3, "Chiefs in Assembly."

47   Ibid.

48   Following his election victory, Trudeau attended an AFN National Chiefs Assembly and said that "we recognize that true reconciliation goes beyond the scope of the Commission's Calls to Action, [and] I am therefore announcing that we will work with First Nations, the Métis Nation, Inuit, provinces and territories, parties to the Indian Residential Schools Settlement Agreement, and other key partners to design a national engagement strategy for developing and implementing a national reconciliation framework, including a formal response to the Truth and Reconciliation Commission's Calls to Action." Quoted in Galloway, "Trudeau Vows to Develop Plan."

49   See https://education.chiefs-of-ontario.org/priorities/lifelonglearning/.

50   See Grand Council Treaty #3, "First Nations Lifelong Learning Table."

51   Ibid.

52   Ibid.

53   Coulthard, *Red Skin, White Masks*, 120.

54   Ibid., 126.

55   Alfred, *Wasáse*, 138.

56   Grand Council Treaty #3, "Treaty #3 Education Gathering."

57   Visit https://www.sac-isc.gc.ca/eng/1308840098023/1531400115587 to see a fossilized collection of "First Nation Education Partnerships and Agreements."

58   Grand Council Treaty #3, "Chiefs in Assembly."

59   For more information on the Lac Courte Oreilles Ojibwe School, see https://www.lcoosk12.org.

60   See Appendix A, sec. 6.1.

61 Grand Council Treaty #3, "Treaty #3 Education Gathering."
62 Kelly, "Pimaatiziwin ~ Kizhewaatiziwin in Treaties."
63 Standing Senate Committee on Aboriginal Peoples, "Reforming First Nations Education," 61–62.
64 See Appendix A, sec. 7.1.
65 Grand Council Treaty #3, "Treaty #3 Education Gathering."
66 Ibid.
67 Battiste, *Decolonizing Education*, 121.
68 Barrett, "Canadian Shield."
69 See Kulchyski, "Bush/Writing."
70 Battiste, *Decolonizing Education*, 121.
71 Grand Council Treaty #3, "Treaty #3 Education Gathering"; see also Appendix A, sec. 7.5.
72 Deloria, *God Is Red*, 87.
73 See Appendix A, sec. 7.25.
74 Ibid., sec. 7.22.
75 Ibid., sec. 15.7.
76 See Appendix A, sec. 12.
77 Standing Senate Committee on Aboriginal Peoples, "Reforming First Nations Education," 64.
78 Wilson-Raybould, *Indian in the Cabinet*, 147.
79 See Appendix A, sec. 7.13.
80 Ibid., sec. 7.17.
81 Cardinal, *The Rebirth of Canada's Indians*, 222.
82 Simpson, *Dancing on Our Turtle's Back*, 127.
83 Ibid.
84 See Appendix A, sec. 13.0.
85 Ibid., sec. 13.3.
86 Goulet and Goulet, *Teaching Each Other*, 53.
87 See Appendix A, sec. 17.
88 Ibid.
89 See Grand Council Treaty #3, "Law-Making Process."
90 United Nations, UNDRIP, Article 19. See also International Covenant on the Rights of the Child, International Covenant on Economic, Social and Cultural Rights, Expert Mechanism on the Rights of Indigenous Peoples Human Rights Council, Convention on the Rights of the Child, and World Declaration on Education for All.
91 Grand Council Treaty #3, "Notes to the Elders Gathering on Education."
92 Grand Council Treaty #3, "Chiefs in Assembly."
93 Ibid.
94 Grand Council Treaty #3, "Law-Making Process."
95 Longboat, "First Nations Education Law," 8.
96 Ibid.
97 Ibid.
98 Grand Council Treaty #3, "Chiefs in Assembly."

99 Ibid.

100 Kelly, "Executive Summary and Elements."

101 Simpson, *Dancing on Our Turtle's Back*, 66-67.

Chapter 4: Reconciliation as Recognition and Affirmation

1 Borrows, "Earth-Bound," 53.

2 See Hegel, "Lordship and Bondage."

3 Fanon, *The Wretched of the Earth*, 14.

4 Cardinal, *The Rebirth of Canada's Indians*, 152.

5 Simpson, *As We Have Always Done*, 101.

6 Mills, "What Is a Treaty?," 244.

7 See Valaskakis, Dion Stout, and Guimond, *Restoring the Balance*.

8 Alfred, *Peace, Power, Righteousness*, 154.

9 In February 2020, members of the Mohawk Nation set up a rail blockade in Tyendinaga in support of the Wet'suwet'en hereditary chiefs who oppose the construction of a natural gas pipeline scheduled to be built across Wet'suwet'en traditional territory. This action was followed by similar protests in other parts of Canada. See Tunney, "OPP Arrest 10 Demonstrators."

10 Coulthard, *Red Skin, White Masks*, 172.

11 Ibid., 166.

12 Alfred, *Peace, Power, Righteousness*, 100.

13 Memmi, *The Colonizer and the Colonized*, 127.

14 See Payton, "First Nations Get Broad Promises on Indian Act Development."

15 My speech at the Truth and Reconciliation national event occurred on 23 June 2012. It can be viewed on the National Centre for Truth and Reconciliation website at https://nctr.ca.

16 See "AFN Chiefs March on Parliament."

17 See "Idle No More."

18 Cardinal, *The Rebirth of Canada's Indians*, 21.

19 Turner, *This Is Not a Peace Pipe*, 96.

20 See Appendix B.

21 Quoted in Williams, *Linking Arms Together*, 121.

22 Morris, *The Treaties of Canada*, 66; emphasis added.

23 Talbot, *Negotiating the Numbered Treaties*, 78.

24 Foucault, *The Archaeology of Knowledge*, 74.

25 Ibid., 104–05.

26 Coyle, "As Long as the Sun Shines," 61; emphasis in original.

27 Tully, *Strange Multiplicity*, 211.

28 Asch, *On Being Here to Stay*, 94.

29 See Appendix B; emphasis added.

30 Starblanket and Stark, "Toward a Relational Paradigm," 196.

31 Turner, *This Is Not a Peace Pipe*, 96.

32 Coulthard, *Red Skin, White Masks*, 13; emphasis in original.

33 Tully, "Reconciliation Here on Earth," 86.

34 Simpson, *As We Have Always Done*, 154.

35 See Longboat, "First Nations Education Law," 12.

36 Ibid., 11.

37 Borrows, *Law's Indigenous Ethics*, 43.

38 Longboat, "First Nations Education Law," 12.

39 Ibid., 13.

40 Standing Senate Committee on Aboriginal Peoples, "Reforming First Nations Education," 62.

41 Cardinal, *The Rebirth of Canada's Indians*, 52.

42 See Appendix A, sec. 8.4.

43 Ibid., sec. 8.2.

44 Assembly of First Nations, "Tradition and Education," 2.

45 See Appendix A, sec. 11.3.

46 For a more comprehensive account of this history, see Long, *Treaty No. 9*.

47 See Appendix A, sec. 11.2.

48 Forsythe, "In Search of Indigenous Education Sovereignty," 131.

49 For more on the criminalization of Indigenous resistance, see Pasternak, *Grounded Authority*.

50 Wilson-Raybould, *Indian in the Cabinet*, 24.

51 RCAP, *Final Report*, 2: 240.

52 Mills, "Rooted Constitutionalism," 157.

53 See Appendix A, sec. 12.1.

54 Ibid., sec. 11.7.

55 Ibid., sec. 11.16.

56 Cote-Meek, *Colonized Classrooms*, 157.

57 See Appendix A, sec. 11.18.

58 Borrows, *Otter's Journey through Indigenous Language and Law*, 45.

59 See Appendix A, sec. 11.8.

60 Cardinal, *The Rebirth of Canada's Indians*, 75.

61 Goulet and Goulet, *Teaching Each Other*, 5.

62 There is a certain inevitability, on the basis of need, that some non-Anishinaabe teachers and staff will be hired, and preference should be given to those who have knowledge of the Anishinaabe worldview or a basic understanding of Anishinaabemowin and Anishinaabe protocols and customs.

63 Goulet and Goulet, *Teaching Each Other*, 77.

64 Bevan-Brown, "Improving Special Needs Education for Māori Children," 385.

65 Goulet and Goulet, *Teaching Each Other*, 111.

66 See Appendix A, sec. 10.1.

67 Cote-Meek, *Colonized Classrooms*, 33.

68 Donald, "Homo Economicus and Forgetful Curriculum," 120.

69 Ibid.

70 Borrows, *Law's Indigenous Ethics*, 150.

71   Coulthard, *Red Skin, White Masks*, 171.

72   Johnston, "Is 'Space' the Final Frontier?," 485.

73   See Appendix A, sec. 10.9.

74   Borrows, "Earth-Bound," 56.

75   The treaty curriculum is based upon an initiative developed by the Federation of Saskatchewan Indian Nations, First Nations University of Canada, Office of the Treaty Commissioner, Curriculum Sub-Committee for the Shared Standards and Capacity Building Council, and Ministry of Education back in 2013 and adapted to meet the needs of teachers and students in Treaty #3 territory. See Saskatchewan Ministry of Education, "Treaty Education Outcomes and Indicators."

76   Bimose Tribal Council, "Manitou Mazinaa'igan Gakendaasowin."

77   See Appendix A, sec. 10.10.

78   See Highway, *The Rez Sisters*.

79   See Culleton Mosionier, *In Search of April Raintree*.

80   Kuokkanen, *Reshaping the University*, 69.

81   See Appendix A, sec. 17.5.

82   For more information on Nanabush, see Benton-Banai, *The Mishomis Book*; Copway, *The Traditional History and Characteristic Sketches*; and Johnston, *Ojibway Heritage*.

83   Deer, "Confronting Indigenous Identities in Transcultural Contexts," 244.

84   Deloria, *God Is Red*, 274.

85   LaRocque, *When the Other Is Me*, 137.

86   Simpson, *As We Have Always Done*, 198.

87   See Appendix A, sec. 4.0.

Chapter 5: Reflections

1   Cardinal, *The Rebirth of Canada's Indians*, 87.

2   Derrida, *Given Time*, 61.

3   See Trudeau, "Prime Minister Justin Trudeau Delivers a Speech."

4   *R. v. Badger*; emphasis added.

5   *R. v. Van Der Peet*, para. 31.

6   Asch, *On Being Here to Stay*, 79.

7   Quoted in Dart, "First Nations Schools Are Chronically Underfunded."

8   Jai, "Bargains Made in Bad Times," 148.

9   Ibid., 144.

10   Treaty Relations Commission of Manitoba website, https://trcm.ca/.

11   Turner, *This Is Not a Peace Pipe*, 121.

12   Standing Senate Committee on Aboriginal Peoples, "Reforming First Nations Education," 66.

REFERENCES

Legislation

Canadian Charter of Rights and Freedoms, Part 1 of the *Constitution Act, 1982*, being Schedule B to the *Canada Act 1982* (U.K.), 1982, c. II, at s. 25.

Hudson's Bay Company Charter, 1670.

Indian Act, R.S.C. 1985, c. 1–5.

Royal Proclamation of 1763, reprinted in R.S.C. 1985, App. II, No. 1

The Constitution Act, 1982, being Schedule B to *the Canada Act 1982* (U.K.), 1982, c. II.

The Manitoba Act, 1870, 33 Victoria, c. 3.

United Nations Declaration on the Rights of Indigenous Peoples Act, S.C. 2021, c. 14.

Legal Sources

Calder v. British Columbia (AG) [1973] S.C.R. 313.

Delgamuukw v. British Columbia, [1997] 3 S.C.R. 1010.

Jones v. Meehan, 175 U.S. 1 (1899).

R. v. Badger, [1996] 1 S.C.R. 771.

R. v. Marshall, [1999] 3 S.C.R. 456 *(Marshall I)*.

R. v. Sioui, [1990] 1 S.C.R. 1025.

R. v. Sparrow [1990] 1 S.C.R. 1075.

R. v. Taylor and Williams, [1981] 3 C.N.L.R. 114 (Ont. C.A.).

R. v. Van der Peet [1996] 2 S.C.R. 507.

St. Catharines Milling and Lumber Co. v. R, [1887] 13 S.C.R. 577.

Primary Documents

Grand Council Treaty #3. "Chiefs in Assembly: Draft Record of Decision on the Making of a Written Law in Kinaamatiwin." 2008.

———. "First Nations Lifelong Learning Table." 2018.

———. "Law-Making Process." N.d.

———. "Notes from Education Conference," 1989.

———. "Notes to the Elders Gathering on Education." 2007.

———. "The Creator Placed Us Here." N.d.

———. "Treaty #3 Education Gathering." 2018.

Kelly, Fred. "Eternal Law and Traditional Law: The Source of the Anishinaabe Constitution." N.d.

———. "Executive Summary and Elements of the Constitutional Government of the Anishinaabe Nation in Treaty #3." N.d.

———. "Implications of an Oral Constitution." N.d.

———. "Pimaatiziwin - Kizhewaatiziwin in Treaties." Treaty #3 Youth and Elders Gathering, 2019.

———. "A Treaty-Based, Community-Driven Model of Self-Government in Education and Language and Culture." 1994.

Published Sources

Absolon, Kathy, and Cam Willett. "Putting Ourselves Forward: Location in Aboriginal Research." In *Research Is Resistance: Critical, Indigenous, and Anti-Oppressive Approaches*, edited by Leslie Brown and Susan Strega, 97–126. Toronto: Canadian Scholars Press, 2005.

Acoose, Janice. *Iskwewak: Neither Indian Princesses nor Easy Squaws*. Toronto: Women's Press, 1995.

Adams, Howard. *Prison of Grass: Canada from the Native Point of View*. Toronto: General Publishing, 1975.

"AFN Chiefs March on Parliament." 14 December 2012. *The Nation* Archives. https://www.nationnewsarchives.ca.

Alfred, Taiaiake. *Peace, Power, and Righteousness: An Indigenous Manifesto*. Don Mills, ON: Oxford University Press, 1999.

———. *Wasáse: Indigenous Pathways of Action and Freedom*. Toronto: University of Toronto Press, 2009.

Althusser, Louis. *On the Reproduction of Capitalism: Ideology and Ideological State Apparatuses*. 1970; reprinted, London: Verso Books, 2014.

Armstrong, Jeannette. *Slash*. Penticton, BC: Theytus Books, 1988.

Asch, Michael. *Aboriginal and Treaty Rights in Canada: Essays on Law, Equality, and Respect for Difference*. Vancouver: UBC Press, 1997.

———. "Confederation Treaties and Reconciliation: Stepping Back into the Future." In *Resurgence and Reconciliation: Indigenous-Settler Relations and Earth Teachings*, edited by Michael Asch, John Borrows, and James Tully, 29–48. Toronto: University of Toronto Press, 2018.

———. *On Being Here to Stay: Treaties and Aboriginal Rights in Canada*. Toronto: University of Toronto Press, 2014.

Ashcroft, Bill, Gareth Griffiths, and Helen Tiffin. *Postcolonial Studies: The Key Concepts*. 3rd ed. London: Routledge, 2013.

Assembly of First Nations (AFN). Policy Statement on Bill C-262. 4 May 2016. https://www.afn.ca/uploads/files/public_statement_bill_c-262-may_4.pdf.

———. "Tradition and Education: Towards a Vision of Our Future, a Declaration of First Nations Jurisdiction over Education." 1988. https://education.chiefs-of-ontario.org/download/tradition-and-education-towards-a-vision-of-our-future/.

Barrera, Jorge. "Trudeau Government Moving Forward on UNDRIP Legislation, Says Minister." CBC News, 4 December 2019. https://www.cbc.ca/news/indigenous/trudeau-undrip-bill-1.5383755.

Barrett, David. "Canadian Shield." *Canadian Encyclopedia* online, 7 February 2006, last edited 11 August 2021. https://www.thecanadianencyclopedia.ca/en/article/shield.

Battiste, Marie. *Decolonizing Education: Nourishing the Learning Spirit*. Saskatoon: Purich Publishing, 2013.

Battiste, Marie, and James Sake'j Youngblood Henderson. *Protecting Indigenous Knowledge and Heritage*. Saskatoon: Purich Publishing, 2000.

Bear Nicholas, Andrea. "The Assault on Aboriginal Oral Traditions." In *Aboriginal Oral Traditions: Theory, Practice, Ethics*, edited by Renate Eigenbrod and Renee Hulan, 13–43. Halifax: Fernwood Publishing, 2008.

Benton-Banai, Edward. *The Mishomis Book: The Voice of the Ojibway*. Minneapolis: University of Minnesota Press, 1988.

Berkes, Fikret. *Sacred Ecology: Traditional Ecological Knowledge and Resource Management*. Philadelphia: Taylor and Francis, 1999.

Bevan-Brown, Jill. "Improving Special Needs Education for Māori Children." In *Indigenous Education: New Directions in Theory and Practice*, edited by Huia Tomlins-Jahnke, Sandra Styres, Spencer Lilley, and Dawn Zinga, 365–404. Edmonton: University of Alberta Press, 2019.

Bimose Tribal Council. "Manitou Mazinaa'igan Gakendaasowin: Treaty Learning." 2019.

Blaut, J.M. *The Colonizer's Model of the World: Geographical Diffusionism and Eurocentric History*. New York: Guilford Press, 1993.

Borrows, John. "Earth-Bound: Indigenous Resurgence and Environmental Reconciliation." In *Resurgence and Reconciliation: Indigenous-Settler Relations and Earth Teachings*, edited by Michael Asch, John Borrows, and James Tully, 49–82. Toronto: University of Toronto Press, 2018.

———. *Freedom and Indigenous Constitutionalism*. Toronto: University of Toronto Press, 2016.

———. *Law's Indigenous Ethics*. Toronto: University of Toronto Press, 2019.

———. *Recovering Canada: The Resurgence of Indigenous Law*. Toronto: University of Toronto Press, 2002.

Borrows, John, and Michael Coyle, eds. *The Right Relationship: Reimagining the Implementation of Historical Treaties*. Toronto: University of Toronto Press, 2017.

Borrows, John, and James Tully. "Introduction." In *Resurgence and Reconciliation: Indigenous-Settler Relations and Earth Teachings*, edited by Michael Asch, John Borrows, and James Tully, 3–28. Toronto: University of Toronto Press, 2018.

Borrows, Lindsay. *Otter's Journey through Indigenous Language and Law*. Vancouver: UBC Press, 2018.

Brant Castellano, Marlene. "Ethics of Aboriginal Research." In *Journal of Aboriginal Health* 1, no. 1 (2004): 98–114.

Cairns, Alan. *Citizens Plus: Aboriginal Peoples and the Canadian State*. Vancouver: UBC Press, 2000.

Campbell, Maria. *Half-Breed*. Toronto: McClelland and Stewart, 1973.

Canada. "Statement of Apology to Former Students of Indian Residential Schools." 2008. https://www.rcaanc-cirnac.gc.ca/eng/1100100015644/1571589171655.

Canadian Press. "Romeo Saganash's Indigenous Rights Bill Passes in the House of Commons." CBC News, 30 May 2018. https://www.cbc.ca/news/politics/saganash-undrip-bill-passes-1.4684889.

Cardinal, Harold. *The Rebirth of Canada's Indians*. Edmonton: Hurtig Publishers, 1977.

Clifton, James, James McClurken, and George Cornell. *People of the Three Fires: The Ottawa, Potawatomi, and Ojibway of Michigan*. Grand Rapids: Michigan Indian Press, Grand Rapids Inter-Tribal Council, 1986.

Copway, George. *The Traditional History and Characteristic Sketches of the Ojibway Nation*. London: Charles Gilpin, 1850.

Cote-Meek, Sheila. *Colonized Classrooms: Racism, Trauma and Resistance in Post-Secondary Education*. Halifax: Fernwood Publishing, 2014.

Coulthard, Glen. *Red Skin, White Masks: Rejecting the Colonial Politics of Recognition*. Minneapolis: University of Minnesota Press, 2014.

Coyle, Michael. "As Long as the Sun Shines: Recognizing that Treaties Were Intended to Last." In *The Right Relationship: Reimagining the Implementation of Historical Treaties*, edited by John Borrows and Michael Coyle, 39–69. Toronto: University of Toronto Press, 2017.

Craft, Aimée. *Breathing Life into the Stone Fort Treaty: An Anishinabe Understanding of Treaty One*. Saskatoon: Purich Publishing, 2013.

———. "Treaty Interpretation: A Tale of Two Stories." 2011. https://papers.ssrn.com/sol3/papers.cfm?abstract_id=3433842.

Culleton Mosionier, Beatrice. *In Search of April Raintree*. Winnipeg: HighWater Press, 1983.

Dart, Christopher. "First Nations Schools Are Chronically Underfunded." N.d. CBCDOCSPOV. https://www.cbc.ca/cbcdocspov/features/first-nations-schools-are-chronically-underfunded.

Daschuk, James. *Clearing the Plains: disease politics of starvation, and the loss of Indigenous life*. Regina: University of Regina Press, 2019.

Daugherty, Wayne. "Treaty Research Report—Treaty Three (1873)." Indian and Northern Affairs Canada, 1986.

Deer, Frank. "Confronting Indigenous Identities in Transcultural Contexts." In *Indigenous Education: New Directions in Theory and Practice*, edited by Huia Tomlins-Jahnke, Sandra Styres, Spencer Lilley, and Dawn Zinga. Edmonton: University of Alberta Press, 2019.

Deloria, Vine Jr. *God Is Red: A Native View of Religion*. Wheat Ridge, CO: Fulcrum Publishing, 2003.

Derrida, Jacques. *Given Time: I. Counterfeit Money*. Chicago: University of Chicago Press, 1992.

———. *Of Grammatology*. Baltimore: Johns Hopkins University Press, 1974.

Doerfler, Jill, Niigaanwewidam Sinclair, and Heidi Stark, eds. *Centering Anishinaabeg Studies: Understanding the World through Stories.* East Lansing: Michigan State University Press, 2013.

Donald, Dwayne. "Homo Economicus and Forgetful Curriculum: Remembering Other Ways to Be a Human Being." In *Indigenous Education: New Directions in Theory and Practice*, edited by Huia Tomlins-Jahnke, Sandra Styres, Spencer Lilley, and Dawn Zinga, 103–25. Edmonton: University of Alberta Press, 2019.

Downie, Gordon. *Secret Path.* Toronto: Simon and Schuster, 2016.

Duncanson, Sander, Coleman Brinker, Kelly Twa, and Maeve O'Neill Sanger. "Federal UNDRIP Bill Becomes Law." Osler, 22 June 2021. https://www.osler.com/en/resources/regulations/2021/federal-undrip-bill-becomes-law.

Eigenbrod, Renate, and Renee Hulan, eds. *Aboriginal Oral Traditions: Theory, Practice, Ethics.* Halifax: Fernwood Publishing, 2008.

Fanon, Frantz. *The Wretched of the Earth.* New York: Grove Books, 1963.

Fiddler, Thomas, and James Stevens. *Killing the Shamen.* Newcastle, ON: Penumbra Press, 1985.

Filice, Michelle. "Treaty 3." *Canadian Encyclopedia* online, 19 August 2016, last edited 22 June 2020. https://www.thecanadianencyclopedia.ca/en/article/treaty-3.

Forsythe, Laura. "In Search of Indigenous Education Sovereignty." MA thesis, University of Manitoba, 2018.

Foucault, Michel. *The Archaeology of Knowledge and the Discourse on Language.* New York: Pantheon Books, 1972.

Freire, Paulo. *Pedagogy of the Oppressed.* New York: Bloomsbury, 2000.

Galloway, Gloria. "Trudeau Vows to Develop Plan to Put Canada on Path to 'True Reconciliation.'" *Globe and Mail*, 15 December 2015. https://www.theglobeandmail.com/news/national/truth-and-reconciliation-head-calls-for-action-as-final-report-released/article27762924/Y.

Goulet, Linda, and Keith Goulet. *Teaching Each Other: Nehinuw Concepts and Indigenous Pedagogies.* Vancouver: UBC Press, 2014.

Grande, Sandy. *Red Pedagogy: Native American Social and Political Thought.* New York: Rowman and Littlefield Publishers, 2004.

Hamilton, Alvin, and Murray Sinclair. *The Justice System and Aboriginal People: Report of the Aboriginal Justice Inquiry of Manitoba.* Vol. 1. Winnipeg: Queen's Printer, 1991.

Harvey, David. *The New Imperialism.* New York: Oxford University Press, 2005.

Hawthorn, Harry Bertram, ed. *A Survey of the Contemporary Indians of Canada: A Report on Economic, Political, Educational Needs and Policies in Two Volumes.* Ottawa: Indian Affairs Branch, 1966.

Hegel, Georg. "Lordship and Bondage." In *Phenomenology of Mind*, 1807; reprinted, Mineola, NY: Dover Publications, 2003.

Highway, Tomson. *The Rez Sisters.* Saskatoon: Fifth House, 1988.

Hubbard, Tasha. "Voices Heard in the Silence, History Held in the Memory: Ways of Knowing Jeannette Armstrong's 'Threads of Old Memory.'" In *Aboriginal Oral Traditions: Theory, Practice, Ethics*, edited by Renate Eigenbrod and Renee Hulan, 139–53. Halifax: Fernwood Publishing, 2008.

"Idle No More: First Nations Protesters Rally across the Country." *Toronto Sun*, 11 January 2013.

Indian Chiefs of Alberta. *Citizens Plus*. Edmonton: Indian Association of Alberta, 1970.

Jai, Julie. "Bargains Made in Bad Times: How Principles from Modern Treaties Can Reinvigorate Historic Treaties." In *The Right Relationship: Reimagining the Implementation of Historical Treaties*, edited by John Borrows and Michael Coyle, 105–48. Toronto: University of Toronto Press, 2017.

Johansen, Bruce, and Barbara Mann, eds. *Encyclopedia of the Haudenosaunee (Iroquois Confederacy)*. Westport, CT: Greenwood, 2000.

Johnson, Harold. *Two Families: Treaties and Government*. Saskatoon: Purich Publishing, 2007.

Johnston, Basil. *Ojibway Heritage*. Lincoln: University of Nebraska Press, 1976.

Johnston, Patricia Maringi G. "Is 'Space' the Final Frontier? Talking Forward Indigenous Frameworks in Education." In *Indigenous Education: New Directions in Theory and Practice*, edited by Huia Tomlins-Jahnke, Sandra Styres, Spencer Lilley, and Dawn Zinga, 483–511. Edmonton: University of Alberta Press, 2019.

Kakeway, George. "Manito Aki Inakonigaawin: Contemporary and Customary Protocols." GK Redstone Copyright, 2016.

King, Thomas. *The Inconvenient Indian: A Curious Account of Native People in North America*. Toronto: Doubleday Canada, 2012.

——. *The Truth about Stories: A Native Narrative*. Toronto: House of Anansi Press, 2003.

Kovach, Margaret. "Indigenous Methodologies." In *Research Is Resistance: Critical, Indigenous, and Anti-Oppressive Approaches*, edited by Leslie Brown and Susan Strega, 19–36. Toronto: Canadian Scholars Press, 2005.

Kulchyski, Peter. *Aboriginal Rights Are Not Human Rights: In Defence of Indigenous Struggles*. Winnipeg: ARP Books, 2013.

——. "Bush/Writing: Embodied Deconstruction, Traces of Community and Writing against the State in Indigenous Acts of Inscription." In *Shifting the Ground of Canadian Literary Studies*, edited by Smaro Kamboureli and Robert Zacharias. Waterloo, ON: Wilfrid Laurier University Press, 2012.

——. "A Considerable Unrest: F.O. Loft and the League of Indians." *Native Studies Review* 4, nos. 1–2 (1989).

——. *Like the Sound of a Drum: Aboriginal Cultural Politics in Denendeh and Nunavut*. Winnipeg: University of Manitoba Press, 2005.

——. "Subversive Identities: Indigenous Cultural Politics and Canadian Legal Frameworks, or, Indigenous Orphans of the State." *E-misférica* 6, no. 2 (2010). https://hemisphericinstitute.org/en/emisferica-62/6-2-essays/e62-essay-ubversive-identities-indigenous-cultural-politics-and-canadian-legal-frameworks-or.html.

Kuokkanen, Rauna. *Reshaping the University: Responsibility, Indigenous Epistemes, and the Logic of the Gift*. Vancouver: UBC Press, 2007.

LaRocque, Emma. *When the Other Is Me: Native Resistance Discourse 1850–1990*. Winnipeg: University of Manitoba Press, 2010.

Lawrence, Bonita. *"Real" Indians and Others: Mixed Blood Urban Native Peoples and Indigenous Nationhood*. Vancouver: UBC Press, 2004.

Lévi-Strauss, Claude. *Tristes tropiques*. Forge Village, MA: Murray Printing Company, 1974.

Lipe, Daniel. "Indigenous Knowledge Systems as the Missing Link in Scientific Worldviews: A Discussion on Western Science as a Contested Space." In *Indigenous Education: New Directions in Theory and Practice*, edited by Huia Tomlins-Jahnke, Sandra Styres, Spencer Lilley, and Dawn Zinga, 453–81. Edmonton: University of Alberta Press, 2019.

Long, John S. *Treaty No. 9: Making the Agreement to Share the Land in Far Northern Ontario in 1905*. Montreal and Kingston: McGill-Queen's University Press, 2010.

Longboat, Diane. "First Nations Education Law for First Nation Governments Template." Ontario Native Education Counselling Association, 2013.

———. "Historical Highlights Leading to the Development of First Nations Education Law in Canada." Ontario Native Education Counselling Association, 2013.

Maaka, Margaret J. "Education through Paideia: The Contested Space of the Indigenous Psyche." In *Indigenous Education: New Directions in Theory and Practice*, edited by Huia Tomlins-Jahnke, Sandra Styres, Spencer Lilley, and Dawn Zinga, 3–38. Edmonton: University of Alberta Press, 2019.

Marx, Karl, and Friedrich Engels. *Capital*. Chicago: Encyclopaedia Britanica, 1952.

Memmi, Albert. *The Colonizer and the Colonized*. Boston: Beacon Press, 1965.

Miller, J.R. *Compact, Contract, Covenant: Aboriginal Treaty-Making in Canada*. Toronto: University of Toronto Press, 2009.

———. *Shingwauk's Vision: A History of Residential Schools*. Toronto: University of Toronto Press, 1996.

Milloy, John. *A National Crime: The Canadian Government and the Residential School System—1879 to 1986*. Winnipeg: University of Manitoba Press, 1999.

Mills, Aaron. "Rooted Constitutionalism: Growing Political Community." In *Resurgence and Reconciliation: Indigenous-Settler Relations and Earth Teachings*, edited by Michael Asch, John Borrows, and James Tully, 133–73. Toronto: University of Toronto Press, 2018.

———. "What Is a Treaty? On Contract and Mutual Aid." In *The Right Relationship: Reimagining the Implementation of Historical Treaties*, edited by John Borrows and Michael Coyle, 208–47. Toronto: University of Toronto Press, 2017.

Mitchell, Joni. "Big Yellow Taxi." In *Ladies of the Canyon*. Reprise Records, 1970.

Morris, Alexander. *The Treaties of Canada with the Indians of Manitoba and the North-West Territories: Including the Negotiations on which They Were Based, and Other Information Relating Thereto*. Toronto: Belfords, Clarke and Company, 1880.

Ningewance, Patricia. *Talking Gookum's Language: Learning Ojibwe*. Lac Seul: Mazinaate Press, 2004.

Palmater, Pamela. *Beyond Blood: Rethinking Indigenous Identity*. Saskatoon: Purich Publishing, 2011.

Parmenter, Jon. "The Meaning of *Kaswentha* and the Two Row Wampum Belt in Haudenonsaunee (Iroquois) History: Can Indigenous Oral Tradition Be Reconciled with the Documentary Record?" *Journal of Early American History* 3 (2013): 82–109.

Pasternak, Shiri. *Grounded Authority: The Algonquins of Barriere Lake against the State*. Minneapolis: University of Minnesota Press, 2017.

Payton, Laura. "First Nations Get Broad Promises on Indian Act Development." CBC News, 24 January 2012. https://www.cbc.ca/news/politics/first-nations-get-broad-promises-on-indian-act-development-1.1152147.

Peterson, Jacqueline, and Jennifer Brown. *The New Peoples: Being and Becoming Métis in North America*. Winnipeg: University of Manitoba Press, 1985.

Pidgeon, Michelle. "Contested Spaces of Indigenization in Canadian Higher Education: Reciprocal Relationships and Institutional Responsibilities." In *Indigenous Education: New Directions in Theory and Practice*, edited by Huia Tomlins-Jahnke, Sandra Styres, Spencer Lilley, and Dawn Zinga, 205–29. Edmonton: University of Alberta Press, 2019.

Ray, Arthur, J.R. Miller, and Frank Tough. *Bounty and Benevolence: A History of Saskatchewan Treaties*. Montreal and Kingston: McGill-Queen's University Press, 2000.

Regan, Paulette. *Unsettling the Settler Within: Indian Residential Schools, Truth Telling and Reconciliation in Canada*. Vancouver: UBC Press, 2010.

Restoule, Jean-Paul, and Angela Nardozi. "Exploring Teacher Candidate Resistance to Indigenous Content in a Teacher Education Program." In *Indigenous Education: New Directions in Theory and Practice*, edited by Huia Tomlins-Jahnke, Sandra Styres, Spencer Lilley, and Dawn Zinga, 311–37. Edmonton: University of Alberta Press, 2019.

Root, Deborah. *Cannibal Culture: Art, Appropriation and the Commodification of Difference*. Boulder, CO: Westview Press, 1996.

Rotman, Leonard I. "Taking Aim at the Canons of Treaty Interpretation in Canadian Aboriginal Rights Jurisprudence." *University of New Brunswick Law Journal* 46 (1997): 11–50.

Royal Commission on Aboriginal Peoples (RCAP). *Final Report*. 5 vols. Ottawa: Government of Canada, 1996.

Said, Edward. *Culture and Imperialism*. New York: Vintage Books, 1993.

———. *The Edward Said Reader*. Edited by Moustafa Bayoumi and Andrew Rubin. New York: Vintage Books, 2000.

Saskatchewan Ministry of Education. "Treaty Education Outcomes and Indicators." 2013. https://edusites.uregina.ca/amh846/wp-content/uploads/sites/58/2020/10/Treaty-Education-Outcomes-and-Indicators.pdf.

Saul, John Ralston. *A Fair Country: Telling Truths about Canada*. Toronto: Viking Canada, 2008.

Seven Generations Education Institute. "Education Guiding Principles." N.d.

Simpson, Audra. *Mohawk Interruptus: Political Life across the Borders of Settler States*. Durham, NC: Duke University Press, 2014.

Simpson, Leanne. *As We Have Always Done: Indigenous Freedom through Radical Resistance*. Minneapolis: University of Minnesota Press, 2017.

———. *Dancing on Our Turtle's Back: Stories of Nishnaabeg Re-Creation, Resurgence and a New Emergence*. Winnipeg: Arbeiter Ring Publishing, 2011.

Standing Senate Committee on Aboriginal Peoples. "Reforming First Nations Education: From Crisis to Hope." December 2011. https://publications.gc.ca/collections/collection_2011/sen/yc28-0/YC28-0-411-3-eng.pdf.

Starblanket, Gina, and Heidi Stark. "Toward a Relational Paradigm—Four Points for Consideration: Knowledge, Gender, Land, and Modernity." In *Resurgence and Reconciliation: Indigenous-Settler Relations and Earth Teachings*, edited by Michael Asch, John Borrows, and James Tully, 175–207. Toronto: University of Toronto Press, 2018.

Stefanovich, Olivia. "Pope Francis Apologizes to Indigenous Delegates for 'Deplorable' Abuses at Residential Schools." CBC News, 1 April 2022. https://www.cbc.ca/news/politics/pope-francis-responds-indigenous-delegations-final-meeting/.

Stonechild, Blair. *The New Buffalo: The Struggle for Aboriginal Post-Secondary Education in Canada*. Winnipeg: University of Manitoba Press, 2006.

St-Onge, Nicole, et al., eds. *Contours of a People: Métis, Family, Mobility, and History*. Norman: University of Oklahoma Press, 2012.

Styres, Sandra. "Pathways for Remembering and (Re)cognizing Indigenous Thought in Education." In *Indigenous Education: New Directions in Theory and Practice*, edited by Huia Tomlins-Jahnke, Sandra Styres, Spencer Lilley, and Dawn Zinga, 39–62. Edmonton: University of Alberta Press, 2019.

Talbot, Robert J. *Negotiating the Numbered Treaties: An Intellectual and Political Biography of Alexander Morris*. Saskatoon: Purich Publishing, 2009.

Tasker, John Paul. "Indigenous Groups Accuse Conservatives of 'Shameful' Stalling Tactics on Rights Bill." CBC News, 10 April 2019. https://www.cbc.ca/news/politics/indigenous-groups-shameful-tory-stall-tactics-1.5092435.

Treaty Relations Commission of Manitoba. https://trcm.ca/

Trudeau, Justin. "Prime Minister Justin Trudeau Delivers a Speech to the Assembly of First Nations Special Chiefs Assembly." 8 December 2015. Canada, Prime Minister of Canada Justin Trudeau. https://pm.gc.ca/en/news/speeches/2015/12/08/prime-minister-justin-trudeau-delivers-speech-assembly-first-nations.

Truth and Reconciliation Commission of Canada. *Final Report of the Truth and Reconciliation Commission of Canada: Honouring the Truth, Reconciling for the Future*. Vol. 1. Toronto: Lorimer, 2015.

———. *A Knock on the Door: The Essential History of Residential Schools from the Truth and Reconciliation Commission of Canada*. Winnipeg: University of Manitoba Press, 2016.

Tuhiwai Smith, Linda. *Decolonizing Methodologies: Research and Indigenous Peoples*. London: Zed Books, 1999.

Tully, James. "Reconciliation Here on Earth." In *Resurgence and Reconciliation: Indigenous-Settler Relations and Earth Teachings*, edited by Michael Asch, John Borrows, and James Tully, 83–129. Toronto: University of Toronto Press, 2018.

———. *Strange Multiplicity: Constitutionalism in an Age of Diversity*. Cambridge, UK: Cambridge University Press, 1995.

Tunney, Catharine. "OPP Arrest 10 Demonstrators at Tyendinaga Blockade Site, Charges Pending." CBC News, 24 February 2020. https://www.cbc.ca/news/politics/tyendinaga-mohawks-removal-blockades-1.5473490.

Turner, Dale. *This Is Not a Peace Pipe: Towards a Critical Indigenous Philosophy*. Toronto: University of Toronto Press, 2006.

United Nations General Assembly. United Nations Declaration on the Rights of Indigenous Peoples (UNDRIP). *UN Wash* 12 (2007): 1–18.

Valaskakis, Gail Guthrie, Madeleine Dion Stout, and Eric Guimond, eds. *Restoring the Balance: First Nations Women, Community, and Culture.* Winnipeg: University of Manitoba Press, 2009.

Vizenor, Gerald. *Manifest Manners: Postindian Warriors of Survivance.* Middletown, CT: Wesleyan University Press, 1994.

Wagamese, Richard. "'All my relations' about respect," *Kamloops Daily News*, 11 June 2013. https://kamloopsnews.ca/kdn-opinion-columnists/wagamese-all-my-relations-about-respect-2/

Walters, Mark. "Rights and Remedies within Common Law and Indigenous Legal Traditions: Can the Covenant Chain Be Judicially Enforced Today?" In *The Right Relationship: Reimagining the Implementation of Historical Treaties,* edited by John Borrows and Michael Coyle, 187–207. Toronto: University of Toronto Press, 2017.

Warren, William. *History of the Ojibway People.* 2nd ed. Minneapolis: Minnesota Historical Society Press, 2009.

White Face, Charmaine. *Indigenous Nations' Rights in the Balance: An Analysis of the Declaration on the Rights of Indigenous Peoples.* St. Paul, MN: Living Justice Press, 2013.

Williams, Paul. *Kayanerenkó:wa: the Great Law of Peace.* Winnipeg: University of Manitoba Press, 2018.

Williams, Robert A. Jr. *Linking Arms Together: American Indian Treaty Visions of Law and Peace, 1600–1800.* New York: Routledge, 1999.

Wilson, Shawn. *Research Is Ceremony: Indigenous Research Methods.* Halifax: Fernwood Publishing, 2008.

Wilson-Raybould, Jody. *Indian in the Cabinet: Speaking Truth to Power.* Toronto: HarperCollins Publishers, 2021.

Zinga, Dawn. "Teaching as the Creation of Ethical Space: Indigenous Student Learning in the Academy/University." In *Indigenous Education: New Directions in Theory and Practice,* edited by Huia Tomlins-Jahnke, Sandra Styres, Spencer Lilley, and Dawn Zinga, 277–309. Edmonton: University of Alberta Press, 2019.

INDEX

Aboriginal, terminology, 13
Aboriginal Affairs. *See* Canadian government
Aboriginal rights, 14, 35, 69, 81, 84, 118, 131, 146
Acoose, Janice, 40
Adams, Howard, 28, 87, 92
addictions, 26, 86, 135
affirmation, defined, 14, 119–20. *See also* recognition and affirmation
alcoholism, 4, 5, 26, 86
Alfred, Taiaiake, 28, 36, 104, 120
Allen, Gary, 6
Althusser, Louis, 24
Anishinaabe (descended people), 13
anishinaabe, etymology, 50
Anishinaabe Enawendiwin (relations), 100
Anishinaabe Gidakiiminaan (connecting to the land), 100
Anishinaabe Inaadiziwin (being), 99
Anishinaabe Inaakonigewin (customary law), 52, 113
Anishinaabe Inendamowin (thinking), 97–98
Anishinaabe Izhichigewin (doing), 99–100
Anishinaabe law: Anishinaabe Inaakonigewin (customary law), 52, 113; developing jurisdiction of governance temporal laws, 53; Kagagiwe Inaakonigewin (sacred law), 51, 113, 131; Kete Inaakonigewin (traditional law), 51, 113; Manito Aki Inakonigaawin (Great Earth Law), 52–53; Ozhibiige Inaakonigewin (written temporal law), 52–53, 82, 88, 116. *See also* Kinamaadiwin Inaakonigewin (Treaty #3 Education Law)
Anishinaabemowin: Anishinaabe law

contained within, 49; and English, 86, 97; fluency and preservation through education, 95, 96, 97, 101, 132; future of the language, 15–16; official language of Draft Record of Decision, 113–14; self-determination via language use, 1; *Talking Gookom's Language: Learning Ojibwe*, 89; translation challenges, 89–90. *See also* English; Kinamaadiwin Inaakonigewin (Treaty #3 Education Law)
anthropocentrism, 138
Armstrong, Jeannette, 32, 140
Asch, Michael, 8, 64, 66, 126, 145
Assembly of First Nations (AFN): endorsement of Bill C-262, 82; formation, 31; on secession from Canada, 133; statistics on attendance and dropout rates, 43; "Tradition and Education: Towards a Vision of Our Future, a Declaration of First Nations Jurisdiction over Education," 131
Assembly of Manitoba Chiefs, 122, 145
assimilation: as altruistic gesture, 18; Anishinaabe law to diminish, 129; Darwin's theories as justification, 20–21; extinguishment of Indian status, 31–32; the Indian Act policies, 29–30, 69; liberalism, 39; and reconciliation, 35; and residential school system, 79; sheer compulsion policy, 70; via public education system, 135

Baskatawang, Annie, 3–4
Baskatawang, Diane, 3, 4, 5
Baskatawang, Leo: about, 3–7; attendance